Land &
Allegiance in
Revolutionary
Georgia

Leslie Hall

The University of Georgia Press

Athens and London

© 2001 by the University of Georgia Press

Athens, Georgia 30602

All rights reserved

Designed by Kathi Dailey Morgan

Set in Adobe Caslon by G&S Typesetters

Printed and bound by Thomson-Shore

The paper in this book meets the guidelines for
permanence and durability of the Committee on
Production Guidelines for Book Longevity of the
Council on Library Resources.

Printed in the United States of America

05   04   03   02   01   C   5   4   3   2   1

Library of Congress Cataloging-in-Publication Data

Hall, Leslie, 1950–

Land and allegiance in revolutionary Georgia / Leslie Hall.

p. cm.

Includes bibliographical references and index.

ISBN 0-8203-2262-8 (alk. paper)

1. Georgia—History—Revolution, 1775–1783.   2. Georgia—
History—Revolution, 1775–1783—Social aspects.   3. United
States—History—Revolution, 1775–1783—Social aspects.   4.
Georgia—Politics and government—1775–1865.   5. Land
tenure—Georgia—History—18th century.   6. Right of
property—Georgia—History—18th century.   7. Allegiance—
Georgia—History—18th century.   I. Title.

E263.G3 H22 2001

975.8′03—dc21   00-041801

British Library Cataloging-in-Publication Data available

Land &
Allegiance in
Revolutionary
Georgia

To my mother,

Ann Cameron MacClellan Hall,

in memoriam

CONTENTS

ACKNOWLEDGMENTS

Among the many tasks that bring a work to its conclusion, acknowledging and thanking those who have helped me is one of the most pleasurable. I express my gratitude to Alan Gallay for the several close readings he gave this study, in its infancy as a thesis under his supervision, and later, in the critical stage of its development, into a lengthier project. His encouragement has been steadfast and much appreciated. I thank the anonymous readers of the University of Georgia Press, whose reports helped me to focus and organize the material. My colleague Evelyn Darrow and my husband, Fred Sodt, both read through the manuscript in its final stage and I thank them for their comments. David Des Jardines, Trudie Calvert, and Kristine Blakeslee, of the University of Georgia Press, guided me skillfully through the various stages of manuscript preparation, for which I am grateful. Family and friends have contributed to my sense of well-being throughout the long process of writing this book, and I cannot thank them enough for their affection and interest.

INTRODUCTION

The story of the Revolutionary War in Georgia can be told in terms of rebels and loyalists or winners and losers, but a more complex and informative story reveals itself when one takes into account those Georgians who did not fall readily into these broad categories. Georgia alone of all the colonies in rebellion had British civil government reestablished during the war, and as a result inhabitants came under unique pressures regarding the pledging of their allegiance. The rival governors, legislative bodies, judiciary systems, and militia and regular troops, as well as the lack of a decisive military victory, motivated many to view the giving of their allegiance with ambiguity and pragmatism. As the war progressed, military and civilian authorities on both sides came to recognize that civilians would give their allegiance if their property rights were protected.

Rebel and royal governments were desperate to earn civilian support, and a flexible loyalty gave civilians some control over the power of government, control they did not have before or after the war. Yeoman farmers, determined not to give up their land, had the opportunity to acquire additional property through booty, plunder, and reward. Many of the more prosperous took the opportunity of wartime to assume ownership of "enemy" estates, sometimes through purchase, other times through plunder, and also through lawsuits. Others, however, lost much, if not all, of their property through debt, plundering, or evacuation.

The various civil governments that operated in Georgia between 1775 and 1782 received help from London and Philadelphia, but they had to rely on themselves for raising much of the needed resources and for developing strategies to secure their position and gain popular support. These civil governments understood that securing civilian property, above all else, provided the key for maintaining their power. During the war these governments sought to maintain orderly property records and allow for the collection of debts and the retrieval of property, all the while confiscating "enemy" property themselves. Both royal and state governments established commissions to administer abandoned property in order to raise money through rental and sale and later to use the property as barter. Although civil authority remained unstable because neither government could maintain law and order, it was resilient. Calls for elections went out numerous times, enjoyed wide participation, and signified civilian desires for a return to stability. Although the settlers may appear inconsistent in their allegiance and fickle in their politics, they were steadfast in their support of civil authority. Throughout the war civil government operated somewhere in Georgia at all times.

Obtaining citizen loyalty was of utmost concern for the competing governments. The state government required oaths of allegiance and forced many loyalists and neutrals to leave the state between 1776 and 1778. After the British reoccupation of lower Georgia, both governments found requiring loyalty from civilians both difficult and unproductive. They shared a desperate need to keep the resident population on the land: without a civilian presence, neither competing government could claim political ownership of Georgia, and without civilian provender, neither government's military forces could remain for any length of time. Government weakness left large areas of Georgia essentially lawless, and citizens took matters into their own hands. Forced by circumstances to respond to revolution in political but nonideological terms, they operated in a practical way and switched allegiance or attempted to remain nonpartisan. In the backcountry area of Georgia, for example, many settlers may have switched their allegiance as many as seven times between January 1779 and October 1780. In the end, pragmatic considerations influenced rebel leaders to offer people what they wanted, land, in exchange for their timely allegiance. Had the royal governor been able to offer land for allegiance, he no doubt would have been as successful as the rebels in attracting recruits.

A good look at Savannah reveals some of the circumstances the residents found themselves facing as a result of royal, then rebel, then royal, then rebel control of the capital. Many residents remained when rebels gained control in March 1776, and they continued their residence after December 1778, when British forces invaded. Others were not so flexible, however, and fled the rebels and returned with the British, or fled the British and returned with the rebels, or fled and returned whenever they thought it necessary or possible. One government would confiscate the property of an "enemy" or "absentee" only to have the next government see that property owner return and regain or attempt to regain his or her estate. The presence of Continental and later British regular military forces created tension in the garrison town through property and authority disputes between military and civil leaders. Under all governments the residents of Savannah had to concern themselves with the infrastructure of the town: road repair, rebuilding the jail and workhouse and maintaining other government buildings, regulating the town market, controlling fugitive slaves, maintaining the night watch and fire brigade, and attending to sanitation. An examination of the ways in which both rebel and royal civil authorities administered the capital of Savannah provides us with a glimpse into the daily life that went on there during the Revolutionary War and illustrates just how firmly reestablished British government became.

Restored royal government very nearly succeeded in Georgia for the respected colonial governor, James Wright, brought advantages that the rebel authorities could not offer the civilian population. The parliamentary stipend once again supported royal civil government, and as a result, Georgia's monetary system, essentially defunct under rebel government, was now backed by the pound sterling, with specie in the form of pay for the troops coming in regularly. Wright brought unified civil leadership, in contrast to the factionalism among rebel authorities. Although he could not achieve the military support he desired, Wright and British military authorities cooperated effectively during times of crisis. Rebel civil and military authorities would not cooperate so closely until late in the war, and only through the intervention of Continental general Nathanael Greene. Wright provided aid to refugees fleeing the depredations in the backcountry as well as to Savannah area planters who could no longer feed their slaves. He provided residents with the opportunity to collect rebel debts and purchase rebel property, thus assisting them in rebuilding or expanding their holdings and reestablishing their credit, but he could not prevent rebels from returning and taking advantage of these economic conditions as well. Much to his regret, Wright's hands were tied by an assembly reluctant to judge the past behavior of any resident. Although not all were able to retain their property at the end of the war, many civilians benefited financially by living under restored British civil government, for they were able to regain their land or a portion of it, purchase additional property, reestablish credit, and collect debts.

The British military evacuation of Savannah resulted in thousands of people having to decide yet again where their allegiance lay. The state encouraged supporters of British civil government to remain in Georgia by joining the militia, and those who did so retained their property. Many, however, evacuated, taking with them as much property as they could, primarily in slaves. The ensuing chaos regarding the ownership of slaves was never resolved. The Board of Commissioners for confiscated properties operated for forty years, 1782–1822, and attempted to settle disputes brought about by the complications of warfare and two competing civil governments. The evacuees tried to make a new start in East Florida, Great Britain, Nova Scotia, and the West Indies, and Georgians struggled to repair their broken agricultural system and establish civil authority in the areas severely beset by plunderers.

The story of how the civilian population responded to the Revolutionary War in Georgia is complex. Although a poor and isolated frontier colony, Georgia offered eighteenth-century families of all social classes the opportunity to obtain free or very inexpensive land and enjoy the status it brought. I hope to show how many of these settlers, motivated to keep their land in the midst of war, transcended political ideology in their resolve to sustain civil authority and thus shaped events of the Revolutionary War in Georgia. With both civil governments dependent on the resident population, many turned the power of allegiance to their own benefit and retained their land.

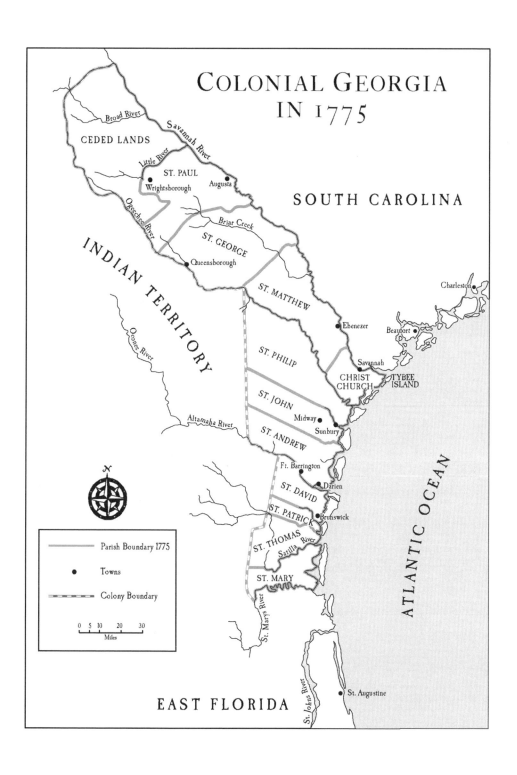

COLONIAL GEORGIA
IN 1775

CEDED LANDS

Broad River

Savannah River

Little River

ST. PAUL

Wrightsborough

Augusta

SOUTH CAROLINA

Ogeechee River

Briar Creek

ST. GEORGE

Queensborough

INDIAN TERRITORY

Oconee River

ST. MATTHEW

Charleston

Ebenezer

Beaufort

ST. PHILIP

Savannah

CHRIST CHURCH

TYBEE ISLAND

ST. JOHN

Altamaha River

Midway

Sunbury

ST. ANDREW

Ft. Barrington

Darien

ST. DAVID

ST. PATRICK

Brunswick

ST. THOMAS

Sarilla River

ATLANTIC OCEAN

ST. MARY

St. Marys River

EAST FLORIDA

St. Johns River

St. Augustine

Parish Boundary 1775

Towns

Colony Boundary

0 5 10   20   30
Miles

CHAPTER ONE

Poor Settlers on the Southern Frontier

Trustee and Royal Georgia, 1733–1776

Most of the inhabitants owed every acre of land they had
to the King's free gift.—Anthony Stokes, Chief Justice of
Georgia, 1769–76 and 1779–82

Georgia was not only the youngest but among the poorest and most sparsely
settled of the thirteen colonies in 1776. Georgians were accustomed to fend-
ing for themselves on a dangerous frontier: outlaws roamed throughout the
province, pirates plundered the coast and tidal rivers, marauders from South
Carolina and East Florida moved across the inland borders, and Native
Americans from the Creek and Cherokee Nations raided along the treaty
lines. While many of the free population were subsistence farmers, they,
along with the more prosperous colonists, benefited from the land grants
and civil authority of royal government. They depended on the courts to
protect their rights as landowners. Many inhabitants struggled to retain or
regain their property during the seven long and difficult years of the Revolutionary War.

A look at Trustee and royal Georgia reveals several characteristics in the
developing province and its population that serve to define it as uniquely
Georgian right through the Revolutionary War. Between 1733 and 1783,
while civil governments changed hands, the population increased, the geographic boundaries expanded, and the economy developed, some things remained the same: the population was generally poor but landholding, frontier conditions prevailed, and civil government, while functional, lacked the
financial resources to sustain itself independently.

Modest Growth Under the Trustees, 1733–1752

Georgia's colonial period was very brief in comparison to that of the other colonies that sought independence from Great Britain. Georgia came into being on paper in 1732 when England's long-held imperial concerns for the defense of South Carolina led the king to approve a plan put forward by a group of philanthropists to establish a charity colony in North America. These men proposed to create a yeoman farmer–based population from the worthy poor Protestants of Great Britain and other parts of Europe who would both defend the new colony and produce exotic exports such as wine, olive oil, and silk. By supporting this venture the king found a means of providing defense for the southern frontier against the Spanish and the French. The philanthropists did not succeed in creating a yeoman-farmer-soldier utopia, but as the Trustees of Georgia, they did succeed in transporting hundreds of "worthy poor" from Great Britain and northern Europe and giving them free land.

James Oglethorpe was almost entirely responsible for the successful defense of the southern frontier and the survival of Georgia during the decade between 1733 and 1743. As the Trustees' representative in Georgia, he tried to put into practice the humanitarian and defensive ideals upon which the colony was founded. His greatest success lay in holding on to the frontier, which he accomplished in large measure by establishing positive diplomatic relations with the Native American population. In particular, Oglethorpe established durable and lasting relations with the Creeks; despite tensions that lasted throughout Georgia's prolonged frontier period, no war occurred with the powerful Creek Confederacy. Additionally, Oglethorpe constructed a series of forts and fortified settlements, brought in a regiment of British regulars, and led several attacks against the Spanish at St. Augustine as well as defended Georgia against Spanish attack. Oglethorpe chose to spend over £90,000 of his personal fortune (all of which Parliament later reimbursed) to protect the southern frontier rather than risk its loss.

Although those who immigrated to Georgia between 1733 and 1752 received their land at no cost and did not pay any tax on it, Trustee land regulations placed many at a disadvantage. Women could neither receive nor inherit land initially, although exceptions to strict male inheritance were made from the beginning. In fact, by 1754, when Georgians were asked to register their land, women registered approximately nine thousand acres, mostly in town lots.[1] The contiguous settlement plan, although important for defensive reasons because it assigned colonists adjacent land, placed those unlucky colonists who received an inferior farm lot at a desperate disadvantage. Despite the poor land, they had to wait for as long as a year to exchange it for a possibly more fertile lot.[2]

Under the Trustees the colony remained economically undeveloped and sparsely settled. Of the approximately 2,840 individual grants given out by the Trustees, all but 329 were for fifty acres or less, indicating that the population consisted primarily of settlers of very modest means. Each head of household received fifty acres and each indentured servant who served his time received twenty to twenty-five acres; the Trustees gave the five hundred–acre parcels only to male adventurers with six indentured servants each. By 1751 the colony had an approximate population of 1,900 whites and 400 blacks. When compared to the estimated total population of 64,000 people in South Carolina in 1750, Georgia under the Trustees had attracted very few inhabitants.[3]

Although small, the population in Georgia was diverse, with varied religious and ethnic backgrounds. This was because the Trustees chose not to establish a legal church in Georgia and by advertising their religious tolerance of Protestants they attracted immigrants from several persecuted groups. They did not welcome Catholics or Jews, however. The population that settled the colony during their administration grew to include a mixture of English, Scots, Irish, and northern European Protestants and Jews, as well as European adventurers and poor settlers from other colonies.

As the need to maintain a significant defensive posture lessened in the late 1740s, in large part through Oglethorpe's efforts, the Trustees began to initiate much needed reforms before the tiny population abandoned their holdings and fled to other colonies. The changes they made laid the groundwork for Georgia's future prosperity, although it was slow in coming. The Trustees began allowing larger land grants in the 1740s, thus providing the means for the plantation system to develop on a modest scale. They also changed the status of grants to that of fee simple in March 1750, which permitted colonists to sell their land and buyers to purchase holdings without limit on the total number of acres. Later in the summer of 1750 the Trustees repealed the ban on slavery, thus enabling the full establishment of the plantation system.

During the twenty years the Trustees controlled Georgia, their agricultural scheme was encumbered by the inexperience of the charity colonists, the ban on slavery, and the smallness of the land grants. In addition, their prohibition against strong alcohol prevented the use of rum as a trade commodity. Although additional charity colonists, indentured servants, soldiers, and independent property holders joined James Oglethorpe and the first group of colonists, the population grew at a very slow rate and consisted primarily of subsistence-level farmers. While the rice planters in South Carolina could imagine potential plantations along the tidal rivers, they would not move to a colony that prohibited slavery and the accumulation of large tracts of land. Many Georgia colonists also felt at a disadvantage, chafed under Trustee restrictions, and sought their fortunes elsewhere. As a group, the Trustees had begun to lose interest in the colony by the mid-1740s, and after Parliament refused their request for funds in 1751, they surrendered Georgia to the Crown in 1752.

Opportunities opened up for the yeoman farmer as well as the elite planter, for the Crown wanted Georgia settled and so made land acquisition easy and slavery legal. While the limited acreage in the coastal area was quickly settled by wealthy rice planters, the king approved additional land cessions in 1763 and 1773, making backcountry land available to farmers at no or little cost. When they received their land, most white males received the vote because property requirements for suffrage were low. This system provided the owner of fifty acres the opportunity to participate in government. Attainable land and the status it brought encouraged many to seek their fortune in the royal colony.

One can catch a glimpse of life in early 1750s Georgia, just as the colony became royal, through reading the correspondence of two Germans who lived there at this time. One man, John Martin Boltzius, had come to Georgia as leader of the persecuted Salzburgers while the other, Johann Christoph Bornemann, came as an independent colonist or "adventurer." Both had been highly educated in Europe yet found themselves committed to life on the primitive southern English frontier. They appeared to enjoy the opportunities and challenges free land and its management afforded them and wrote to European acquaintances of their experiences. Their comments reveal the toil, chance, calculation, and surprise that formed an important part of their daily lives; their observations shed light on how the availability of free land motivated people to immigrate to Georgia.

John Martin Boltzius and his colleague Israel Christian Gronau led the first group of Salzburgers, German Lutheran refugees, to Georgia in 1733, and over the next thirty years Boltzius became an expert on land and agriculture in the province. He learned by bitter experience how devastating poor land could be to settlers, for the original site of the group's town, on Ebenezer Creek, proved unsuitable for habitation. After suffering high mortality rates and two crop failures, the Salzburgers migrated to a new location at Red Bluff on the Savannah River, which they named New Ebenezer. There the settlement prospered, and by 1751 Boltzius could write to a correspondent in Augsburg that the town had two grinding mills, a sawmill, a tanning mill, a rice peeling mill, and a rice stamper.

Responding to a series of questions asked by his Augsburg correspondent, Boltzius described the land and how easy it was to obtain. His ideal plantation contained fertile soil upon which oaks and cypresses grew, as well as rice land, and was located near the Savannah River not far from the capital. He explained that as Georgia had few roads, people relied on the waterways to transport their produce. Although these prime holdings had been "taken up" around Ebenezer and Savannah, Boltzius suggested that new settlers could find similar land thirty or forty miles up the Savannah River. A settler who traveled even further upriver to Augusta could find good wheat land. Those who wished to settle nearer to Ebenezer and Savannah, however, continued to have plenty of land to choose from, although less fertile. He thought that settlers could receive free good land more easily in Georgia than in South Carolina.

While speculators claimed thousands of acres of land in South Carolina "for future sale or rent, also to buy from the poor, who cannot manage in competition with the Negroes, for little money," the Georgia government limited the amount of free land per household to five hundred acres, requiring payment for additional acreage. The government considered everyone, no matter how impoverished, eligible to receive free acreage, and Boltzius noted that white servants "can get free land everywhere; therefore they do not like to serve, but marry soon." He concluded that "even the most lowly peasant is an absolute freeholder in his house and on his land, and cannot complain in the least about any difficulty, oppression and violence, which is exactly the famous English liberty."

In addition to noting that the industrious poor could prosper, Boltzius had advice for Europeans with some financial resources who might wish to emigrate from Europe to Georgia. He cautioned them to establish themselves gradually, for "many a wealthy person who started on too large a scale and wanted to get rich too fast has lost health, life, and fortune." After selecting a good tract of land, Boltzius recommended that the European gentleman build a little house and a separate kitchen and limit his purchases to two male slaves, one horse, six cows and calves, and some chickens. The slaves would first clear the trees and bushes and fence the fields and then work six to ten acres each, planting Indian corn, beans, pumpkins, rice, and potatoes. "With such an initial modest establishment, such a gentleman would come to learn by his own industry and intercourse with his neighbors how to proceed with good success."[4]

Johann Christoph Bornemann and his father-in-law, Johann Heinrich Graeve, both from the duchy of Hanover, fit Boltzius's profile of the successful European settler perfectly. In 1752 they appeared before the Georgia Council requesting land. The party consisted of Bornemann, his wife, Carolina Magdalena, and their infant son Benjamin, Johann Graeve, his wife, and a maid. The council awarded each man five hundred acres and the opportunity to pick the location. Bornemann traveled up the Savannah River and selected his acreage at the mouth of Briar Creek, some miles above the settlement of New Ebenezer. After forcing a squatter off the land, to whom he paid sixteen pounds for having cleared some of the trees and built a hut, Bornemann and his family set to work establishing their home in the Georgia wilderness.

Bornemann wrote to Albrecht von Haller, a scientist at the University of Göttingen and Bornemann's patron, that "the whole country is an unending forest." He compared Savannah to a middle-sized European village, though "all the houses look no better than market booths." This may have been partially a result of the poor wood available for building, for Bornemann noted that a house standing for sixteen to twenty years "is considered old and dilapidated; and few reach this age." Although worse than Savannah, he found Ebenezer to be in better condition than he had expected and noted the "mills, the impressive silk filature, and the beautiful mulberry orchards." To his surprise, Bornemann found no one in great need in Georgia and wrote: "In this country we have almost only poor people, but no beggars." Goods proved expensive, and he found bills of exchange the most convenient way to have his money in Georgia, with Spanish money second best and French money suffering greatly by the exchange rate. "One of the greatest evils of this country" he observed, "is the high price of almost all necessities, [and] the lack of money and useful craftsmen."

By 1754 he could announce to his patron that he was "completely satisfied with my circumstances." This did not prevent him from wishing he had better hunting and fishing skills. He envied the wealthier men of South Carolina and Georgia who produced indigo successfully but chose not to go into debt to procure the necessary equipment. Instead, he grew corn and rice and planted mulberry trees. Plunderers threatened him: "Too many wicked thievish rabble (from whom I have had enough loss in my cattle raising) find their way here from other provinces. We hope meanwhile that the Governor will take measures against them." A model gentleman farmer according to Boltzius, Bornemann began simply and worked hard to acquire a modest estate, which, after his death in 1757, he left to his family.[5]

Royal government worked well in Georgia, and the Crown supported territorial expansion between 1752 and 1776. New settlers received land at no cost until 1773, and with possession of land came the ability for most white males to vote and establish credit to improve their holdings. Few people had access to specie and used their land and their crops to barter or obtain credit for what they wished to acquire, be it more land, slaves, or luxury items. Civil government, dependent on the parliamentary subsidy and administered ably by officials personally interested in Georgia's growth, met the needs of the population for many years. Because of good royal government, especially under the third governor, James Wright, many Georgians sought to maintain the status quo throughout 1775, despite neighboring South Carolina's revolutionary example.

Expansion Under Royal Government, 1752–1775

Grants of land in excess of five hundred acres were awarded for the first time after the colony became royal in June 1752, enabling those with money and slaves to establish themselves on sizable holdings. Rice planters from South Carolina understood the suitability of Georgia's 126-mile-long protected coastline for rice cultivation: numerous freshwater rivers cut through the low country and the Atlantic tides pushed the fresh river water inland from between ten and twenty miles. Little if any ungranted rice land was left in South Carolina, and Carolinian planters such as Jonathan Bryan and Henry Laurens soon established plantations in Georgia. After 1760 little land suitable for rice cultivation remained available and improved rice land on the market was very expensive; Georgia's plantation elite had quickly taken much of the best land for themselves.[6]

This elite group developed over time to include approximately sixty members, each owning a minimum of twenty-five hundred acres and at least forty slaves.[7] Between 1755 and 1770 various men from among this group formed the eleven-member upper house of the Georgia Assembly, or council. Along with the governor, they controlled land regulation and distribution. Georgia's charter entitled each head of household to one hundred acres of land and an additional fifty acres for each member of his household, black or white. To receive land, the petitioners appeared before the council, swore to their household number, and described the land they wanted. The council had the right to delay or refuse any grant and picked those men to whom it wished to grant the best land. Once awarded, the petitioner had six months to register a survey and then received the grant signed by the governor.[8] The council and governor held immense power in colonial Georgia, for everyone wanted land.

Few settlers who came to Georgia had access to the capital necessary to obtain sufficient slave labor to develop coastal holdings. In the 1750s the cost of a country-born or seasoned male slave was between £28 and £36, a female was between £25 and £29, and children from £10 and £35. Although slaves were financially out of the reach of many, it is thought that by the early 1760s at least one-quarter of the households in Georgia owned one slave, and the average number of slaves per household was twenty-three. The 1760 population was estimated at 6,000 whites and 3,578 slaves, with most of the slave population concentrated along the coast. By the 1770s a prime male field hand cost £60, a female cost £30–£50, and children cost £25; settlers began to bring slaves into the backcountry at this time.[9]

Most of the coastal land was taken up by rice and indigo plantations and medium-sized farms, so settlers coming into Georgia between 1752 and 1763 generally received grants along a strip of land extending approximately twenty-five to thirty-five miles inland from the coast, between the Savannah and Altamaha Rivers. Although territory approximately one hundred miles to the northwest of Ebenezer had been settled for some time, particularly around the trading town of Augusta, where James Oglethorpe ordered a fort established in 1736, this had been done without benefit of treaty; most of the land between Ebenezer and Augusta would not be available for settlement until 1763.

Following the Spanish and French departure from the area east of the Mississippi and East Florida at the end of the Seven Years' War, the southeastern Indians became dependent on Great Britain for their trade goods. Taking advantage of this new position, the governors of Virginia, North and South Carolina, and Georgia, along with Indian Superintendent John Stuart, met with approximately eight hundred Indians at the Congress of Augusta to sign a peace treaty. This 1763 treaty also ceded 2.4 million acres

of Creek land to Georgia, opening up for settlement the coastal area between the Altamaha and St. Marys Rivers and north of Ebenezer Creek to
the Little River above the trading town of Augusta. The treaty extended
Georgia's coastal frontier approximately thirty miles, making more rice land
available near the now British-held East Florida. The British presence to
the south better secured Georgia's coastline, and the rice plantations began
to expand their operations and develop in the Altamaha delta and along the
Satilla River.[10] While the coastline of Georgia continued to develop much
as South Carolina's had, with a small number of elite planters establishing
rice plantations worked by slaves, the small farmer also benefited from the
1763 cession.

The Treaty of Augusta opened for settlement the inland area between
the Ogeechee and Savannah Rivers and between Ebenezer and Augusta,
which attracted small farmers. Thought to contain the best ungranted piedmont land in the South, this area brought settlers from Europe as well as
the neighboring provinces of the Carolinas, Virginia, Maryland, and Pennsylvania. The area soon developed substantial farms and small plantations
of corn, grain, and livestock.

Although Georgia had the highest rate of population increase of any
colony during the 1760s, its population continued to be very small in comparison: in 1770 it had an approximate population of 23,400, while North
Carolina had an approximate population of 197,200 and South Carolina
124,200.[11] An estimated breakdown of Georgia's population for 1770 includes between 11,000 and 12,750 whites and 10,625 blacks. It has been suggested that approximately 30 percent of the adult white population in Georgia lived at the subsistence level between 1767 and 1771.[12] Georgia's society
was unusually mobile, for the ready availability of land allowed most men
to advance into political office, if they so desired, and the expanding economy and growing population gave merchants, however modest, the opportunity to expand their fortunes and gain political influence with the
wealthy.[13]

Although settlers arrived in Georgia as family groups or single men, large
contingencies also set up immigrant communities in the piedmont area.
Emigrants from Northern Ireland, totaling approximately seven hundred
people between 1769 and 1773, established the town of Queensborough, located right on the Indian boundary line along the Ogeechee River.[14] In 1767
forty Quaker families from North Carolina settled on land reserved for
them by Governor Wright and the council, approximately thirty miles west

of Augusta near the Little River. The following year the group expanded their holdings and built the town of Wrightsborough. Although the Quakers became a minority in their growing settlement, they retained leadership and the Creeks valued them as neighbors.[15]

Individuals and families involved with the North Carolina Regulator movement began to move into Georgia in 1771, and apparently neither Governor James Wright nor acting governor James Habersham viewed them as desirable settlers. The movement, made up of approximately six thousand backcountry settlers, began in 1766 and demanded that the corrupt local North Carolina government, which cheated them of their land and taxes, be reformed.[16] Their challenge to established government culminated with the Battle of Alamance in 1771, and the defeat they suffered at that time kept political power in the hands of the ruling elite until 1776. The North Carolina Regulator participants who moved into the Georgia backcountry during and after 1771 may very well have brought with them a desire to participate in local civil government, an activity denied them previously.

Outlaws had come into Georgia as soon as it began to be settled: James Oglethorpe complained of outlaws from Carolina coming into Georgia during the 1730s, and Johann Bornemann noted the arrival of thieves from the neighboring provinces in the mid-1750s. By the mid-1760s the neighboring South Carolina backcountry, with approximately thirty-five thousand settlers, had become overrun by bandits as a result of inadequate civil authority.

The Cherokee War of 1760–61 had devastated the province's backcountry, an area to the northeast of Georgia's backcountry at that time. Outlaw bands formed in the depopulated area over the next five years and by 1767 dominated the territory. Property owners joined forces and established themselves into a group called Regulators, in what has been called the first organized manifestation of the American vigilante tradition. Their objective was to punish the plunderers and their supporters while at the same time seeking a more efficient judicial system from the royal government in Charleston to protect their property. After two years of effort, using arbitrary and violent means to drive the renegades out, the Regulators, now joined by the Moderators, received improved civil authority from the South Carolina government.[17]

Some of the outlaw activity spilled over into the Georgia backcountry. Horse stealing had become common in the Augusta area by 1763, and a gang of approximately twenty horse thieves operated there in 1767, apparently relying on support from local residents. The Regulators' efforts to protect their property in South Carolina and their success at obtaining improved civil authority probably pushed more bandits and squatters across the Savannah River and into Georgia than might have come on their own. Nonetheless, Georgia backcountry settlers did not experience civil unrest during the 1760s.

Anthony Stokes, chief justice of colonial Georgia between 1769–76 and 1779–82, described the outlaws coming into Georgia as "a swarm of men from the western parts of Virginia and North Carolina, distinguished by the name of Crackers." He noted that "these Crackers were very troublesome in the settlements, by driving off gangs of horses and cattle to Virginia, and committing other enormities: they also occasioned frequent disputes with the Indians."[18] The Creeks also viewed these squatters as troublesome and wished the royal government would stop them from trespassing on their land. When the "Crackers," or "Virginians," as the Creeks referred to them, ignored the boundary between Georgia and Indian Territory that had resulted from the 1763 Treaty of Augusta, they threatened the peace.[19] The squatters despised the Indians and the British policy of upholding Indian treaty rights.

In an effort to attract the "middling sort" of settlers to Georgia, those preferred by Governor Wright, new land had to be obtained. He wanted people with some assets to move in to Georgia and farm, not on a subsistence level but to establish prosperous holdings. He hoped they would have a surplus of produce to sell and contribute to maintenance of civil authority in their area by participating in the militia and local politics. The vacant lands remaining from the 1763 cession held little to attract these preferred settlers, for the acreage lay in small tracts in the interior, along narrow streams and rivulets leading into pine barrens. Rice land remained available, but the resources needed to develop it exceeded those a "middling" farmer had at his disposal.[20]

An opportunity to expand the territory of Georgia occurred when a group of Cherokees decided to pay their debts to Indian traders through the cession of a portion of their territory, some of which belonged to the Creeks. In 1771 they asked Governor Wright to bring their request before the king and assured him they would convince the Creeks to go along with the land cession should it receive royal approval. While on leave in London during 1772, Wright sought and gained the approval of King George III and the Board of Trade for the cession. Rather than the Indian traders receiving the land as payment for tribal debts, Wright arranged for the province of Georgia to obtain the land and pay the traders with money from the proceeds of the resultant land sales. This meant that for the first time acreage in Georgia would be sold for a price rather than given for free. In the eventual cession, both the Creeks and Cherokees ceded over two million acres of land north and west of Augusta.[21]

Governor Wright was ordered to secure the land cession and met with the Creeks and Cherokees at Augusta to do so in June 1773.[22] The surveying party immediately started out from Augusta to mark the boundary line with William Bartram, a naturalist, as one of its members. Bartram recorded in his journal his impressions of the terrain and his fascination with numerous Indian ruins, which included a stupendous conical pyramid, vast tetragon terraces, sunken areas surrounded by banks of earth, deserted settlements elevated above the riverbanks, and ancient cultivated fields and orchards. He observed bears, panthers (which were called tygers in the South), wolves, wildcats, beautiful butterflies, and an infinite variety of insects.[23]

Anxious to see this new part of Georgia for himself, Governor Wright made a tour through the lower part of the ceded territory. In a letter to the Earl of Dartmouth written on December 27, 1773, Wright described the countryside as hilly, with good soil, plenty of water and "much like many parts of England."

Although many people applied for tracts in the ceded lands, quite a few required three years to pay the purchase money and either settle there or bring in settlers, while others could not pay at all. Wright reported to London in December 1773 that after three months 55,650 acres of land had been properly purchased in the ceded lands and the population would increase by 1,413 white men, women, and children and 300 slaves. James Habersham had reported that 3,000 people already lived in the ceded land area in 1772, thus bringing the population figure to an approximate total of 4,713 people. Wright had hoped for more settlers, but this was a good start. The presence of so many farming families with legitimate titles to the land would tend to drive off the Cracker squatters and thus reduce conflict with the nearby Creeks and Cherokees, while at the same time the heads of these families would join the militia and provide a defensive force against potential Indian raids.[24]

The population continued to grow as predominantly small farmers moved across the Savannah River into the newly opened backcountry. By the beginning of the Revolution an estimated 14.5 percent of Georgia's population lived in the backcountry. In 1773 Governor Wright reported the overall population of Georgia to be approximately 18,000 whites and 15,000 blacks, and he predicted that an additional 10,000 people would emigrate to Georgia by January 1775. While Wright predicted a population of 43,000 by 1775, estimates for 1776 range from 33,000 (17,000 whites and 16,000 blacks) to between 45,000 and 50,000. Most slaves lived along the coast and their number nearly equaled that of the white population in 1776, yet compared to South Carolina's estimated black population of 110,000, they were few indeed.[25]

The isolation of the new homesteads in the ceded lands, the animosity that Indians felt for the squatters, and the hatred many settlers felt for the Indians added up to potential conflict, if not war. In 1773 gunmen from the surrounding Creek, Cherokee, Choctaw, Chickasaw, and Catawba tribes numbered 10,050 while the entire fighting force of Georgia equaled 2,828 militia.[26] Although the Indians along the southern frontier never created a united front, the British worked to establish unity among them during the Revolution.

Between late December 1773 and the end of January 1774 Creek and Cherokee parties raided in the ceded lands along the northern branch of the Ogeechee River. They murdered various members of two settler families. The incident began when several of William White's horses were stolen and he and William Sherrill captured them back from two Creeks, wounding or killing one of the Indians. The Creeks retaliated by killing White and his family, which included his wife and either two or four children and Sherrill and his family, which included his wife and daughter, two slaves, and possibly two additional whites. The local militia, joined by a troop of rangers, went to the area in response to these attacks; they fled when ambushed by a group of Indians, abandoning several men who had fallen.[27]

Some time later, a detachment returned to the scene of the ambush and found that the Creeks and Cherokees had hideously tortured one of the men they had left, a Lieutenant Grant.[28] They reported the scene to the rest of the militia, who immediately deserted. As the news of the torture spread to the inhabitants along the frontier, "the people everywhere abandoned their settlements, many left their wives and children who crowded down to Augusta for protection." Settlers as far away as Virginia apparently fled their homesteads and "abandoned their all."[29]

Governor Wright understood why the militia, rangers, and settlers re-

sponded to the Indian attacks with such terror. As he explained in a letter
to Lord Dartmouth on January 31, 1774, Georgia was "a province without
men or money" enough to defend itself from an Indian war. No Indian war
occurred, however, and the settlers returned to their homesteads.

As a result of these attacks on settlers in the ceded lands, Wright held a
preliminary conference with the Upper Creeks in Savannah on April 14,
1774. While accepting symbolic gifts from the Creeks, Wright expressed
his displeasure at the killing of the settler families. He asked the Creeks
to locate and execute at least some of the people responsible for the murders and return all slaves and horses taken from the settlers since the
December 25 attack. Until they did so, he suspended all trade with the
Creeks.[30]

John Stuart, Indian superintendent, expressed his concern in a letter to
the Earl of Dartmouth on May 6, 1774, that if the Creeks did not follow the
stipulations set out at this conference, British troops would have to be called
in "for the province of Georgia is not in a situation to defend itself." Governor Wright and representatives of the Upper and Lower Creeks signed a
treaty in Savannah on October 20, 1774, that restored the peace. The exchange of goods between traders and Indians now resumed and settlers
returned to their homesteads in the ceded lands.

The return to peace did not eliminate conflict, however. Many people
held a variety of grievances against each other and the royal government
that sprang primarily from the land cession of 1773. Traders discovered that
they did not benefit directly from land sales as they had anticipated and
resented the restrictions imposed on them by the cession. These men, primarily from Carolina, had long enjoyed unregulated trade, private land acquisition, and personal influence over the Indians. Centered at Augusta,
they sent their agents into the Creek and Cherokee Nations with goods
from Charleston and shipped deerskin and peltry downriver, undisturbed
by Trustee and later colonial regulations. John Rae, George Galphin, and
Lachlan McGillivray dominated the trade throughout the colonial period
and generally promoted stable relations with the Indians.

Many Creeks had not supported the land cession in the first place and,
once it was implemented, found not only that they did not benefit from
gifts as they had anticipated but that whites continued to encroach on their
land. Not all Georgians were satisfied with the amount of land ceded in 1773
and wanted more Indian land made available for settlement. The assembly
recommended to Governor Wright that he require the Creeks to cede land

along the Oconee River as a term of peace in October 1774, which he did not do. The cession of 1773 had become complex indeed.

Although royal government land policies certainly attracted men of prosperity to Georgia, as late as 1757 the province did not have ten residents worth £500 each. This fact shaped the interaction between the government and colonists in several significant ways.

The provincial government could not raise any significant amount of revenue through the collection of duties or taxes. The assembly warned the first royal governor of Georgia, John Reynolds (1754–57), that although it would try to defray the contingent expenses of government, "our present situation and circumstances are such that we shall be able to contribute very little to that purpose." The second governor, Henry Ellis (1757–60), encumbered "every fund or means of raising money," and the third governor, James Wright (1760–82), found that he would have to do the same. He wrote to the Board of Trade: "What can be done where there is in general such wretched poverty and an absolute necessity of raising money on the most urgent occasions, even for immediate defence and preservation." As a result, the salaries of the provincial officials came from an annual subsidy awarded Georgia by the British House of Commons.[31]

This financial situation enabled the government officials to remain independent of the assembly while the province relied on Parliament to provide for its survival. The colony's dependency on Great Britain would make a break with that country difficult to contemplate. Another result of the impoverished condition of most inhabitants was that, despite attempting to do so, the government failed to establish a quitrent tax law.[32] All landowners in Georgia benefited from this situation, from the elite planter with thousands of acres to the subsistence farmer with twenty-five or fifty acres, for no one had to pay tax on the land.

A factor contributing to this situation was the lack of circulating specie in the colony and the conservative and modest issues of provincial paper currency. The colony's agent in London had access to the annual parliamentary appropriation in pounds sterling, which gave the local Georgia pound high value. It commanded a high exchange rate with the Spanish dollar, the coin that determined the value of all colonial currencies. Thus royal Georgia's paper currencies did not depreciate, despite the fact that most Georgians had no money at all.[33] The result of this lack of money, either paper or specie, was that Georgia's private debt structure rested on land.

Establishing a two hundred-acre plantation with forty seasoned slaves cost an estimated £2,476 and most people did not have this amount of capital or credit. Some borrowed from the great planters such as Jonathan Bryan or their local merchants to get started.[34] Others, including those intent on establishing and improving smaller holdings, used the loan office, or land bank. This lending institution, in existence between 1755 and 1762, allowed people to receive loans on mortgage security, and it also formed the basis for the colony's bills of credit.[35] With land readily available, the status gained by improving their holdings was within the reach of many.

Both rich and poor also bartered, with rice forming a medium of exchange for the planters. Acting governor James Habersham sent barrels of rice to Governor Wright and his daughters Bella and Nancy as well as to his own son Joseph while they were all in London to serve as presents for their friends. William Bartram noted that "the planters chiefly rely upon [rice] for obtaining ready cash, and purchasing family articles."[36]

Land not only provided the means for people to obtain credit in Georgia, but it enabled most white males twenty-one years of age and older to vote and participate in civil government. Suffrage required fifty acres, identical to the requirement in North Carolina, and less than the one hundred–acre freehold of South Carolina. Georgians needed to hold five hundred acres to qualify as representatives to the assembly. In South Carolina the property qualification to hold a seat in Commons included a minimum of twenty slaves or personal wealth equaling £1,000.[37] Although theoretically this requirement excluded small landholders from holding office, many wealthy planters in South Carolina also found political power difficult to obtain. They were excluded because of the districting system that favored particular geographic areas and the familial politics that kept power in the hands of relatively few families. Jonathan Bryan, though a wealthy planter, had difficulty obtaining political position in South Carolina, whereas in Georgia his wealth and status virtually guaranteed him access to political offices. Georgia, a new colony, had yet to develop networks of family power that might exclude the propertied and talented.

In the colonial period, assembly seats were available for the middling men of property who would not have been able to hold office in South Carolina.[38] On the eve of the Revolution Georgia's political system maintained, if not increased, its broad representational nature. As land cessions occurred, the number of yeoman farmers qualified to vote increased and Governor Wright extended representation to the new districts, a phenomenon at odds with trends in both North and South Carolina.

Royal Georgia enjoyed unusually equitable representation in the assembly. In 1770 the ratio of representatives to adult white male Georgians was 1:62, while in South Carolina it was 1:192 and in North Carolina 1:315. The South Carolina government could provide representation to the majority of its population, who lived in the backcountry, only by taking representatives away from the coastal parishes, which it refused to do. North Carolina's provincial representation discriminated against the heavily populated western piedmont, and the endemic corruption among government officials disinclined them to attempt reapportionment. Although the Georgia parish of Christ Church sent more representatives to the assembly than any other parishes, this reflected the denser population of the parish and the location of the primary port, Savannah, rather than any significant imbalance of political power. During the 1770s conservative and radical factions emerged in Christ Church and St. John Parishes, respectively, and power in the assembly became an issue.[39]

The British government responded in unique fashion to Governor Wright's requests to add additional representatives to the Georgia Assembly. Wright pushed the Board of Trade to allow him some leeway in late 1768 when he informed them he had exceeded the nineteen-member limit by allowing a total of twenty-five representatives and wished to add to that number by having the four southern parishes represented. He also wanted the gentlemen and merchants living in Savannah who owned several town lots to be allowed to vote, even though they did not own fifty acres of land. The assembly pressured Wright to add representatives in 1771; the four southern parishes eventually sent representatives to the assembly, and Wright received permission to establish representation in the 1773 ceded lands but did not implement this reform before his departure in 1776.

By allowing him to increase representation by executive order whenever he saw fit, officials relaxed the restrictions they had placed in 1767 on the expansion of all colonial representation. Perhaps British officials approved additional representation for Georgia's newly settled territory because they understood that Wright controlled the provincial assembly, whatever its size. The resultant expansion of representation showed the inhabitants of Georgia that British officials supported the growth of their civil government.[40]

Although the yeoman farmers and backcountry settlers had representation in the assembly or were close to achieving it, the political power of the colony continued to rest comfortably with the coastal elite. More precisely, Christ Church Parish representatives dominated the assembly throughout the colonial period. Chief Justice Anthony Stokes recalled: "Before the Civil War, the Commons House neither received nor claimed wages; but affected great popularity, although, at times, they did some things with a high hand; and it required a great address in the Governor to keep them in tolerable temper after the Stamp Act passed."[41]

When news arrived in the spring of 1765 that Parliament had imposed a stamp tax on the colonies, Georgia politics began to factionalize. The stamped paper had to be purchased with specie, thus limiting the number of people able to do so to an extremely small number, despite the fact that the stamps would be required on all legal documents, newspapers, pamphlets, and ships' clearance papers. While all could agree on the impracticality of the stamp tax, the conflict lay in how to oppose the tax: through petition to obtain repeal or through the use of physical violence to prevent the stamp collector and the stamped paper from entering the colony and the tax to be collected.

During the following year Governor Wright maintained his authority by using his discretion in applying the law and deftly accommodating opposing factions. Although mobs protested the Stamp Act, they never became violent because Wright had the support of a sufficient number of influential men to control them. (Leadership for those opposed to the Stamp Act remains unknown.) An informal agreement between the Liberty Boys and the merchants enabled the stamped paper to be sold, and Wright opened the port of Savannah after a little more than a month's closure. Savannah thus had a distinct advantage over other colonial ports regarding trade. It also proved an embarrassment when Parliament repealed the stamp tax, for the other colonies then ridiculed Georgia. Governor Wright, alone of all the colonial governors, had upheld parliamentary law; in the process, he lost the unanimous support of his colonists.

Factional politics remained alive and stymied royal government during the next seven years but without great effect. The governor and the assembly did not work well together between 1769 and 1771, nor did they cooperate with acting governor James Habersham while Wright took leave between July 1771 and February 1773.[42] Habersham called for an election to be held in March 1772 and predicted accurately to Wright that "a Majority of the last Assembly may get reelected, if they chuse it, as the common People, who are the principal Electors are too easily blinded and imposed upon by the specious Pretence of Liberty and patriotism."[43] Habersham dissolved this assembly and called for new elections in December 1772. Members of the opposition faction, in and out of the assembly, included Jonathan Bryan, Noble Wimberly Jones, William LeConte, David Zubly, Benjamin Andrew, Thomas Carter, John Baker, Josiah Powell, and Henry Bourquine.[44]

During the years of Governor Wright's absence the northern colonies increased their protests against parliamentary legislation. Georgians learned about such activities by reading colonial newspapers, in particular Peter Timothy's *South Carolina Gazette*. This newspaper published whig writings under the close supervision of the South Carolina Commons, one of the most powerful of the colonial lower houses. Charleston was only an overnight passage by sea from Savannah, and the South Carolina papers arrived within several days of their publication. Although the colony had a newspaper called the *Georgia Gazette*, established by James Johnston in 1763, Johnston remained doggedly neutral and impartial in his publication.[45] As the events leading up to the Revolutionary War began to unfold, Georgians sought their information in South Carolina publications.

James Wright returned to Georgia in 1773 a successful man, not only having obtained King George's approval to carry out the land cession above Augusta but also having been knighted and made a baronet. He returned to a functioning assembly, which, although it contained an opposition faction, had nothing much to protest that attracted support. After years of neglect, the legislature addressed the muddled revenue situation and passed the first tax bill since 1770. By the following year, however, assembly factions began to exert some pressure on the governor and revolutionary protests outside Georgia began to influence the population.

The assembly and the council bickered over who had the right to nominate the colonial agent during the first half of 1774, and this quarrel emphasized their lack of cooperation with each other. John Stuart described the debilitating effect the quarreling had on civil government in a letter to the Earl of Dartmouth on May 6, 1774: "Whatever the abilities or inclinations of this province may be, the divisions in the legislature and the pretensions of the Commons House of Assembly are such that until they are composed and decided no hearty concurrence in the pursuit of any object of whatever consequence or utility can be expected or hoped for." In the end, neither house could agree and the lower house alone renewed Benjamin Franklin's appointment as agent for the colony (he had been agent since 1768).

Georgians responded modestly to calls for protest in 1774. The young lawyers George Walton and John Houstoun joined with several others in advertising a meeting at Tondee's Tavern on July 27, 1774, to consider the effect on Massachusetts of the "Intolerable Acts," issued by Parliament in response to the Boston Tea Party of December 1773. Although several meetings were held during July and August, poor attendance and conservative opposition prevented the group from resolving to send delegates to the first Continental Congress. A radical faction developed from these meetings, however, led chiefly by men from St. John Parish.[46] George Walton and others issued a set of resolutions protesting the Intolerable Acts. Because they relied on the British to provide them with soldiers in case of an Indian uprising, the potential Creek war in the backcountry was of more concern to Georgians than events in Massachusetts.[47]

On September 7 the *Georgia Gazette* published a response to the resolutions formulated by Walton and others, signed on August 30 by 103 people. The *Gazette* informed the public that the resolutions to the Intolerable Acts should not be considered as representing the sentiments of a majority of Georgians. Although some of the signers later became rebels, at this point they described themselves as "impressed with a deep sense of gratitude to the Crown, and to the Parliament of Great Britain."[48] Most Georgians understood that their colony needed the yearly stipend awarded by Parliament and the protection of British troops.

Governor Wright blamed the influence of South Carolina's newspapers for inciting the "Liberty people" in Georgia, as he had blamed the Charleston Liberty Boys for fomenting action in Georgia during the Stamp Act crisis nine years earlier. In late August he complained to Lord Dartmouth that Lieutenant Governor William Bull of South Carolina appeared to allow the Sons of Liberty to do whatever they pleased, which incited the Georgians. Wright found himself unfavorably compared to Bull and noted in a letter to the Earl of Dartmouth on August 24, 1774, that people said, "'Why should our governor do so and so when the people in Carolina have gone greater lengths than we have and the governor has not taken any notice of it?'" Wright clipped and mailed articles from the South Carolina papers to his superiors in London and warned them that temporary solutions to the issues would not last, for "the flame will only be smothered for a time and break out again at some future day with more violence." Although Wright described his situation to the Earl as "everything unhinged and running into confusion so that in short a man hardly knows what to do or how to act," he attempted to fulfill his duty as royal governor for the next year and a half.

The Beginning of the End of Royal Authority, 1775–1776

Examining the final period of royal government before the Revolutionary War reveals how reluctant many Georgians were to establish rebel control of the colony. Despite the fear of a race war and the pervasive influence of rebellious South Carolina, Georgians took their time and responded to conditions in their own way. Royal and rebel men of authority shared the desire to maintain civil peace.

Georgia politics reached a new level of complexity when both the royal colonial assembly and the rebel provincial congress met in Savannah during January 1775. Conservative Christ Church Parish rebels lowered the voting requirement in the hope of attracting a broader electorate. Radical St. John Parish leaders, although interested in taking political power away from these men, chose not to participate in this conservative-dominated effort. They did so in part because the other parishes, unlike St. John, had not signed the Continental Association. This was a policy established by the first Continental Congress to enforce nonimportation and nonexportation to and from Britain, Ireland, and various British possessions through local committees. Five parishes sent delegates to the provincial assembly, and at least six delegates attended both the provincial and royal legislatures.

The provincial congress adjourned in disarray on January 25, having adopted the Continental Association, with reservations, and selected delegates to attend the next Continental Congress. Uncertain of its legitimacy, perhaps in part because of the forty-five delegates only sixteen had previously served in a legislative capacity, the provincial congress asked the royal assembly to approve what it had done. Wright prorogued the royal assembly before any action could take place. The royal assembly refused to meet on the next scheduled date of May 9, and by November 9, 1775, Wright had to cancel the assembly because his civil authority had been so greatly eroded. The royal colonial assembly did not meet again until May 1780.

On the very day of the Battle of Lexington, James Habersham wrote to the Countess of Huntingdon of his fears should the British government not reconcile with the colonies: "I expect no less than an open Breach amongst us, Father against Son, and Son against Father, and the dearest Connections broke through by the Violent Hands of Faction and Party." The news of Lexington reached Savannah on the evening of May 10, and Habersham gave up all hope of reconciliation. He died soon afterward, spared the knowledge that his own sons would join the rebel cause.[49]

News of the Battle of Lexington had reached Charleston two days earlier, on May 8, just after the reception of a letter from Massachusetts colonial agent Arthur Lee. Lee reported from London that the ministry appeared interested in a plan to start a slave insurrection in the South. This combination of news created the idea in the minds of many South Carolinians that the British would meet colonial resistance with an armed force of slaves. This terrifying vision soon expanded to include the British arming the Indians as well. The fear of a racial war quickly spread down the coast to Savannah.[50]

John Stuart, Indian superintendent, was at home in Charleston during May and became the embodiment of rumored British policy. Stuart's support of British administration in Indian territory had made him unpopular with elites who wished to develop frontier land without government restrictions. Additionally, backcountry settlers viewed British authority in general and John Stuart in particular as favoring Indians and Indian trade over themselves. Stuart's well-known influence over the Indians and the ability of the British government to arm them made many southerners understandably nervous of Indian attack. In this charged atmosphere, William Henry Drayton, a member of the elite whose land lease proposal Stuart had opposed, used his position on the South Carolina rebel Committee of Intelligence to label Stuart the man who would carry out the rumored British policy. The superintendent fled to Savannah in fear of his life.[51]

Stuart's safety in Savannah was short-lived, however, for reports from South Carolina followed him, as did members of the Charleston rebel party. Governor Wright reported to the Earl of Dartmouth on June 20, 1775, that the South Carolinians "so inflam'd & enrag'd our People, that he [Stuart] did not think himself safe," and Stuart fled to St. Augustine on board an armed schooner. The rumored British policy to arm slaves and Indians in an attempt to subjugate the South brought out the inherent fear of a race war held by most colonists. Georgians responded by becoming more directly involved in the revolution already begun in New England and now carried to the South.[52]

Citizens made their last attempts to work within the structure of royal government in June 1775. Thirty-four prominent Savannah citizens met on June 13 and agreed to voice their objections to parliamentary revenue raising through a petition to the king, to keep the peace, and not to harass individuals or molest their property as long as they expressed their opinions decently. At another meeting in Savannah, citizens formalized an agreement between various parishes to accept and enforce the resolutions passed by the Continental Congress and the provincial congress, to gain dominance over parliamentary oppression, and to secure reconciliation between America and Great Britain. This group also called for a meeting of the provincial congress in July and set about to elect representatives from all the parishes. A council or committee for safety began to function during the summer, apparently to enforce the recent Savannah agreement.

The second provincial congress, held in Savannah during July, was attended by over one hundred representatives from all but two parishes, and of these delegates only thirty-five had legislative experience. Although the conservative faction dominated many of the committees and the council of safety, the congress selected radical Lyman Hall as a delegate to the Continental Congress and adopted the Association. Following the lead of Christ Church, the provincial congress lowered the voting requirement for the entire province to payment of tax on ten pounds worth of possessions and determined the number of representatives at ninety-six, with the ceded lands receiving representation for the first time and St. John Parish receiving more equitable representation. Governor Wright described the people active in rebel government to Lord Dartmouth on December 19, 1775: "The parochial Committee are a Parcel of the Lowest People Chiefly Carpenters, Shoemakers, Blacksmiths & with a Few at their Head in the General Committee and Council of Safety, there are Some better Sort of Men and Some Merchants and Planters but many of the Inferior Class."[53] The lowering of the franchise swelled the radical ranks.

Georgia's rebel government would form more slowly than that of any other colony in the South despite the powerful example of neighboring South Carolina. South Carolinians quickly formed a rebel government during May and June and began to organize for defense. They were the first to do so outside of New England before the Continental Congress appointed an overall Continental general. Elite slave owners, formerly reliant on British civil authority to provide law and order in their white minority colony, now viewed Britain as promoting that which they most feared: the rising up of the slaves. While Governor William Campbell of South Carolina fled to the safety of a warship on September 15, 1775, following the examples of Virginia governor John Dunmore and North Carolina governor Josiah

Martin, who sought the protection of warships during the summer, Governor Wright did not board a warship until February 11, 1776.[54] During the time remaining to him as governor, Wright and the Georgia colonists continued in their attempt to avoid a complete break with royal authority.

The "liberty people" turned to him on various occasions as a ceremonial gesture. In July the second provincial congress requested that Wright appoint an official day of fasting and prayer for reconciliation of America and Great Britain. He did so and received the favorable comments of John Hancock. Archibald Bulloch, serving as a delegate to the Continental Congress, referred to Wright as the governor of Georgia that September. Yet though they hesitated to break completely with him as an individual and as the representative of the Crown in Georgia, Governor Wright's ability to govern steadily weakened during 1775.[55]

He requested a sloop of war and a minimum of five hundred troops from Lord Dartmouth but received no reinforcements. Wright endured further frustration when he learned that the Charleston "liberty people" read his official mail before he did.[56] He had legislative information published in the *Georgia Gazette* during November and December and met with the council through November 7. Continuing this semblance of regularity, Wright appointed John Hume to replace James Habersham as secretary, council member Lewis Johnston to succeed Noble Jones as treasurer, and recommended Josiah Tatnall, Sir Patrick Houston, Lachlan McGillivray, and Charles William MacKinen to fill the vacancies caused by these deaths and Grey Elliot's leave of absence. Wright lamented to Lord Dartmouth, however, that the rebels had "not yet attempted to obstruct the Court of Chancery, but Except that, I have scarce any Power left, but Proving Wills and Granting Letters of Administration."[57]

During the summer of 1775 rebel recruiters came into Georgia from the Carolinas. In early July Barnard Elliot, a captain in the South Carolina militia, recruited in the backcountry. In August, a rebel recruiter named McCarthy appeared in Savannah. Unable to arrest him for recruiting, Anthony Stokes jailed him without bail on a charge of attempted murder. A mob released McCarthy, and he openly went about his recruiting business the next day, beating his drum as he passed both Wright's and Stokes's homes.[58] While toying with the dignity of the governor and chief justice, the council of safety appeared to hold Wright and Stokes in respect.

During the summer and fall of 1775 royal officials lost control of the judicial system. The newspaper published lengthy and numerous lists of those who neglected their summons for jury duty, and at the general court in October, most of the jurors present refused to be sworn in. Chief Justice Anthony Stokes ordered them into the marshal's custody but had to release them on a technicality. His assistant judges left him, "menaces" prevented one of his marshal's bailiffs from summoning jurors, extralegal committees took the law into their own hands, and attorneys supported a resolution of the third provincial congress to shut down the royal courts by deliberately delaying their cases. The provincial congress ordered royal attorney general James Hume "out of the Province within a month" for not acknowledging its authority and served Stokes with a resolve when complaints were lodged against him for declaring he would strike delinquent attorneys off the roll.[59]

Tension mounted as Stokes struggled to keep the legal system out of rebel hands. On December 12 he asked James Johnston to print the "Rule of the General Court" in the *Georgia Gazette*. This rule stated that any attorney obstructing the courts by deliberately delaying their case would be struck off the roll or lose his license. Johnston cautioned Stokes against this action, for it would "not only subject some of the King's officers to insult and ill treatment, but may involve all his Majesty's well-disposed subjects here in much trouble." Stokes, respecting Johnston's assessment of the rebel mood, withdrew the rule from publication and declared he would "lodge it with the Prothonotary."[60] On December 20, 1775, the council of safety, angered at Stokes's action, searched unsuccessfully for the rule in the prothonotary's office. The council viewed Stokes's intent to proceed against the lawyers and his vilification of the provincial congress as derogatory, arbitrary, and illegal.

Soon after, on January 10, 1776, Stokes announced at the court of sessions of oyer and terminer and general gaol delivery that he would cease to exercise his office as chief justice. He would resume it when his majesty's government was restored and the courts freed from the control of unlawful bodies of men. He chose to withdraw rather than risk unleashing violence aimed at loyal citizens in an attempt to maintain some semblance of control over the courts. Perhaps, as with James Wright, the rebels felt they knew his character well enough to count on him to back away from perpetrating civilian violence.[61]

Governor Wright played a diminishing role in the defense of Georgia as the rebels took control of the militia. The council of safety gained initial support with a portion of the Grenadier Company and the Light Infantry, stationed at Savannah. When the governor ordered the Grenadiers to pro-

tect him from a rumored kidnap attempt in June 1775, the officers refused
to obey. In July, they participated in taking the British ship *Phillipa* for its
gunpowder.[62] In early August the council of safety ordered the Grenadiers
north to Augusta to protect the trading town from a threatened attack by
loyalist Thomas Brown. Brown, who was recovering in South Carolina
from injuries suffered at the hands of Augusta rebels, threatened to return
with several hundred men but did not. Viewing himself as still in charge of
the militia, Wright protested that they had not requested his permission to
leave Savannah. If the council of safety controlled the Savannah militia, it
did not control Lieutenant Colonel James Grierson of the Augusta militia,
for he reported to Wright that he had refused to follow the council's
orders.[63]

The council of safety applied to Wright in mid-August to dismiss commissioned militia officers it deemed unpopular but whom Wright knew to
be loyal to the Crown. Pointing to the "relaxed" powers of government and
the disruption of normal legal proceedings at a time when Georgia was
threatened by Indian, Spanish, and slave attack, the rebels claimed the inhabitants needed militia leaders they respected to defend the province.
Governor Wright did not comply with the rebel council of safety's request,
but this made little difference. By September most loyalist officers had been
replaced by those in support of the rebel council of safety.[64] Although the
rebels tried initially to use Wright as a figurehead to gain support for their
military plans, perhaps in acknowledgment of his reputation, they went
forward with their reorganization without him.

Governor Wright used what little power he had left in an attempt to
prevent a potential war with the Creek Indians during the fall of 1775. The
gunpowder and ammunition sent to Georgia for the Creeks had been stolen
by the rebels, leaving the agents with nothing to give them. Wright requested five hundred pounds of gunpowder from Governor Patrick Tonyn
of East Florida, and then he and the royal council decided to inform the
Creeks of the lack of available powder. He asked David Taitt, British com-
missioner to the Creeks, to prevent them from coming to Savannah in
search of powder. Two members of the council of safety attended a conference called by Wright in late October, and Wright believed that they
reached an agreement to supply the Creeks with their accustomed gunpowder and ammunition, thus reopening trade and averting a war.[65] Whether
or not Wright played a pivotal role in reinstating the supply of gunpowder
and ammunition to the Creeks, the rebels did not hinder his efforts.

The rebels recognized the value of the defense measures Wright had initiated to protect the backcountry settlers against Indian attack. In mid-October Wright told Lord Dartmouth that the council of safety, upon learning that a group of backcountry settlers had captured a small stockade formerly garrisoned by a party of loyal rangers, ordered them to return the fort to the rangers and to disperse to their homes.[66] The rebels needed the backcountry fortified and could not afford to lose protection of any kind.

While Georgians continued to maintain a semblance of the status quo during the summer and fall of 1775, South Carolinians formed opposing loyalist and rebel militia units and engaged in battle. A loyalist force of twelve hundred men, led by Thomas Fletchall, laid siege to Fort Ninety-Six in an attempt to recapture ammunition rebel forces held there. The one thousand besieged rebels, led by William Henry Drayton, signed a truce with the loyalists on September 16, 1775, but hostilities continued. Lacking the support of royal governor Campbell, now on board a British warship in Charleston Harbor, the loyalist forces dissolved before the onslaught of an enlarged rebel force. Approximately four to five thousand men, led by Colonel Richard Richardson, scoured the backcountry seeking them. They captured the remnants of the loyalist force on December 22 at Great Cane Break and took approximately 130 prisoners.[67] South Carolina's history of internal violence over the past fifteen years had included an Indian war, subsequent anarchy in the backcountry, and the formation of the Regulator and Moderator movements. Now, many citizens joined opposing militia units and fought each other in a civil war. Georgia's sparse population did not form into opposing militia units at this time, nor would it ever engage in civil war as intense as that in South Carolina.

Georgia's small population and relative lack of sectional and class tensions while a royal province helped to keep it free from pre–Revolutionary War violence. While a small group of elites dominated the civil government of Georgia, as was the case in North and South Carolina, Georgia differed from these two colonies in its availability of land, lack of a quitrent tax, fair representation, and solid civil government. The coastal and backcountry areas of Georgia developed at a relatively close pace. Because suffrage was within reach of nearly all white adult males and much of the colony was represented in the provincial assembly, many individuals had the opportunity to prosper and rise to officeholding positions.[68]

Class lines had not sufficiently hardened in Georgia to cause discontent, in part because the colony was so young. Throughout the short history of

Georgia, the ownership of land had formed the base on which colonists built their status; cheap, readily available land continued to provide the means for economic, social, and political advancement. Some of the earliest colonists were still alive in 1775, and their rise from poverty to prominence provided an example of social mobility to all. Noble Jones had been aboard the first Trustee ship of charity colonists and James Habersham came in 1738. Both men arrived in Georgia nearly penniless, achieved prominence, and died in 1775.[69] The citizens of Georgia remained less polarized than their neighbors to the north.

Governor Wright retained enough authority as an individual to be acknowledged by the rebel government as a valuable man. He retained more than his ceremonial stature during 1775, contesting the growing rebel control over civil and military affairs by exerting his own at every opportunity. Perhaps some of the rebels might have wished to use his experience in governmental matters and his expertise on the affairs of Georgia when they formed their own government, had he been willing to guide them. Wright, in a letter to Lord Dartmouth, explained that he had not taken advantage of the leave of absence granted him because both "Kings Officers and Friends to Government" as well as "Several of the Liberty People" wanted him to remain in the province for the present. Wright added that "at the same time many on both sides think I might be of more Service in England than here."[70] Additionally, Georgians did not yet want to cut all their ties with the royal government in 1775, for reconciliation remained a possibility.

In mid-January 1776, British warships appeared at the mouth of the Savannah River, and armed conflict became a distinct possibility. In a letter to Lord Dartmouth, Wright recalled how, before the arrival of the warships, "the Lives of the Kings Officers & Friends to Government" did not appear to be in danger and "they Enjoyed the Possession & use of their Property." This situation changed on January 18, when the council of safety sent Joseph Habersham at the head of the Grenadiers to place the royal council and Governor Wright under arrest.[71] Had the British ships not anchored off Tybee Island and occasioned their imprisonment, parole, and subsequent flight, Governor Wright, royal officials, and supporters might have continued to meet and walk the streets of Savannah undisturbed for some time to come.

The fabric of civil government stretched tightly between the time Georgians set about creating a provincial government in the summer of 1775 and the effective end of royal government in January 1776. While pulling authority away from the royal government, the rebels simultaneously maintained a connection with the resident officials of Britain. These royal officials, also maintaining a connection with the rebels, tried to tug their usurped power back into place. When the breaking point came, it was not accompanied by a violent parting. The final snap of separation occurred in an atmosphere of wary tension, an achievement that did credit to both parties. Rebel and royal officials acknowledged the shifting of power and made every attempt to keep the peace; neither wanted to risk precipitating politically motivated violence by the population. This stance of maintaining the civil peace became the modus operandi for civil governments as they competed for authority in Georgia during the Revolutionary War.

Rich or poor, the inhabitants of Georgia lived on a dangerous strip of frontier, with powerful enemies in all directions. These enemies changed over time, from the Spanish and French in the early Trustee period to various parties of British, Continental, and French regulars, loyalist and rebel militia, and loosely aligned roving bands during the Revolutionary War. Political threats also existed from within: the specter of slave insurrection haunted white Georgians. Moreover, throughout Georgia's first fifty years, Native Americans attacked encroaching settlers in the backcountry, and marauders and pirates plundered the coastal area. Easily obtainable land provided white male Georgians of all classes with economic and social opportunities, but they had to survive a hostile environment in order to take advantage of them.

The population lay sparsely scattered across the territory and unable to defend itself from surrounding enemies. Settlers looked to Great Britain for protection and aid throughout the Trustee and colonial periods and to the Continental Congress when Georgia was under rebel state government. The British had provided troops, conducted diplomacy, and organized militia to secure Georgia from its enemies before the Revolution. During the long years of the war, however, British and rebel governments repeatedly proved unable to provide adequate protection. People formed their own strategies to cope with the threats that war brought to their families and property: many left temporarily, to return at what they hoped would be a safer time to pick up the pieces of their property and lives; others left permanently, forfeiting their holdings to begin life anew in some other place. Many, however, clung to their land and defended it with their wits, cunning, and strength of arms.

The poor settlers of Georgia, lacking neighbors, towns, and leaders, responded to the Revolutionary War in their own distinct fashion. They did not have to flee to save their lives, as did known royal officials during the first part of the war and known rebel officials during the second. Nor did they have to decide what role to play in the new political landscape, as did the more prosperous and well-known "middling sort." With few regular troops, tenuous local authority, and widespread plundering, Georgia's settler population could easily have slipped into anarchy and civil war by robbing and killing for personal gain. Instead, many chose to swear allegiance to any politicized group that asked them to do so and to support any form of available civil authority that presented itself locally. They did this because they wanted government established to protect their property rights. Political ideology might have concerned them, but the retention of their land took precedence over the winds of political change. Largely as a result of their active participation, civil government of one kind or another functioned at all times in Georgia throughout the Revolutionary War. The subsistence settlers, having benefited from a remarkably broad franchise, equitable representation, and easy availability of land under royal government, continued to gain further civil rights when the state government initiated almost universal manhood suffrage and a highly democratic legislature, as well as continuing a generous land policy during the Revolutionary War. The settlers had everything to gain by seeking the maintenance of civil authority, both state and provincial. Many emerged from the Revolutionary War with their land intact and their civil rights secure, a remarkable achievement for a poverty-stricken and dangerous frontier.

CHAPTER TWO

Rebels Take Charge

Georgia State Government, 1776

It [government] was the only alternative of anarchy and
misery.— Georgia Council of Safety, April 30, 1776

The fledgling rebel government attempted to gain the allegiance of a majority of Georgians beginning in 1775, but this task was difficult to achieve
for several reasons. To begin with, until February 11, 1776, the popular royal
governor, James Wright, lived in Savannah. Although the rebels' power reduced his importance, he remained a presence, and there were those who
did not want an irrevocable break with him and what he represented. When
Wright left, it was to join a fleet of warships that had the power to reduce
Savannah to rubble, destroy the rebel government, return him to his former
authority, and provide defense. Unless a citizen fervently embraced the
rebel cause, and certainly many did, he tended to take a temperate stance
under these ambiguous conditions and avoid committing himself to rebel
authority until events compelled him to do so. The proximity of a respected
royal governor as well as British warships stymied rebel efforts to gain
allegiance.[1]

In addition, Georgians involved in trade tended to ignore the Continental Association, and this hindered the establishment of rebel authority. The
Association was a policy of nonimportation and nonexportation to Britain
and the West Indies established by the Continental Congress. Adopted by
the provincial congress in July 1775, it was ostensibly concerned with using
economic means to achieve political ends. Georgia's geography played a
decisive role in this situation, making it all but impossible for the tiny rebel
navy to patrol the many rivers, inlets, and islands along the coast.

Beginning in 1775, the council of safety made a superficial attempt to
control the civilian population by requiring oaths, backing up the call for

allegiance with threats of violence, and attempting to run loyalists out of the state. The council of safety targeted individuals for rough treatment throughout the summer and fall of 1775, long before it received the resolution from the Continental Congress "to arrest and secure every person . . . whose going at large may in their opinion endanger the safety of the Colony or the liberties of America." Elizabeth Lightenstone Johnston noted in her memoirs how "all, gentle and simple," were made to declare their support for the rebels. "If a Tory refused to join the people, he was imprisoned, and tarred and feathered."[2]

The council also coerced Georgians into at least giving the impression of support for the Association by requiring them to sign it. On August 7, 1775, Governor Wright described to Secretary of State Dartmouth how people throughout the province had signed, many after having their property threatened.[3] Wright noted that the signing placed the individual under the authority of the provincial congress.[4] Cooperating with rebel authorities by signing the Association provided a way for many to remain on their land while keeping thoughts about allegiance to themselves.

Despite pressure from the rebel council, many citizens continued to sell their rice to East Florida.[5] Even Georgia delegates to the Continental Congress in September 1775 petitioned for permission to sell cargoes that had been shipped before adoption of the Association, as well as permission to export certain articles.[6] In December the council of safety set up committees to intervene physically in the illegal exportation activities taking place along the coastline. Governor Wright noted in a letter to Dartmouth on January 3, 1776, a public announcement that private citizens must either sign the Association or leave the province while at the same time royal officials would be prevented from leaving.

Four days later, the council received information that two British warships and a transport were headed for Georgia seeking supplies. They anticipated that the British would plunder livestock along the coast or, worse yet, succeed in getting merchants to sell them foodstuffs, thus breaking the Association. Over the next two weeks the council prepared for rebel government's first major crisis by initiating a series of measures aimed at organizing the militia, holding elections for the next assembly, and reasserting Georgia's support for the Association. These simultaneous activities in the face of potential British threat revealed the weakness of rebel civil authority.

The council had to send militia into the upper three northern parishes to assert authority regarding militia quotas and election procedures. They also noted a reluctance on the part of St. Philip Parish to organize its militia. The council of safety needed every parish to have its militia organized and duly elected representatives in place so the government could be viewed as legitimate.

On January 13 the British ship *Tamar* was sighted off Tybee Island, and on January 18 additional ships appeared, spurring the council to take action. Joseph Habersham and twenty armed men took the royal council prisoner, arresting Governor Wright, Anthony Stokes, and Colonels John Mullryne and Josiah Tatnall. They ordered those who had not signed the Association disarmed unless they gave their parole, or pledge, not to support those aboard the British ships. The council further ordered the troops, which had been sent to bring the upper parishes under control, back to Savannah as soon as possible, along with one-third of the local militia and any volunteers.[7] The council perhaps anticipated the need for greater defense after arresting the royal governor and thought it more expedient to have troops in Savannah than in the three upper parishes.

These troops from the outlying areas brought their complaints with them, however. In late February, the council of safety appointed Archibald Bulloch, George Walton, and William LeConte to "enquire into the cause of the discontent among the County Militia now in Town." Discontentment among the militia continued throughout the war, for many did not want to leave their farms and families unprotected, received little if any money for their efforts, were poorly supplied, and lacked leadership.

Citizens responded to the call for elections during this time of crisis, and they would do so repeatedly throughout the Revolutionary War. The fourth provincial congress met on January 20 and several days later took over the courthouse as a meeting place. Members considered the selection of officers for the Georgia Continental battalion, and this issue exposed the partisan conflict among them. Those assembled chose the compromise candidate, Lachlan McIntosh, over the radical candidate, Button Gwinnett and the conservative choice, Samuel Elbert. What unity had existed within the rebel ranks while laboring to build a power base in opposition to the royal governor now came to an end in Georgia; factionalism would cripple rebel civil and military authority for years to come.[8]

At least five men-of-war and various support ships, including the *Tamar, Raven, Cherokee, Scarborough, Hichinbrook,* and *St. John,* with approximately 200 troops aboard two transport ships and more than 390 seamen, anchored at the mouth of the Savannah River by late February. Captain Andrew Barclay, the British naval commander, had been ordered from Boston by Major General Sir William Howe to purchase rice and other provisions for the garrison. Governor Wright twice tried to persuade the council of safety to allow Barclay to purchase rice, but its members refused.[9] If they had done as Wright suggested and thus broken the Association, the rebel government of Georgia would have all but ceased to exist.

Governor Wright was under the impression that the British forces had come to assist him in reestablishing authority and that the *Raven* was to be stationed at Savannah. He went down to the British ship *Scarborough* with his son, two daughters, and various council members during the night of February 11 fully expecting to return to town in forty-eight hours. Council member Lewis Johnston joined the Wrights, and eventually so did Lieutenant Governor John Graham and John Lightenstone, commander of the scout boat.[10] Colonel Lachlan McIntosh predicted that, with Wright aboard, the British "meant to land at or near the town, destroy it, and carry off about twenty sail of shipping." Both men were wrong, for Captain Barclay wanted only rice.[11]

Several weeks passed without action, and during this time McIntosh noted that the British ships had encouraged slaves to desert to them as well as pilfering nearby islands for provisions.[12] This confirmed a general consensus among Georgia slave owners that, given the opportunity, many slaves would run away and join the British army. In September 1775 John Adams noted in his diary that Archibald Bulloch and John Houstoun estimated that should a force of one thousand regular British troops land in Georgia and announce that all slaves who joined them would be free, twenty thousand slaves from Georgia and South Carolina would join them in a fortnight. The slaves would not distinguish between rebel and loyalist owners: Bulloch and Houstoun at least could take some pleasure in the fact that "all the Kings Friends and Tools of Government have large Plantations and Property in Negroes" and would lose their slaves to the British army along with the rebels.[13]

Governor Wright recalled in a letter to Lord George Germain on June 6, 1779, that after he sought asylum on board the *Scarborough*, "betwixt two and three hundred Negroes who sayd 'they were come for the King'" came on board the various ships of the convoy. The slaves remained and the British offered no compensation to the owners, loyalist or rebel, when they sailed away.

In addition to anticipating that slaves would run to British forces, slave owners feared that a British invasion force might arm the slave population. Slave labor formed the basis of Georgia's economy, and slave ownership reflected an individual's social and economic status. The possibility of the irretrievable loss of slaves through flight, absorption into the military, and possible manumission by the British, not to mention their potential threat as armed enemy soldiers, caused grave concern among the white population for their way of life.[14]

The rice the slaves cultivated formed the basis of planters' wealth; the question of whether to sell rice to Captain Barclay brought the rebel council of safety to a standstill. Council members could not agree on whether to extend the Association. Meeting on February 20 and 21, the council heard members of the South Carolina Council recommend that the date to release the shipping be extended from March 1 to May 1. They responded to the suggestion by postponing consideration of the issue. Some members of the council must have wanted the rice-laden ships released on March 1, for the council did not reconvene to resolve the issue. Lachlan McIntosh commented that this behavior on the part of the council only added to the anarchy and confusion.

Battle of the Rice Boats

With March 1 rapidly approaching, Captain Barclay could anticipate purchasing rice from the outgoing ships now at anchor in the Savannah River. In a show of strength, the British ship *Cherokee*, two transports, and various armed vessels came upriver within two and one-half miles of Savannah. McIntosh had placed a detachment of 150 men nearby on shore. He recounted: "The enemy were parading with their boats for several days within gunshot of our sentinels, who, though they were ordered not to fire unless they were fired upon first, or they attempted to land, gave them several shot, but were not returned."

With no civil authority active, Colonel McIntosh held the responsibility for the defense of Savannah. Describing it as an "open, straggling, defenceless, and deserted town, with numberless avenues leading to it," he estimated that he had at his disposal three to four hundred Georgia militia and perhaps one hundred from South Carolina.[15] Probably at his instigation, the council of safety met again.

The council resolved on March 1 that the Association was to be extended to May 1 and the ships would not sail. In an effort to keep people in Savannah to defend the town and also to protect the shipping from local sabotage, the council initiated various resolves on March 2. Believing an attack on the town was imminent, the council announced that it would destroy Savannah and the shipping in the river before surrendering to the British. It proclaimed that those who had signed the Association and owned property in Savannah would have their property valued and appraised for future indemnification, in case of damage or destruction. To qualify, however, these "associates" had to be seen defending the town, their property, or both in case of attack. The council ordered the shipping crippled: the rudders unshipped and the rigging and sails removed in hope of inhibiting any of the rice boat captains or seamen from attempting to join the British. These measures arose from the fear that "many householders in the town of Savannah, and the hamlets thereunto belonging, have basely deserted their habitations since the commencement of the present alarms." The council had abandoned its responsibilities during a crucial week and now found itself compelling citizens to defend their property through the threat of its destruction.

The council of safety did not initiate these measures in time. Before the rice boats could be crippled, various British ships moved up behind Hutchinson Island on the night of March 2 and landed soldiers, howitzers, and fieldpieces. The British force could now reach the rice boats easily. McIntosh reported that the British accomplished this maneuver "with the assistance and contrivance of all our own seafaring people, and many from the town, [who] crossed the Island and hid themselves aboard of our merchant ships."[16]

Unaware of this development, the next morning the council of safety sent Captain Joseph Rice to cripple the rice boats. The British took Captain Rice prisoner, and later that day they also captured Captain Raymond Demere and First Lieutenant Daniel Roberts. The British sailed down the Savannah River the evening of March 3 with between ten and fifteen rice boats containing sixteen hundred barrels of rice and promised to cease hostilities.[17]

Although the rebel leaders had failed to stop the British from seizing the rice, they used what authority they had to arrest several known Crown supporters: Captain Hugh Inglis and Captain Wardell, who had lent their ships to aid British maneuvers during the Battle of the Rice Boats; royal council members James Edward Powell, a member since its inception, Josiah Tatnall, a new member who had assisted Wright in escaping downriver, and Chief Justice Anthony Stokes; and prominent planters John Mullryne, Captain William McGillivray, who had connections with one of the rice ships, and his cousin, Lachlan McGillivray, longtime Indian trader, whom Wright had nominated to serve on the council.[18] Governor Wright reported to Lord Germain on March 10, 1776, that the rebels had searched unsuccessfully for Lieutenant Governor John Graham and several others "and that several Merchants & other Friends to Government," aware that they had become "very obnoxious to the Rebels," left Savannah to seek refuge aboard the British ships.

The ailing Stokes wrote to Colonel Lachlan McIntosh protesting his arrest and treatment and warned, "I ask no favor of you; but remember that you are men, and for your own sakes, do not disgrace human nature by cruelty and oppression." Georgia had been spared political violence while Wright was governor, and Stokes urged McIntosh to consider the ramifications of his actions. Perhaps rebel authorities arrested the leading loyalists three days after the Battle of the Rice Boats to protect them from angry rebels as well as to use them as a means of exchange for Rice, Roberts, and Demere.

Over the next few weeks numerous letters passed between the council of safety and the British command anchored at the mouth of the Savannah River, but they failed to arrange an exchange of prisoners. Stokes reported that two of his fellow prisoners had been sent into the country and the rest of them would soon follow. He learned later that if an exchange had not been effected, they would have all been sent "to the Northward," possibly Cambridge, Massachusettes.[19] With so many loyalists in and about Savannah and British ships nearby, the rebels sought to prevent loyalists from communicating with the naval force and Governor Wright off Tybee Island. The council of safety declared, according to Wright, that all those who had gained protection aboard the British ships and all those who would do so in the future would be "deemed Enemies to the Cause of American Liberty" and outlawed.[20]

On March 25, rebel leader Archibald Bulloch and between fifty and one hundred men dressed as Indians, accompanied by several Creeks, attacked Tybee Island, where people from the British ships took recreation. They probably hoped to capture slaves who had escaped to the British or important hostages such as Governor Wright. South Carolina rebels had made a similar raid on Sullivan's Island off Charleston in December 1775 to capture runaway slaves, and Colonel Stephen Bull may have suggested this action to the Georgians. They surprised six marines and a carpenter from one of the British ships. After killing and scalping one man and wounding several more, they burned three houses and captured several men from town who were on the island and twelve or thirteen slaves.[21]

If they had hoped to gain important hostages, they came away disappointed. The attack may have had an effect, however, for two days later an exchange took place. The British released Captain Joseph Rice, First Lieutenant Daniel Roberts, and Captain Raymond Demere. In exchange, the council of safety released the loyalist prisoners from house arrest and granted the requests of council member Lewis Johnston and Lieutenant Governor John Graham that they be allowed to leave the *Scarborough* and return to their families near Savannah. Stokes, and it may be presumed the others released by the rebels as well as Johnston and Graham, gave his parole to the rebel government not to communicate with the "King's vessels and soldiery" without permission and was put at liberty to leave the province with his family, personal effects, and servants.[22]

A month after the exchange of prisoners, Lachlan McIntosh reported to George Washington that two British ships of war remained at Tybee Island while several "armed Vessels infest our other Inletts to the Southward, and made several captures which we cannot prevent." The ships were after provisions, and citizens drove them off without benefit of any rebel naval vessels.[23]

Georgia's defenses remained fragile because there were too many enemies and too few soldiers. McIntosh, in addition to needing naval vessels, needed soldiers to protect the settlements in the ceded lands from the Creeks, now that Governor Wright's ranger unit no longer patrolled this area. He also needed a troop of horse to prevent the British in East Florida from stealing cattle in southern Georgia. But McIntosh understood how unattractive it was to join Georgia's battalion because of the low enlistment bounty, the low pay for officers, and the high price all Georgians paid for manufactured goods. In fact, McIntosh did not know how he would be able to afford clothing and weapons for those soldiers he did have.[24]

Taking a broad view, McIntosh suggested to George Washington that "this colony should have a considerable Force to defend and secure it, as its safety is of the utmost consequence to the great cause of the Continent."[25] The Continental Congress, Major General Charles Lee, and later General Robert Howe of the Southern Military Department all acknowledged the need for more troops to defend the Georgia frontier and did their best to provide them. The factionalized civil government in many cases hindered military efforts, however. In the end the state military was essentially left to provide what defensive measures it could against the many enemies that crossed the southern and northwestern frontiers and raided along the coast.

The threatening presence of British warships anchored at the mouth of the Savannah River from January through April of 1776 did not result in a concerted effort at defense by the inhabitants of Georgia. Nor did the British command take the opportunity to use the forces so handily gathered to reestablish control of the colony and end rebel government. While the rebel leaders quarreled among themselves regarding the issue of the Continental Association and control of the militia and Continental troops, many civilians ran away from their homes and businesses rather than defend Savannah. Others showed their apathy by reluctantly supporting the council of safety's attempts to call out the militia, if at all. To prevent further erosion of civil authority, in April the assembly established a temporary but workable constitution.

A More Formal Government

Since Savannah remained vulnerable to attack from British ships after the Battle of the Rice Boats, the provincial congress next met in Augusta, on March 8. An additional motivation for meeting there was that the upper part of Georgia had not responded with alacrity to the call for the defense of Savannah and, with the assembly meeting in Augusta, settlers in the backcountry would understand that civil authority extended throughout Georgia, not just along the coast. Royal government had come to an end, and the council of safety would need to be replaced with a more regularized provincial government. The assembly formulated and adopted a set of "Rules and Regulations" on April 15, which went into effect on May 1, 1776.

This more formalized governmental structure established its authority over the various committees and councils that had attempted to govern Georgia during the past year. The provincial assembly retained its power to legislate and had control over the executive and judiciary. The assembly elected the president and members of the council every six months and appointed judges for the general court. The president and council appointed magistrates for the parishes. Colonial laws remained as long as they did not prove inconsistent with those of the Continental Congress or the provincial congress. The first land legislation, passed on July 12, 1776, promised one hundred acres to anyone who would sign up for three years of military service or until peace was declared. The assembly elected Archibald Bulloch president under this new government.[26]

The council wrote an address to Bulloch on April 30, describing the "Rules and Regulations" as "the only alternative of anarchy and misery, and by consequence the effect of dire necessity." It expressed the hope that he would enforce the "Rules and Regulations" in an unbiased way, a significant comment considering the dissension between conservatives and radicals in Georgia's government. The council also warned him of the consequences if he did not gain the support of the inhabitants, many of whom remained neutral: "For no Government can be said to be established, while any part of the community refuse submission to its authority." This address by the council suggests that it encouraged a coercive approach in dealing with the neutral and unaligned population of Georgia.

The government of Georgia looked to the Continental Congress for guidance. Georgia's government subordinated itself to the Continental Congress for several reasons. It was important to be in good standing with that governing body in order to receive supplies, money, and armed forces from it. In addition, the state government relied on the Continental Congress's authority to supplement its own. Samuel Adams described Georgia in April 1776: "I have not mentioned our little Sister Georgia; but I believe she is warmly engaged in the Cause as any of us, & will do as much as can be reasonably expected of her." Weak, young, and poor, Georgia was in need of protection and possibly not up to the tasks required of it.[27]

The council established government throughout the spring and summer of 1776. The council commissioned officers and regularized militia duty. Unsuccessful in forcing non-Associates out of Georgia in the past, the council pragmatically ordered them to pay fines. The courts of Georgia were literally put back in order in late May, when the chief justice, John Glen, requested the retrieval of the jury box from the town of Ebenezer and had it reinstalled in the courthouse in Savannah. The building needed to be vacated by the guard, cleaned, and repaired so that the court of general sessions could meet. The Council appointed constables, justices of the peace, and magistrates for the various parishes. The council found itself in a similar position to Governor Wright's in 1775: it lacked strong military support to defend Georgia from its many enemies.

The revolutionary council of safety inherited a legacy of planter indebtedness to merchants, little or no specie, more imports than exports, a modest currency emission, little or no tax collection, and a vast area of unsettled land in the public domain. The loss of external markets, the burden of preparing for war, the need to defend the East Florida border and the seacoast, as well as initiating three invasions into East Florida all weakened the financial resources of the state between 1776 and 1778.

In addition to increased expenditures required for defense, prices began to climb in 1776 and Georgia's currency depreciated. The Continental Congress did not assume even partial expense for the Georgia Continental troops until late in 1778, and this neglect contributed to the depreciation of state currency by forcing Georgia to continue to issue paper money to pay the troops. The state issued paper currency in the form of interest-bearing treasury notes and bills of credit until September 1778.[28]

Georgia, along with Delaware and New Jersey, issued less paper money than the rest of the states during the war. Georgia and Delaware were the only two states to offer security for the first emission of their state currency, and in Georgia's case this security came from the projected proceeds of the sale of confiscated loyalist estates.[29] Although this plan for providing security for the bills of credit failed, Georgia continued to issue paper currency in the form of bills of credit in an attempt to meet the fiscal needs of the state.

Because little or no taxes were being collected, paper currency was depreciating, and sparse proceeds were coming in from the eventual sale of confiscated loyalist estates, the land in the public domain would provide the only means by which the state could attempt to build a fighting force. Beginning in 1776 the state offered soldier land bounties of varying amounts and immigrant land bounties with the hope that people would either enlist in the army or come to Georgia as settlers and join the militia.[30]

Civil government attempted to gain as much authority as it could by responding to citizens seeking redress for a variety of property violations. Land and property left by royal officials and Crown supporters during the spring of 1776 created ample opportunity for property violations to occur. This happened because of the simultaneous activities of state militia requisitioning property, people leaving without paying their debts, and only a rough court system to maintain order. Citizens expected the civil government to uphold authority in these areas, and it had to do so to prove its legitimacy.

The council responded to a variety of situations. In early January it sent armed men to retrieve loyalist William Manson's one hundred indentured servants who had been kidnapped and enlisted into the rebel army of South Carolina.[31] The council directed officers of the militia to stop and secure the property of people leaving Georgia. It ordered the militia to return slaves belonging to the estate of Clement Martin, a member of the royal council who had died in debt, to the executors. It stopped the sale of former royal attorney general James Hume's estate because he was heavily indebted. The council ordered Captain William Bryan to return various items, including nails and hoes, that had been inappropriately taken from a plantation, presumably by the militia. A Mr. Hazard claimed that a Negro woman and two children, taken with a group of slaves near Wright's Fort for the use of the province, were his property, and the council decided that they could not be sold along with the other slaves. With the courts closed, Quinten Pooler took into his possession slaves from the late William McDaniel's considerable estate, under claim of deed; in response, the council eventually ordered the provost marshal to take Pooler into custody, locate the slaves, and turn them over to the executor.

The rebel government needed to consider the complex and important issues of property and allegiance. Of vital concern were the legal confiscation of abandoned loyalist property, the proper application of resultant monies to the maintenance of the provincial government, and the protection of remaining citizens' property. The civil government, however, took some time to organize itself on these issues.

Rebel officials dealt with eighteen prominent Crown supporters arrested and placed on parole at various times between January and the end of March 1776 with some ambiguity. These men included Governor Wright, Lieutenant Governor Graham, Chief Justice Stokes, nine royal council members (James McKay, James Edward Powell, John Hume, James Hume, James Robertson, Lewis Johnston, James Read, Henry Yonge, and Josiah Tatnall), two ship captains (Captain Wardell and Captain Hugh Inglis), three prominent planters (John Mullryne, Captain William McGillivray, and Lachlan McGillivray), and John Lightenstone, a royal official.[32] The rebel government would not initiate confiscation or banishment legislation until 1778.

Governor Wright sailed with the British warship *Scarborough* in April, eventually proceeding to England to take his leave of absence.[33] Wright did not enter into negotiations with the rebel government regarding his immense holdings. He reported in a letter to Lord Dartmouth on March 10, while still off Tybee Island, that a considerable part of his property had been seized and his slaves employed in pioneer work for the rebel army. The rebel government noted formally on May 1, 1776, that it began to use some of his slaves for road work. Wright, in anticipation of confiscation, had his lands appraised in early 1776, and lawyers acted on his behalf after his departure.[34]

Lieutenant Governor John Graham returned to Savannah from the *Scarborough*, and during early May the council of safety determined what to do with his extensive property. He was allowed to depart with his family, necessary servants and provisions for the voyage to England. Though he was initially required to leave his property behind for the security of his creditors, the council later ordered him to give a bond of £10,000 as security to the public and told him that he could return to Georgia. In a memorial to Lord George Germain, Graham noted that before he left Savannah the rebels had burned four hundred barrels of his rice and nearly destroyed his valuable house in town. He claimed to have left a fortune of £50,000 sterling, consisting chiefly of slaves, and expected that it would be disposed of by the rebels and lost to him.[35]

Chief Justice Anthony Stokes sought permission to leave Georgia with his family in early May. Through his correspondence with Edward Langworthy, secretary to the council of safety, he sought the definition of the word "servant" as used in the "Resolutions and Stipulation" issued by the council. This document outlined the terms under which he would be released from house arrest and allowed to remain in or depart the province. Eventually, President Bulloch issued a permit giving him permission "to take with him John Poulain, his overseer, and five negroes, his furniture, sundry trunks, containing his books and apparel; and likewise necessary provisions for his voyage." Stokes chartered a ship to England "with some other gentlemen" (possibly Graham and other council members James Edward Powell and James Read). Before sailing, Stokes received a complimentary letter from rebel council member John Wereat, who asked, as a personal favor, that Stokes deliver several letters for him once in England. Wereat wrote: "I am very sorry that this province is deprived of so upright a Magistrate as our late Chief Justice, and sincerely wish you health, peace, and freedom; for the last of which America is contending, and will contend at every hazard."[36]

John Lightenstone, commander of the scout boat, fled to the *Scarborough* after barely escaping arrest and remained on board once it sailed. He disembarked in Halifax and made his way to New York. His daughter Elizabeth Lightenstone Johnston eventually received his property when she petitioned the Board of Commissioners, sometime in 1778. She noted in her memoirs that "one or two cases besides mine show that they did give the property to wives and children whose husbands and fathers had been forced away as mine had."[37]

Various others left the colony. Council member James Edward Powell returned to England at some time, probably as soon as possible considering his lengthy service to the Crown, and accepted appointment as lieutenant governor of the Bahamas in 1781. Attorney General James Hume, Wright's nephew, left Georgia in early January 1776 for London; rebels occupied his house in Savannah during the Battle of the Rice Boats. Secretary John Hume, being a relation, may very well have fled Savannah with Wright and his children in February. James McKay, despite being a council member from the earliest days and having communicated with Wright while he was aboard the *Scarborough*, was neither arrested nor placed on any later confiscation lists by the rebel government. Perhaps he as well as council member James Read, a staunch supporter of Wright who was neither arrested nor included on any future confiscation lists, joined Wright on board the warship. John Mullryne and his cousins Lachlan and William McGillivray all left Georgia, although William McGillivray delayed in Charleston. Of this group of eight, all but Read, McKay, and Lachlan McGillivray would have their lands confiscated two years later.[38]

Various others remained in Georgia. Lewis Johnston returned to his house in Savannah while Josiah Tatnall and Henry Yonge lived on their plantations. James Robertson, whom Wright had appointed attorney general in January 1776, also lived quietly in the country. Although it is not known if Captain Wardell continued to transport goods in the area, Captain Hugh Inglis certainly did, for he participated in a partnership with rebel merchants James and Joseph Habersham and Joseph Clay into the spring of 1777. Tatnall, Yonge, and Robertson would have their lands confiscated two years later.[39]

The rebel government generally enforced oath taking but only occasionally forced individuals to leave the state during 1776. The assembly took years to pass legislation banishing former Georgians and confiscating their property. The population and geography combined to create an environment in which rebels, neutrals, loyalists, and the apathetic lived side by side.

In late June 1776 the council listed forty-three individuals as people whose going at large was dangerous to the liberties of America, no doubt in response to the imminent attack on Charleston's defenses by fifty British warships and accompanying soldiers. The July 1 council minutes indicate that two individuals listed, Dr. John J. Zubly, a Savannah minister, and Edward Telfair, a Savannah merchant, had been arrested and then improperly released by the chief justice, and the council ordered them taken into custody once again. Both later served as delegates to the Continental Congress. Responsive to military threat, the council eased up as soon as the British forces left the South Carolina coast in defeat. Most "dangerous" people on this list remained at liberty or went to the British colony in East Florida.[40] The government did not have the power to drive large numbers of suspected loyalists out of Georgia, let alone the capacity to determine who and where they were.

For those loyalists who remained in Georgia, the political environment became more complex. John Jamieson and James Robertson, both of whom were on the list, stayed in Georgia and took an oath of neutrality in June 1776. This oath, administered to many people about the time of the Declaration of Independence, required faithfulness to the cause of America; signers could take no part against the rebels or hide weapons. Robertson, who had refused to attend the rebel provincial congress in 1775 although elected a delegate and who later had been appointed attorney general by Wright in 1776, was jailed and took the oath of neutrality to obtain his release. He justified his actions by the fact that the oath did not contain an abjuration, or renunciation, of the king. John Jamieson, a merchant whose business had failed by 1775, took the oath of neutrality to save his property and life because he suffered poor health and could not travel. He had been a member of the royal assembly and published his opposition to rebel activities in the 1774 Georgia newspaper.[41] Acknowledgment of the government's authority to demand from them an oath of neutrality provided these men with a way to remain in Georgia without sacrificing their personal politics.

The government continued to pressure individuals to take oaths. On July 26, 1776, the council ordered that a test oath be given to all male inhabitants of Savannah. Many others not on the list of forty-three "dangerous" individuals were asked to take the oath of neutrality and support the Association. James Butler, considered a substantial man and one of the "best" planters in Georgia, lived along the Great Ogeechee River. He took oaths in 1776 after having been imprisoned and then let out on parole. Loyalist Georgians described him as having temporized at this time. Josiah Tatnall, member of the royal council and a planter and sawyer living near

Savannah, refused the Association and oath, although it was frequently tendered him. Basil Cowper, a merchant and planter, joined the rebel assembly and remained a member until Governor Wright left in January 1776. Loyalist Georgians described his actions as being motivated by a desire to protect his property, by principles of moderation, and by the idea that he could keep the port of Savannah open and prevent violence. He fled to Jamaica in 1776. James Johnston, the only printer in Georgia and publisher of the newspaper, stopped his press on October 7, 1776, and moved to the backcountry with his wife and children. He later went to St. Vincent in the West Indies, even though the state government offered to protect him and his property if he set up shop again. His older brother, royal council member Dr. Lewis Johnston, never took an oath although frequently asked to do so.[42] As was true of his brother James with his printing skills, Lewis's expertise as a physician no doubt made him valuable to the state and outweighed his loyalism. Generally, civil authorities pressured suspected loyalists to leave Georgia or to join the rebel cause by threatening imprisonment and by physical harassment.

In due course Georgia became one of the thirteen independent states, with representatives in the Continental Congress. The Continental Congress declared independence for Georgia, and the council of safety learned of this in a letter received from John Hancock on August 8, 1776. In response, the council ordered a public ceremony and militia officers "to assemble the people accordingly."[43] In late summer President Bulloch called elections for a new assembly, one that would have the opportunity to write a state constitution. That fall an alliance between low-country and backcountry radicals took control of the assembly away from the Christ Church conservatives. The radicals, led by Button Gwinnett, began to intrigue against the conservative officers in the military.[44] The presence of neutrals, loyalists, and rebels, many of whom were closely related to each other, as well as pervasive factionalism among state civil and military officials, combined to muddy the waters of allegiance.

The Case of George McIntosh

The case made against George McIntosh for exporting goods to East Florida reveals the complex social fabric of Georgia during 1776 and 1777. George McIntosh, the younger brother of General Lachlan McIntosh, was a member of the council of safety and a prosperous landowner along the

Sapelo River in St. Andrew Parish.[45] In June 1776 he purchased a small brigantine, the *Betsey and Nancy,* with his neighbors Robert Baillie, a professed tory, and Sir Patrick Houstoun. They planned to load the brig with rice and sail it to Surinam, returning with Dutch goods to sell in Georgia. William Panton, a well-known Georgia trader, came up the Sapelo River at this time. He had moved his headquarters to St. Augustine and established a trading post on the St. Johns River, acting as Thomas Brown's agent for handling British presents to the Creeks and Cherokees. Learning of the brig, Panton proposed that he become the fourth partner and handle the trading details by taking charge of the brig and cargo. They agreed. George McIntosh gave a bond of £1,000 sterling for the voyage, had the ship cleared for Surinam, and remained in Savannah to attend council of safety meetings. That he took William Panton, Robert Baillie, and Patrick Houstoun as partners suggests that McIntosh had no qualms about doing business with loyalists.[46]

In August he learned that the *Betsey and Nancy* had gone to St. Augustine to sell the rice instead of to Surinam and was now in the St. Johns River, loading for the next voyage out. His brother General Lachlan McIntosh had recently led a rebel force down to the St. Johns, and perhaps someone from this group spotted the brig and spread the word. Although for McIntosh, Houstoun, and Baillie shipping rice from St. Andrew Parish to East Florida was not breaking the parish law, the sighting of the brig in the St. Johns River proved unfortunate for the partners.[47]

The affidavit of James Johnston, master of the brig, described the voyage. Johnston stated that William Panton placed his brother Thomas Panton in charge of the brig. Thomas Panton ordered Johnston to sail from the Sapelo River to the St. Johns River to obtain a clearance from Florida as protection from the British men-of-war cruising the coast. Once the ship was in the St. Johns, sixteen armed men sent by the privateer George Osborne boarded it. They remained in control while Panton went to St. Augustine to obtain a new set of registration and clearance papers for the island of Tobago. During the five weeks this trip apparently took, the brig sat inactive, except for the unloading of ten barrels of rice for William Panton's Indian store. The brig set sail for Tobago on August 9, 1776, but eventually sailed to Jamaica by way of Antigua. There Johnston sold the rice and purchased sugar, rum, and coffee for the return trip to St. Augustine. The brig arrived on January 6, 1777.[48]

The St. Andrew Parish committee of safety placed no legal restraints upon residents for shipping rice to East Florida in return for goods, in direct disobedience of the Continental Association, which forbade all trade with British colonies and which the state government of Georgia supported and tried to enforce.[49] Possibly influenced by the brig's sighting in East Florida waters or the July 26 order by the council that all males in Savannah be given the test oath or taken into custody if they refused, the St. Andrew parochial committee published a list of loyalists in early September 1776. Acknowledging that they had shown greater leniency and indulgence to loyalists than any other parish from the hope that "those we once called our Friends, Neighbours, and nearest Connections" might come to support the state, the resolve stated that those listed would be taken into custody and made to take the test oath or give security to the president and council of Georgia. The list included Robert Baillie and Sir Patrick Houstoun but not George McIntosh.[50] He, unlike his partners, represented the parish on the council of safety, and this position may have protected him. His trading activities soon destroyed his reputation among rebels, however.

On January 8, 1777, John Hancock, the president of the Continental Congress, wrote a letter to Archibald Bulloch, president of Georgia, informing him that George McIntosh was guilty of treasonable conduct. The proof, which he enclosed, was a copy of an intercepted letter from Governor Patrick Tonyn of East Florida to Lord George Germain, written on July 19, 1776, while the brig *Betsey and Nancy* rode at anchor in the St. Johns River. In the letter Tonyn discussed his success in supplying East Florida with food from Georgia, through the help of William Panton. He also correctly surmised the danger to George McIntosh, should he be linked with East Florida trade in such a conspicuous way.[51]

In March 1777, Button Gwinnett, newly appointed president of the council upon Archibald Bulloch's death, acted independently of the council in ordering McIntosh arrested and placed in irons in Savannah's common jail. Gwinnett refused him bail, and McIntosh claimed he did not know the charges against him. Personal feelings may have been involved for George McIntosh had cast the only negative ballot against Gwinnett's succession to the council presidency, and his brother Lachlan had received command of the Georgia brigade over Gwinnett. The assembly and council divided over his imprisonment, and violent factionalism occurred throughout the state.

For whatever reason, regular legal procedures were not carried out. Although common acts of treason during the Revolutionary War included giving substantial aid to the king's forces, trading with the enemy was not regarded as a treasonable action. In addition, accused traitors had a copy of the indictment against them, as well as counsel. The indictment was carried out in a regular fashion, and the law required multiple witnesses to the treasonable actions of the accused.[52] George McIntosh's treatment was irregular, to say the least.

The council released George McIntosh the next day and helped to pay his bail of £20,000. Because the amount was considerable and most Georgians had little if any money, McIntosh clearly had the support of wealthy rebels. In Governor John Adam Treutlen's later account of the incident to John Hancock, who had recommended that George McIntosh be jailed, he noted that most of the council members were related to McIntosh.[53] Between leaving jail and appearing before the Continental Congress in October, McIntosh apparently lived as a refugee, "wandering from place to place through the woods like a vagabond and an outlaw." He claimed that Governor Treutlen ordered his plantation on the Sapelo River destroyed.[54]

The House of Assembly struck out on its own course regarding George McIntosh. His supporters published a pamphlet, which was countered by radical Lyman Hall's attempt to convince the house to arrest them. The house did not do so, according to John Wereat, because "there was too much truth in it to be controverted." Apparently emotions ran high, for Wereat commented: "I never observed so much rancor in the conduct of any man, as appeared visible in the Doctor [Lyman Hall] upon this Occasion." Nor would the house sanction the governor or the council in their conduct regarding George McIntosh, despite the latter's threat of resignation if the house did not support them. The house refused to issue a bill for the restitution of George McIntosh's estate.[55]

George McIntosh owned extensive property. In response to a suit of equity brought against Lachlan McIntosh by George's son John in 1793, Lachlan McIntosh described George's estate at the time of his death, probably in 1779. It consisted of approximately 13,080 acres of land contained in forty-five tracts in Liberty, Glynn, and Camden Counties and a town lot in Savannah. In addition to this real estate, George McIntosh owned a considerable number of slaves, who were appraised in 1784 at £3,762.[56] He probably had owned more slaves in 1777, before the British invasion of Georgia. If the radical faction plundered his estate in 1777, as McIntosh and his supporters claimed, it had attacked a significant landholder.

Defense of the Southern Frontier

In addition to Georgians attacking Georgians, the royal colony of East Florida threatened the state's already weak defenses with debilitating raids and plundering along the coast and southern border. Governor Patrick Tonyn invited loyalist refugees from other colonies to come to East Florida in 1775. Rich and poor alike took him up on his offer. Among them was Thomas Brown, formerly of Georgia, whom Tonyn ordered to raise a regiment of mounted Rangers. This regiment, composed generally of men of property from Georgia and South Carolina who were expert frontiersmen, worked well with the Indians. Their main purpose over the next six years would be to secure the East Florida border and feed the garrison at St. Augustine.[57] Although Georgia and Continental troops retaliated, their limited presence in combination with frontier conditions forced many settlers to take care of themselves in the face of a formidable enemy.

As the only British port between New York and Jamaica, St. Augustine harbored many ships, including British warships, small coasting vessels, and privateers. The British colony, with its garrison of soldiers and expanding settlements of refugee loyalists, depended on outside sources for food. The port offered trade opportunities for anyone who could bring in livestock, slaves, and produce. Heavily armed vessels captured rebel ships sailing the southern coast and brought their merchant and military cargoes to St. Augustine. Privateers made their way behind the islands and up the rivers of Georgia's plantation belt and plundered slaves and other tradable goods. Coasting vessels rendezvoused with individuals interested in selling rice or indigo or slaves for shipment to St. Augustine. A member of the Continental Congress noted the presence of these ships and their various activities along the southern coast in late 1778: "St. Augustine during the Continuance of this war (from Her Scituation) will constantly have it in her power, not only to distress our *poor frontier State Georgia,* by land, but to embarrass and Almust ruin the trade of the four Southern States by their Privateers."[58]

One troublesome pirate, George Osborne, received letters of marque from East Florida governor Patrick Tonyn in 1776, authorizing him to capture enemy merchant ships and cargo. He apparently both raided independently and served the British navy as needed, first in his ship *Governor Tonyn* and later in the sloop *Ranger.* Osborne, or as some called him "The famous privateer Man Captain Ozburn," terrorized the coastline between

East Florida and South Carolina until October 1781, when he was captured and killed, probably by Georgia militia.[59]

Another pirate, Captain Oldis, operated in the same coastal area as Osborne with an armed schooner and sixty men. The Georgia council learned of his presence on board Osborne's vessel at Cockspur Island in late August 1776. Inhabitants apparently sold hogs and sheep to the pirate ships, as well as to British men-of-war. McIntosh learned from a deserter that Oldis and his men were "Renegades from our own Province." Apparently Oldis, like Osborne, ranged up along the South Carolina coast, for McIntosh continued: "I am astonished the Armed of Carolina don't rout those Little petty pirates."[60]

Isolated planters and settlers along the Georgia coast found protecting their valuable slaves and produce from the depredations of sea raiders difficult. With little military support available, inhabitants relied on themselves and each other. James Baillie, manager of Henry Laurens's plantation near Darien, took precautions against Osborne by separating his slaves, moving the women and children to Cathead and the men to New Hope, where they slept outside. Lachlan McIntosh Jr., son of General McIntosh and an officer in the Continental army, led a detachment of twenty men from the Georgia Battalion to a post near Darien on the Altamaha River and wrote his father about Baillie's actions: "I fancy Osburn can do him no other Damage than Burning the Houses upon the Island, which I shall endeavour to hinder, if I have the least Warning of his being there."[61]

The islands at the mouth of the Savannah River afforded ships in support of the British cause a haven in which to replenish their supplies, make repairs, communicate with each other, and receive intelligence regarding the rebels. Well aware of this activity, the rebel government did its best to prevent contact with these ships. By the end of August the council proclaimed that "there will be no license or pass granted to any person whatsoever, for the purpose of going down to the said ships of war, except to those who are about to leave the Province never to return."

Georgia's navy consisted of five galleys, eight row galleys, and two sloops. In addition to attempting to protect coastal and island settlements, at least one state-owned ship made several voyages to the West Indies to obtain clothing and "necessaries" for the troops. Despite the small number of naval vessels, General Lachlan McIntosh tried to put them to use chasing the pirate Captain Oldis. He commented to President Archibald Bulloch that to protect the settlements and retaliate against the plunderers, the galleys and armed boats needed to be better positioned, "instead of Lying Idle in and about Sunbury."[62]

In addition to struggling to defend the coastline, Georgians attempted to maintain control of the border they shared with East Florida. This border, generally considered to be the St. Marys River before 1776, stretched south to the St. Johns River in August, only to pull north to the Altamaha River by October. The land in between these rivers provided pasture for enormous herds of cattle owned by both Georgians and East Floridians.[63] Because legal trade was no longer possible between the neighbors, military units from East Florida drove off the free-roaming cattle to provision the garrison at St. Augustine. Georgians retaliated by crossing the St. Marys and driving cattle back into Georgia. As these raids escalated, the border area became increasingly violent. Combined state and Continental troops invaded East Florida during August and September, and although this first attempt failed, General Lachlan McIntosh and his troops wrought significant devastation, and retaliation followed.[64]

McIntosh struggled to defend the Barrington area from the East Florida rangers, battling not only the enemy but apathy among the general population and his soldiers. McIntosh wrote that he "end[eavoured] to raise some Militia in Saint Andrew's parish to Little purpose," finding only ten men at Sunbury, thirty at St. Catherines Island, and about the same number on Ausabaw Island. When a large party from East Florida attacked Fort Barrington later in October, the post had only eighteen men to defend it; the neighboring militia units were unavailable because "they are [bus]y moving theire families." McIntosh ordered Major Leonard Marbury and his men to join him in the Barrington area, and Marbury responded that his officers would not leave their homes unguarded in the backcountry.[65] Men appeared unwilling to leave their families and property unprotected whether or not they were in the militia.

In mid-October McIntosh learned from a prisoner that the East Florida rangers expected Creek warriors to join them. He pulled what serviceable troops he had north behind the Altamaha River and declared to General Howe: "We have not above 200 well men of our Battalion and very few of the others to occupy the various posts necessary to be defended on our frontiers." Royal governor Tonyn of East Florida knew that "the Americans [were] a thousand times more in dread of the Savages than of any European Troops." McIntosh pragmatically decided that the Altamaha River now formed Georgia's border with East Florida.[66] After November those civilians caught between the rivers had three choices: leave their land and take what property and slaves they could and go north; leave their land and take what they could south; stay on their land and endure repeated plundering raids by both sides for many long years to come.

McIntosh sensed a mood of apathy among the citizens and soldiers of Georgia. He tried to defend the state with an army that did not want to fight and had little to fight with. Short of military stores, which McIntosh described as "Scant Indeed!," he sent General Howe an account of Georgia's ammunition and supplies in mid-November. All had been provided by the state, and he commented that "few as they are, by far too few for such [an] Exposed State as ours, every Inlet of which will [a]dmit Ships of almost any burthen." He knew Georgia was vulnerable to attack and believed one would come during the winter. He complained that "it [is] impossible to rouse our people to a Sense of it." [67]

Although civil authority, primarily in the form of the council of safety, and military authority, in the form of the Georgia Battalion, local militia units, and a small navy, were established and maintained in 1776, there was no cohesive civil or military leadership. Citizens and soldiers alike protected their homesteads first, and many ignored the Association and continued to trade with the enemy. Active rebels dickered over power while the infrastructure of the state began to collapse. Georgia remained the isolated and impoverished frontier it had always been but now with the addition of a complex political environment.

CHAPTER THREE

Things Fall Apart

Georgia State Government, 1777–1778

> We are in general Novices as to the knowledge of Gov-
> ernment, both Civil and military, and have little means of
> obtaining information among ourselves.—Joseph Clay, mer-
> chant and deputy paymaster general for the Continental
> Army in Georgia

Although uncertain of defense, the state proceeded to strengthen civil
authority through the creation of a constitution. Although adopted on
February 5, 1777, the document was delayed by a military crisis and did not
go into effect for four months. East Florida raiders came as far as the Altamaha River in late February, and the council of safety gave full executive
power to President Archibald Bulloch; Button Gwinnett became president
of the council of safety and commander in chief following Bulloch's sudden death.[1] Despite these emergencies, civil government made a successful
transition from president and council of safety to governor and House of
Assembly on May 8, when the assembly elected John Adam Treutlen governor. Georgia state government operated under this new constitution for
the next ten years.[2]

The constitution effectively silenced the voice of the conservative elite
and placed the government in the hands of essentially the entire adult white
male population of Georgia. The potential for this transformation had been
remarked upon by royal governor Wright in December 1775 when he wrote
to Lord Dartmouth that few men of ability or property had joined the rebel
committees. Loyalist Elizabeth Lightenstone Johnston commented in her
memoirs that in 1776 "everywhere the scum rose to the top."[3] According
to Joseph Clay, Savannah merchant and conservative rebel, "the principal

People" did not participate in state government because they were either "Tories" or fearful of consequences and had thus lost influence. He continued in his letter of July 2, 1777, to the firm of Bright and Pechin, that in his opinion, "Rule & Government has got into the Hands of those whose ability or situation in Life does not intitle them to it."[4]

With the sovereignty of the people as its primary principle, the constitution created a unicameral legislature, called the House of Assembly, and gave it all governing power. It renamed the parishes as counties and based their representation on the size of the electorate residing in each. The broad franchise included essentially all white male Protestants aged twenty-one years or older who had lived in Georgia for six months and had either ten pounds worth of possessions or followed the mechanic, or skilled craft, trades; representatives had to meet the property qualification of 250 acres or £250 worth of personal property. A man with a title of nobility had to give it up if he wanted to vote, be elected, or hold a post in the government; no civil or military officers, except justices of the peace and militia officers, could sit in the House of Assembly, nor could a clergyman. Members, unpaid under royal government, voted themselves wages, and annually appointed delegates to the Continental Congress.[5]

The governor, elected by the legislature for a one-year term, could act only upon the advice of the executive council, which the legislature elected from among its members. He could appoint militia officers and issue civil and military commissions, as well as fill vacancies occurring between elections, reprieve a criminal, or suspend the payment of a fine until the assembly met. The governor had to live where the assembly told him to, and he and all state officials could be called to account before the assembly.[6] Neither the governor nor the council had veto power over assembly acts. The governor, designated commander in chief by the constitution, held a potentially powerful position only during time of war.

Judicial power rested in the hands of individual counties, and juries possessed unusual latitude to define the law. Annually, the legislature appointed one chief justice for the state and four assistant justices for each county. Each county had a superior court of final jurisdiction which the chief justice attended on circuit, and this promoted some uniformity in the interpretation of the law. But because there was no state supreme court until 1845, each county interpreted the law as it chose. Judgments could be stayed until the first Monday of March, and court costs could not exceed three pounds, nor could cases remain on the docket for more than two sessions. While the governor had no judicial power, the assembly had the power to pass final judgment on pardons and the remission of fines.[7]

Joseph Clay observed that Georgians took state offices for economic gain alone. Although he was not a member, he described the legislature in a letter to Henry Laurens on October 16, 1777: "We chiefly meet to carve out some way of Fleecing the State, accomplish it in the best manner we can and then break up[,] go home and live on the spoils of our Country." Urged to accept the post of deputy paymaster by Laurens, now a delegate to the Continental Congress from South Carolina, Clay reluctantly accepted this paid position in Georgia's government out of concern that the position might go instead to an individual whose "levelling Principles and Conduct" made him as much an enemy to the state as the British. Writing to Brigadier General Robert Howe on October 15, 1777, regarding his duties, Clay expressed the hope that Georgia's reputation with the other states would improve, explaining that for the present, "We are in general Novices as to the knowledge of Government, both Civil and military, and have little means of obtaining information among ourselves."

Financial Instability

The state had dire financial problems, in part because its paper money steadily depreciated. Joseph Clay wrote to a business acquaintance, Josiah Smith, on May 15, 1777, that Georgia's depreciating currency was a result of large emissions "to pay the several Troops in this State" on the Continental payroll. In August Governor Treutlen wrote to the president of the Continental Congress, John Hancock, stating that Georgia had no Continental currency. To repay several officers who had spent large sums of their own money to recruit soldiers, the governor requested $20,000 in Continental currency, which he did not receive.[8]

Soldiers did not want to take the state money, preferring the scarce Continental currency, and merchants and farmers grew less willing to accept Georgia money as payment for goods and services the army required. To obtain what they needed, the government and military began to requisition goods and services in 1777. Trying to keep approximately three or four hundred men mounted and protecting the borders of Georgia proved very difficult for Continental commander Colonel Lachlan McIntosh, not only because horses were hard to come by and very expensive but because on twelve dollars a month in 1777, no soldier could afford either to purchase or maintain one.[9] As a result of Georgia's poor buying power, enlistments remained low and desertion and the threat of mutiny seriously hampered the state's ability to defend itself.

During 1778 the state loaned bills of credit to the Continental army in Georgia while at the same time attempting to meet its monetary obligations to the Continental Congress by passing tax legislation. The subsequent British reoccupation and the disappearance of rebel government until mid-1781 no doubt prevented all but the initial collection of this tax.[10] Joseph Clay blamed the continued currency depreciation and rising prices on the large emissions of bills of credit as well as lack of trade. He pointed a finger at "Jews and others worse than Jews" who raised prices and accused them of doing more harm than the British army.[11]

The inability of the Continental Congress to provide monetary support for the troops in a timely way undermined its reputation among the soldiers and civilians in Georgia. Soldiers, unpaid for eight to nine months, deserted or threatened mutiny. Civilians, approached by the military for goods, did not want to accept payment in Georgia script. Officers such as Joseph Clay felt their reputation as trustworthy gentlemen was in danger of being destroyed through nonpayment of debt accrued by the army under their name. They went to great lengths to borrow money from friends and acquaintances to keep the army's credit, and hence their own, sound. Although the Continental Congress eventually sent money, it arrived too late, just before the British reoccupied the state.[12]

The state might not have sufficient money, but it did have land. It opened a land office on June 7, 1777, and each county set up a committee to inquire into the confiscation of royalist property. Unlike the royal council, the state land office did not give preferential treatment to the landed elite, and some absentee landholders feared that the legislature would sell all of the confiscated and absentee estates, regardless of who owned them.[13]

Henry Laurens, one such absentee landholder, possessed extensive lands in Georgia and held a firm commitment to champion the state. He wrote to John Wereat, a Savannah merchant, conservative republican, and Continental prize agent, on August 30, 1777, complaining of the "evil consequences" that must follow the opening of the land office. He then wrote to Joseph Clay expressing his fears that his property in Georgia would be confiscated under this new law and due process ignored. As a member of the Continental Congress, Laurens had abandoned these lands only because his property, including a considerable number of slaves, had been attacked by plunderers and the state of Georgia could not provide him with any protection. He asked Clay to intervene and protect his property from confiscation.[14]

Joseph Clay responded to Laurens on October 16, 1777, that the plan to sell the confiscated and absentee estates had been formally withdrawn from the legislature. Although many had already selected their lands, the legislation died because of "the numberless Acts of Injustice" potentially committed by selling what belonged to "Widows, Orphans, Minors, Friends" and those away in the army. The land-hungry legislators acknowledged the necessity of due process, if only at the last minute.

On a more practical note, the state attempted to attract soldiers and settlers to the virgin public domain land in Wilkes County through land bounties and headright land grants, respectively. Anxious to settle the backcountry and establish militia units there, early in June 1777 and again in March 1778 the state offered settlers from other states land bounties if they served in the militia. Families received headright land grants through measures passed in June and September 1777 and January 1780. The minimum headright was two hundred acres, doubling the amount previously allotted, with an additional fifty acres for each family member and up to ten slaves. The headright limited the amount of land the owner of more than ten slaves could receive, giving the advantage to small and subsistence farmers for the first time. Most of those immigrating to Georgia during the war came from North Carolina and Virginia; no doubt the poor families clung to their two hundred acres of backcountry land as tenaciously as they could while political pressures and violence rose and fell around them.[15]

Since the earliest days, the private debt structure in Georgia had rested primarily on land. As a merchant, Joseph Clay involved himself with private debt, his own as well as others'. With the state bills of credit depreciating and the uncertainty that war brought making repayment unpredictable (and, in the case of British debts, impossible), Clay recommended that debts held by his merchant house be invested in land. There was some urgency in this recommendation, for in March 1778 the Georgia Assembly nearly passed a law requiring people holding money belonging to British merchants or loyalists to pay it into the state treasury. Clay wrote to Ralph Izard Jr. on March 12, 1778, of the opportunity to discharge debts through the purchase of land. This had to be done in a timely manner, however, for Clay anticipated an attack on Georgia, which would "be the means of depriving us and many who are indebted to us of the means of paying any thing to those we or they are indebted to."[16] Erasing the debt on paper by investing in land helped all parties for it offered something for the debt on paper and eliminated responsibility for carrying the debt through uncertain times.

Political Instability

Lack of money did not pull civilian and military authorities together, unfortunately. Once appointed president in February 1777, Button Gwinnett set upon a path of personal aggrandizement that further weakened an already factionalized leadership. On March 4, the council gave him the authority to attack St. Augustine with Georgia militia. Gwinnett arrested George McIntosh for treason on March 14, and members of the council helped to pay his bail. George McIntosh appeared before the Continental Congress, which released him because of insufficient evidence in early October. Gwinnett then suggested to General Howe that George McIntosh's brother Colonel Lachlan McIntosh be transferred out of state. Although originally friends, Gwinnett and McIntosh became rivals for positions of military authority as well as members of opposing political factions. Their rivalry reflected the factionalism in politics that hindered the development of state government. Gwinnett and his followers next began publicly to equate conservative faction members with tories and Gwinnett targeted General Howe as an enemy for rejecting his plan to invade East Florida.[17]

In a letter to John Hancock on March 28, 1777, Gwinnett explained that "Tory Friends in this State" had supplied the garrison at St. Augustine with rice, corn, and cattle, thus enabling the British to remain in East Florida. He wanted to stop the debilitating incursions into Georgia and so launched the second East Florida expedition between March and June. It was ill-equipped, short of men, and poorly led and failed to curb the depredations. President Gwinnett and Colonel Lachlan McIntosh refused to cooperate with each other and the council recalled them to Savannah. After Gwinnett died on May 19 from wounds suffered in a duel with McIntosh, the radical faction, calling itself the Liberty Society, set about to remove Lachlan McIntosh from command of the Continental forces in Georgia.[18]

A total of 574 men eventually signed a circular letter supporting the general's removal. According to John Wereat, radical leaders such as Lyman Hall, Joseph Wood, Governor Treutlen, and Colonel George Wells used coercion to obtain many of the signatures.[19] George Walton, one of Georgia's delegates to the Continental Congress, had anticipated this response to Gwinnett's death. In a letter to George Washington he stated that he had feared Gwinnett's followers would "again blow up the embers of party and dissention, and disturb the harmony and vigour of the Civil and military authorities." Walton's support of Lachlan McIntosh helped convince George Washington to order him to headquarters for service in the North, where he served at Valley Forge and later commanded the Western Department.[20]

Subversive activities disturbed civil order in Savannah during the spring and summer. During the period of time George McIntosh eluded capture, civil authorities quarreled over his treatment and an assassination attempt was made against William Farrel, officer of the guard. It failed, and the council offered a reward of one hundred pounds Georgia currency to anyone who could locate the offenders. Daily rioting and disturbances required Governor Treutlen, in mid-July, to issue a proclamation prohibiting those activities. He called the assembly into an emergency session and on August 19 urged the members to rid the state of active loyalists. He warned that should internal enemies remain in Georgia, "all your outward operations will prove ineffectual, [and] you will remain a weak and feeble body, because of those Vermin in your Bowels."

He elaborated on the state's dire situation. In strong, simple language he listed the problems: there was no money to pay the soldiers or maintain the government; the orders and resolves of the assembly were held in contempt; a circuit court law was needed and the functions of the probate office had to be regularized; and the state was not only surrounded by enemies but infested with tories and tory sympathizers. He concluded by urging the legislature to act.

Treutlen, as governor under the new constitution, had limited power to initiate action. The council had limited power as well, and both branches of the executive were subservient to the House of Assembly. Twice, however, the council gave Treutlen authority to assume control over it during times of imminent danger. In this way Treutlen gained considerably more power than the house intended the governor to have during normal conditions. Under the constitution the governor had the right to assume the authority of commander in chief, and during this time in Georgia conditions demanded a strong executive.

John Wereat wrote to George Walton at the end of August that he began "to tremble for the fait that awaits this devoted Country." Radicals gave anyone not in support of their party the "hatefull name of Torey and to hold him up to the resentment of the people, as an Enemy to his Country." Wereat feared Georgia could not exist as a state for more than a year without the "immediate interposition of Congress." Because of "being oppressed, and plundered of their little means of subsistance," people from the southern part of Georgia moved to East Florida or to South Carolina. He thought that "we shall in a short time be joined to Carolina or Florida, God avert the latter the former would be infinitely preferable to our present Sitution, when neither Liberty, or property are secure."[21]

As a conservative rebel, Wereat felt growing concern for the stability of government. A union with South Carolina had been proposed by that state, and William Henry Drayton and John Smith presented the proposition to the Georgia Assembly in January 1777. Drayton and subsequent letters and petitions he had circulated in Georgia caused enough of a furor by July for the assembly to offer a £100 reward for his capture or that of anyone working for him. Although Drayton stayed out of Georgia and avoided arrest, he claimed he had support among some of the more socially prominent citizens.[22]

However inexperienced the state government officials and representatives might be and however factionalized their leadership, settlers in distress turned to them for help in protecting their land. The council received reports of depredations in Effingham County perpetrated by disaffected individuals, Indians, and the Florida Scout. These depredations occurred along the Ogeechee River on the western frontier, near enough to Savannah for residents to fear that their slaves and horses would be stolen. The council sent available militia troops and recommended that the commander in chief of the Continental troops garrison forts along the southern and western frontiers.

Governor Treutlen announced the appointment of Colonel Samuel Elbert as commander of the Continental troops stationed or sent to the westward in late August 1777 "to punish those faithless and cruel savages and to protect our back inhabitants against the excursive and rambling enemy." In late August the East Florida Scout and their Seminole allies had operated along the Ogeechee River and ridden through Augusta and gone within five miles of Savannah. Elbert visited various forts in the Ogeechee and Little River areas to the south and north of Wrightsborough in September. He reported no signs of Indians at that time, but the settlement forts were "crowded with the inhabitants."[23]

Although he found no Indians, Elbert was disappointed in the condition of the troops. He reported many men ill, those healthy enough for duty spread out among the forts and unable to join forces quickly in case of an attack, and at least twenty desertions since his arrival in the area earlier in the month. He observed that the Light Horse officers had little authority over their men and did not severely punish those caught deserting. Among the five forts Elbert visited in 1777, Creek Indians attacked Robert Carr's Fort in 1778 and 1779, Indians destroyed Zachariah Phillips's Fort in 1780, and Taitt's Indians destroyed Well's Fort in 1779 and attacked Benjamin Fulsam's Fort in 1778 and destroyed it in 1779.[24] These forts offered little protection to the inhabitants against a serious Indian attack and there was insufficient military force to maintain them.

The Florida Rangers or Scout as well as roving bands of banditti continually aggravated property holders throughout Georgia. Joseph Clay wrote to Henry Laurens on September 29, 1777, stating that "for though we have had generally for some Months past from 10 to 1200 Men on the Continental Establishment besides what we have on the Pay of the State, not the smallest Check has ever been given to these People." It was not for lack of trying, however. Colonel Elbert recommended a defensive posture because "we have too many Secret Enemies amongst us who Keep up a regular correspondence with our Florida Neighbors." Out on a scouting mission with troops up the St. Marys River to keep "those Rascals out of Georgia," Elbert hoped not only to prevent them from getting food supplies but to keep them so busy defending themselves that they could not care for their crops of corn and indigo. He suggested that the assembly provide assistance in helping cattle owners remove their stock from below the Altamaha River. In mid-July, troops covered the cattle drivers as they brought approximately a thousand head of cattle up from the Satilla River area and north across the Altamaha.[25] Despite these efforts, however, the rangers and banditti continued to plunder well up into Georgia between the Canoochee and Ogeechee Rivers.

In response to the continued depredations along the frontiers of Georgia as well as closer to Savannah, on September 16, 1777, the General Assembly adopted a resolution entitled "An Act for the Expulsion of the Internal Enemies of This State." The legislature wanted Georgians aiding and abetting Indians and Florida banditti expelled.

Georgia had been slow to enact legislation of this sort. The political climate of the state made the issue of loyalty to either the conservative or liberal whig factions of vital concern. This highly charged environment may have allowed the greater issue of loyalty to either England or the United States to slip into the background. Additionally, the complex family relationships among the well-established landholders probably created a tolerance for quiet loyalism. Elite rebels were reluctant to enact laws that would strip their former social equals, if not their relatives and friends, of their property, despite the fact that they were loyalists. Richard Howley offered General Horatio Gates insights into Georgia's political situation in 1777. Referring to the highly democratic constitution created by the radical faction in opposition to the elite faction formerly in control of Georgia government, he wrote: "The form [of radical government] gave umbrage to Some persons in the State, and the Decisive laws they Enacted against the friends of the king of Great Britain, who were Inhabitants, and compelled to Retire, hurt their feelings."[26] Not only did this law break up the old elite planter community, but it indirectly threatened them with the possibility that their land might be taken as well. Property was possibly a more concrete social bond than loyalty for many Georgians.

Each county appointed a committee of twelve to meet on the first and third Tuesday of every month, or more often if necessary, to enforce the expulsion act. They had the authority to send for people and papers. The individual summoned by the county committee had to be a white male twenty-one years or older. If he could appear before the committee with two or more undoubted friends to the American cause to vouch for him, and if the committee found his friends acceptable, he next took an oath. The oath promised allegiance to Georgia and the renouncing of allegiance to King George III; it entitled him to all of the privileges, protection, and immunities of the state. Inability to comply with these requirements resulted in the individual leaving Georgia within forty days, under penalty of death, and the state confiscated half of his property under the supervision of commissioners. Failure to appear when summoned by the committee resulted in the individual's expulsion from the state and the forfeiture of all his property. The expulsion act contained a sentence of execution upon conviction for those caught returning to Georgia without permission or found fighting against the states.[27]

This process created a variety of paperwork: summons to the committee, the oath itself, the order declaring that the individual summoned to say the oath had refused to do so and was ordered out of the country, permits to remain in Georgia longer than at first specified by the committee, and, in a short-lived gesture of generosity on the part of the republican government, the right to leave a power of attorney to sell half of the property with the other to remain on pledge.[28] Prudent, well-organized loyalists petitioning the Royal Commission after the war offered the act itself, along with the above-mentioned paperwork, as evidence of their losses and services.

The Reverend John Joachim Zubly, a learned Swiss minister of the Independent Meeting House and the German Calvinistic congregations in Savannah, fell out of favor with the state government when he refused to support independence while a delegate to the Continental Congress. He was arrested on July 1, 1776, when named as one dangerous to the liberties of America but immediately released by Chief Justice John Glen. After being named in the expulsion act over a year later, he came before the Chatham County Grand Jury in October 1777. Zubly published a broadside on October 8 in which he described his opinion of the proceedings.

He found the establishment of the Chatham County committee and the requirement to swear an oath alarming and unconstitutional. Vested with discretionary powers, the committee deprived men of their liberty and property without due course of the law: "A power to tender an oath to deprive a man of half his estate, and banish him from every endearing connection, is lodged in seven men, without appeal, without check, without challenge." The charge brought against Zubly, that of not signing the Association before going as a representative to the Continental Congress, he sarcastically called "great and mighty." He objected to "swearing myself a subject, till the Assembly had reconsidered whether we ought to be subjects or freemen." He found the requirement that two people vouch for the individual called before the committee insulting and saw no reason to swear allegiance to other states when they were not bound by oath to Georgia. Zubly refused to swear that he had never received protection from the king because he had. Instead, he offered to swear to do his duty as a good and faithful freeman, not to give intelligence to or take up arms to assist British troops, and to swear he had not received letters of protection since the war. He ended the broadside by stating his interest in knowing upon what principle he, a man trusted for his veracity and accused of no crime, had been condemned as an internal enemy of Georgia. Banished and half of his estate confiscated, Zubly went to South Carolina.[29]

As county committees administered oaths to suspected loyalists over the next year, numerous loyalists found the oath of allegiance to the American cause and the abjuration, or renouncement, of allegiance to George III impossible to make. Peter Dean arrived from England in 1774 and had supported royal government in Georgia until Governor Wright left, then hid in the countryside. He would not swear the oath when brought before a committee. Banished in October 1777, he sold half of his property, and the other half was held as security that he would not bear arms against the state. He went to the West Indies. James Robertson had taken the oath of neutrality in 1776 but would not swear the oath when called upon to do so in October 1777. Ordered to leave Georgia within forty days, he sailed for the Bahamas with a permit from the whig governor dated December 10, 1777, and eventually went to St. Augustine in 1778. Josiah Tatnall, who had not sworn any previous oaths, refused this one as well. When summoned before the committee, "he told them that he despis'd them and their Oath." He received permission to take longer than the original sixty days given him to leave Georgia, and in December 1777 he sailed to the Bahamas. His time of travel was singularly unfortunate, for an English privateer seized Tatnall's ship en route to the Bahamas. Later, Count D'Estaing's fleet captured his ship traveling from the Bahamas to England and escorted it to Philadelphia. Tatnall eventually reached England in December 1778. These individuals risked the uncertainty of sea travel as well as considerable financial loss to remain loyal to the king. Zubly noted in his broadside that the state made no provision for transporting loyalists out of Georgia who did not have the means to pay for it themselves, implying that the state expelled only loyalists of certain means.[30]

Other suspected loyalists besides John Zubly remained closer to home. John Jamieson had taken the oath of neutrality in 1776 but would not swear to the oath of allegiance and abjuration in 1778. In ill health, as he had been two years before, he traveled only as far as South Carolina after leaving Georgia. There he took the South Carolina oath so he could collect his debts and slaves. Later, he petitioned the Georgia council without success to return for a short time to settle his private concerns in the state. Another loyalist, Colonel John Philips of South Carolina, refused this oath in the spring of 1778. Imprisoned in Augusta and condemned to hang in December 1778, he waited fifteen days "with the Gallows before the Window." That month British forces retook Savannah and part of Georgia, and Philips lived because rebels feared British retaliation for his death.[31]

Others had no trouble taking this oath. John Henderson apparently took every oath offered him and gave a bond for £15,000 that he would take no active part against Americans. He felt that taking the oath was of much less consequence than taking part with the rebels, and he did not consider the oaths as lawful for they were tendered to him by people in rebellion. Basil Cowper, former member of the rebel congress who fled in 1776, came back from the West Indies in 1777, took the oath in 1778, and was placed on parole.[32] These men worked the political system, meeting the requirements of civil authorities so they could remain in or return to Georgia.

The council received reports on February 9, 1778, regarding contempt of this order. The Chatham County committee reported that many of those required to leave the state had not done so. Unable to depend on oceangoing vessels to transport them from Georgia within the appropriate time period, those who did obey the order had to make their way to East Florida. Colonel Samuel Elbert noted that this movement southward enabled royal governor Tonyn to obtain current information on Georgia from loyalists forced into exile.[33] Regardless, the council ordered the county sheriff to obtain a list of the offenders, arrest them, and send them out of Georgia. The act could not be efficiently carried out to rid the state of loyalists and at the same time prevent the spread of military information into East Florida.

Nearly seven thousand refugees from Georgia and South Carolina ended up in East Florida as a result of the expulsion laws in each state. Although some arrived with the means to build homes and establish plantations, others remained dependent on public funds until they could find employment or join a military unit. Brigadier General Augustine Prevost, in East Florida, asked for an increase in the budget to meet the needs of these "unfortunate refugees from the neighboring colonies."[34] The expulsion act failed to remove all loyalists from Georgia because the population did not support it.

Civilian and military authorities found that, despite hostility, they had to cooperate in order to combat the terrorist incidents in Savannah. In late September 1777, the council discovered that the militia and the Continental forces on duty in Savannah did not know each others' parole or countersign. Fearful that this might cause confusion, if not death, they asked Continental general Lachlan McIntosh to come to them to discuss the matter, which he refused to do. By December both civilians and military personnel accused each other of aggressive behavior. Colonel Elbert, McIntosh's replacement, established a curfew for the military in Savannah at this time.[35] Cooperation became imperative as the Florida banditti raided closer to Savannah during 1778.

In October and again in December, Colonel Elbert directed his attention to breaking up groups from East Florida that were plundering cattle high up the Canoochee River. The inhabitants of this area were believed to be supportive of the Florida Scout, if not related to them. Elbert cautioned his expedition: "March all night, and then secrete yourself in the day, or they will get intelligence."[36] In August 1778 the council ordered the nearby area along the Ogeechee River cleared of the small settlements established by the wives of the Florida Scout; they not only provided their husbands with a safe haven in the midst of enemy territory, but they gathered and passed along information regarding rebel activities.

By December 1777 raiders had pushed the border between East Florida and Georgia from the Altamaha north to the Ogeechee and threatened to push it even farther north. Elbert suggested to General Howe on December 5 that South Carolina soldiers help Georgia guard against the "thieves of Florida" crossing the Savannah River, for it "would require an army of ten thousand men" to guard all of its fording places.[37]

Isolation and a Weak Defense, 1778

During February 1778 Savannah entertained two visitors, General Howe, in command of the Southern Department, and Ebenezer Hazard, a northerner from Philadelphia in charge of establishing a national postal service in the South. (He later became postmaster general of the United States.) Each formed impressions of the state's isolation and its dangerous situation as a result of military unpreparedness. In Savannah during an assembly session, they met at dinner on February 19, 1778.[38]

Hazard had traveled to Savannah from Purrysburg, South Carolina, by boat, and lodged at Mrs. Minis's. He described the capital as "a small Town, situated on the Top of a Sand-Hill; the Sand is so deep as greatly to incommode and fatigue a Person in walking." The few good houses were constructed "mostly of wood and much scattered." Over the next few days he attended to business, appointing William Hornby postmaster at Savannah and conferring with a committee from the assembly. He found the company of the men at the "'smoking Club'" to be agreeable, willing to drink moderately and converse on any subject.

Hazard wrote some strong comments in his journal after he left Savannah. He expressed his dislike for the effects of slavery on the personalities of slave owners, or "country gentlemen," in the South, saying that, "accustomed to tyrannize from their Infancy, they carry with them a Disposition to treat all Man-kind in the same Manner they have been used to treat their Negroes."[39] He added that the three states of North and South Carolina and Georgia were so similar as to be considered the same in customs, manners, geography, and produce. Clearly they were different from the North, and Georgia, as the furthest south and the frontier state, was the most isolated of all from the rest of the country.

While in Savannah, General Howe addressed the assembly and the governor about Georgia's weak defensive posture. He expressed his concern for a variety of issues, including the lack of good health among the soldiers. In early February Howe urged Governor Houstoun to expedite the building of a barracks in Savannah, as well as a hospital. With a quarter of the soldiers in Georgia ill, he believed that "the want of proper Barracks, Hospitals, Clothes, Blankets and Medicines must undoubtedly in a great measure ocasion it, as no better Winter country than this can possibly be." Appealing to the politicians' humanity, he urged them to offer "every aid and assistance that either they or you can give me to alleviate or remove the inconveniencies and distresses under which the Soldiers labor." The government responded by erecting brick barracks in Savannah.[40]

Lack of supplies and frontier posts also alarmed General Howe, who asked the Georgia Assembly to procure enough powder and lead to meet the needs of the army and to repair its cannon. Georgia lacked sheets of tin, rope, cordage, carts, carriages, matches, and other articles necessary to ignite armaments. The state had no furnace to cast shot and no traveling forges to supply the artillery with balls. Georgia also needed iron, steel, and all sorts of tools, particularly to build trenches. Howe suggested building frontier posts, and he offered to locate and supervise their construction.[41]

Howe also blasted the practice of enlisting minute battalions and allowing the men to decide whether they wished to fight and where. These unreliable battalions sapped the state of needed money and rations. Howe believed them "Soldiers only from Courtesy" who burdened the state with expense without adding to its strength. In addition, men who might otherwise enroll in the regular battalions would not do so because they could enlist in these minute battalions and stay in their local area, anxious as they were to protect their families and property from the Florida Scout and the Indians.[42] Howe's unflattering yet pragmatic review of Georgia's defenses may have contributed to the already unfavorable opinion many held of him.

In response to continuing depredations in the vicinity of the capital, civil authority began to regulate the presence of strangers. A plan formulated by the council on February 23, 1778, involved both civil and military authorities in policing the town of Savannah and the surrounding area because of "frequent robberies and other enormities committed . . . by persons in disguise who are suspected of being or acting in concert with the Florida Scout." Regulations stipulated that strangers report immediately upon their arrival in town to either the governor or the military. A "Town Major" determined the daily countersign and sent it to the civil and military authorities and examined any persons "not known as a reputable Inhabitant of the State" brought to him by a constable. Two members from a group of twenty "respectable inhabitants" of Savannah rotated duty each night between nine o'clock and daybreak, interviewing and detaining or discharging individuals who, not knowing the countersign, had been brought to them by "Centinels" patrolling the town and environs.

Three weeks later, the plan encompassed all of Georgia by incorporating "Well affected Inhabitants of this State" to apprehend and detain strangers whose business was either not known or approved of or who did not have a pass from either the governor or their own state. County magistrates determined if the individual should be released or sent to the governor. Additional changes to the plan in Savannah involved the role of the "Town Major." He no longer assigned but now received the daily countersign from the governor or other commander in chief and appointed new members to the group of twenty men rotating night duty. The government no doubt set up this plan to monitor the presence of strangers in response to groups of South Carolina loyalists traveling through Georgia at this time. Despite curfews, countersigns, and citizen arrests, the state failed to monitor the movement of people within its borders.

The state continued to demand the loyalty of its citizens. The assembly passed a resolve on March 1, 1778, requiring all white male inhabitants of the state aged sixteen years and older to take the oath of abjuration if they had not already done so and had the *Georgia Gazette* publish the names of the five magistrates for each county who would take the oaths. This call for more oath taking indicates that numbers of men had neither taken it previously nor been compelled to do so. Civil authority attempted to strengthen its hold over the population during the spring of 1778.

On March 1, 1778, the assembly issued an act of attainder to bolster depreciating state notes by obtaining hard cash.[43] This act set up a complex mechanism whereby the state could obtain collateral through confiscation of the real and personal property of 117 individuals. Attainted of high treason, these people, including high-ranking royal officials such as Governor Wright, Lieutenant Governor Graham, and Chief Justice Stokes, would suffer death if they returned to the state or took up arms against the rebel states.

Lesser folk were named as well, and ten individuals who filed claims listed in *The Royal Commission on American Loyalists* can be traced. Of these, George Barry, John Lightenstone, John Murray, and Alexander Wylly left Georgia in 1776 without taking any oaths. Peter Dean, John Simpson, and Josiah Tatnall remained in Georgia until 1777 and refused all oaths. John Jamieson and James Robertson remained and took the neutrality oath in 1776 but refused to take the oath of allegiance and abjuration in 1777, and both were gone by 1778. Basil Cowper left Georgia in 1776, returned in 1778, and left again in 1779. James Johnston, listed on the bill of attainder in 1778, unlike those above, did not file a loyalist claim after the war but remained in Georgia. All of these men, with the exception of George Barry, returned to Georgia when it was retaken by the British and actively defended Savannah during the siege or were a part of the royal government under Wright.

The case of John Murray sheds light on the state government's treatment of loyalists during 1778. He had applied for and received permission to leave Georgia in May 1776, and while he was in England the state attainted his property. Sometime in the late summer of 1778 he arrived in Charleston, South Carolina, and got a permit to enter Georgia. While there, he petitioned the government to be taken off the list of attainder and be allowed to live on his land. He subsequently misplaced this petition to the rebel Georgia governor and so could not present it as evidence before the Royal Commission. He claimed that it stated only that he had done nothing against the rebels. The council reviewed his petition on August 31 and determined that not only could it not reverse the attainder but that Murray broke the law by returning to Georgia. He asked the Georgia government to put him on trial, and "they refused to try him and a Mob carried him off and set him down on the Carolina side of the river."[44] This action indicates that the government was serious about keeping attainted loyalists out of Georgia. Perhaps he was not executed because he had acknowledged the government's authority by requesting a permit to leave and later enter Georgia and present his case.

The assembly established boards of commissioners in each county to examine the legal claims against these attainted estates, determine the property already removed from them by those who felt it their legal right to do so, and determine if anyone, such as a child or wife or relative of the attainted individual, had the right to claim the estate. After taking an inventory, the commissioners were to sell the property; all money accrued would go to the government. The sale of slaves took particular care: not more than twenty-five slaves over the age of fifteen could be purchased by one buyer and they could not be removed from the state. No one from out of state who did not immediately settle in Georgia could participate. Until the sale took place, all the money the estate earned through produce and rent went to the government.

Georgia lagged behind most of the states in enacting legislation against royalist property holders. The social revolution between the poor and the elite regarding land acquisition had created a climate of insecurity. Opposition to the act of attainder was general, and citizens did not cooperate with the commissioners, many of whom resigned or were inactive. Some commissioners, noted Joseph Clay, "began as is generally said to Act as if the Estates had been confiscated for their sole benefit instead of the States."[45] The slowness, or reluctance, to legislate and the subsequent ineffectiveness of the act to raise cash through the sale of confiscated property was in large part caused by the government's failure to function well enough for the citizens to accept its authority. Part of this dysfunction had to do with the depreciating Georgia currency: little money existed to pay anyone for anything. Rents and profits from those confiscated estates under cultivation were collected in kind, and the military requisitioned property from the estates as needed.[46]

Lack of cooperation between military and civil authorities also contributed to the dysfunction of government and is exemplified in the third attempt to invade East Florida. The attempt was undertaken between April and July, and, according to Colonel William Few, the troops met defeat "not by the sword of the enemy, but by the dissension of the Governor [John Houstoun] and General [Robert Howe]." Houstoun and Colonel Andrew Williamson of the Carolina militia did not recognize Howe, commander of the Southern Military Department, as their superior officer. Commodore Oliver Bowen refused to take orders from any of them. Houstoun's determination to have the military be subordinate to the state government led eventually to Howe's removal from command of the Southern Department and Bowen's dismissal. The loss of these experienced men further eroded what defenses existed.[47]

Civil and military authorities in Savannah showed that they could work together, however. Citizens and soldiers battled a fire, possibly deliberately set, on Sunday, March 22, 1778, that threatened to destroy the town. Not only did the governor and council express their great thanks, but they ordered a quarter cask of rum and a barrel of beer given to the soldiers for their services in extinguishing the blaze. Citizens of Savannah no doubt felt relief from the strain of housing the Continental troops when the soldiers moved into the newly completed barracks.[48]

Fear of an Indian war in the late summer of 1778 brought about coordination among militia units. Houstoun warned Laurens that the Creeks had now aligned with the British and "that Eight Towns have declared for War against us. . . . So that in addition to other Misfortunes we may consider ourselves as fairly in for an Indian War." From above the Broad River to the north, in the ceded lands, to the St. Johns River in East Florida, Seminoles and Upper and Lower Creek bands varying in size from a few to over two hundred attacked white settlements and forts and drove off cattle and horses. These raids ceased in late August, when the South Carolina and Georgia state governments called out the militia to protect the frontiers.[49] Successful collaboration did not continue, however.

East Florida troops had received hundreds of volunteers during April when disaffected South Carolinians traveled through Georgia to East and West Florida. They had been spurred south by contact with Thomas Brown's Florida Scout reconnaissance parties who had come into Georgia and South Carolina in March. The Scout had come to determine the number of Crown supporters and decided that more than six thousand South Carolinians would rise up and join the British, given the opportunity.[50] The ease with which the loyalist groups traveled south clearly shows how indefensible the frontier areas were.

Most of the men who reached East Florida joined the South Carolina Royalists under the command of Major James Mark Prevost. They, along with General Augustine Prevost's British regulars, combined forces and numbered about twelve hundred men. Joined by Indians, they maintained two strong posts on the St. Johns River and the south side of the St. Marys River.[51]

Two expeditions went into Georgia in November to forage. The first, led by Major James Mark Prevost, went as far north as Midway to collect cattle to feed the garrison at St. Augustine. The second, led by Colonel Lewis Fuser, traveled by ship to Sunbury along the inland passage to draw attention away from Prevost's foraging expedition. They arrived off Sunbury in early December and left as soon as they learned that Prevost had completed his task. Fuser landed some troops on St. Simon's Island to repair the fort and dispatched a troop composed of South Carolinians to convey to Florida the slaves, cattle, and other valuables taken as booty.[52] The British came to within about thirty miles of Savannah.

Although lacking a circulating medium, Georgians had sufficient surplus of crops to export as well as for the British to plunder. Merchants such as Joseph Clay obeyed the restrictions placed on exports by the Continental Congress and the state. In July 1778 the Continental Congress prohibited the exportation of various food supplies, including wheat flour, rye, Indian corn, rice, bread, beef, pork, bacon, and livestock because the British captured so many vessels carrying provisions that they were able to supply their own troops with the rebel food. Georgia supported this embargo on provisions and initiated several of its own, including that against exporting salt, in January 1778, and corn, in June 1777. The state renewed the provision embargo shortly before the British invaded Georgia. Although Georgia's agriculture apparently produced enough extra foodstuffs and livestock to export, no one wanted it to be captured by the British.

In October, the state government initiated a program to provide stores of provisions in each of the upper six counties. The government appointed individuals to spend a specific sum of money to purchase particular items at set prices and arrange for their delivery when needed. The provisions included salted pork and flour to be immediately stored and rice, live cattle, corn, and peas to be delivered as required. There did not appear to be any difficulty in locating these provisions, only in adjusting the set price to accommodate the higher market price. Georgia had enough surplus produce to provision the small number of troops within its borders. Despite the steady plundering and illegal exporting of produce and slaves, Georgia's agriculture appears to have adequately met the needs of the citizens between 1776 and 1778.

Although rumors of an invasion of South Carolina and Georgia had circulated for years, the British made specific plans only during the fall of 1778. The Carlisle Peace Commission, of which General Sir Henry Clinton was a member, devised an overall plan that encompassed several strategies. East Florida and New York forces, led by General Augustine Prevost and Lieutenant Colonel Archibald Campbell, respectively, would invade Georgia by land and by sea. As they did so, Indian superintendent John Stuart would send Creeks toward Augusta. These invading forces would rely on loyalist support to supplement their numbers and assist in the reestablishment of civil government. The commission, thwarted in its attempt at reconciliation by the French-American alliance of February 1778, viewed the retaking of the South in this manner as a potential bargaining chip in future negotiations.[53] The weak state government, contentious relationship between civil and military authorities, and dispersal of armed forces along the frontier prevented Georgians from paying much attention to rumors presaging the arrival of British invasion forces.

Henry Laurens took the rumors seriously and tried to get the attention of military and congressional leaders. He alerted General George Washington and Richard Caswell, delegate from North Carolina, in late September to the potential benefits the British would achieve by taking the South.[54] In mid-November he asked Patrick Henry, Virginia delegate to the Continental Congress, to send relief to the southern troops for "there is still great reason to believe an Embarkation has been made at New York intended at least for subduing the latter [Georgia]," and he feared Creek participation. (British Indian superintendent John Stuart was ordered to mobilize the Creeks to begin a joint offensive upon the arrival of British troops but failed to do so.)[55] Eventually Congress requested Virginia and North Carolina to send troops to aid South Carolina and Georgia.

No doubt in an effort to gain the attention of delegates, probably sometime in late December 1778, Laurens compiled a list of plunder the British could hypothetically capture. He listed as ostensibly available for the taking twenty thousand barrels of rice; two hundred thousand pounds of indigo; galleys and other shipping; between one thousand five hundred and three thousand horned cattle; enough Indian corn, peas, and potatoes to feed the British troops and fleet for two or three months; sufficient naval supplies for the British fleet; and wood and lumber. He also listed not fewer than five thousand slaves as plunder for the British army.[56] This estimate might have been based on the slave population of coastal rice plantations, knowledge that Laurens probably had because of his own landholdings in Georgia. These slaves, as well as much of the plunder, would be close to hand for the British in Savannah and easily transported by water.

Although by late November the citizens of Charleston had become persuaded that the British might invade Georgia, the time had long passed for Georgians to defend themselves adequately. The Continental officers had nothing to work with: no assistance to build defensive works, few supplies and little ordnance or usable fieldpieces, and a reluctant militia.[57]

The fleet carrying invasion forces under the command of Lieutenant Colonel Archibald Campbell set sail from New York on November 17, 1778. It arrived off Tybee Island on December 23, and the troops landed unopposed below Savannah on December 28. Lack of cooperation between the civil and military authorities in Savannah, including Continental commander Robert Howe, Governor John Houstoun, and Colonel George Walton of the Georgia militia, contributed to the easy capture of Savannah by the British invasion force.

State and local government and military officials, as well as other prominent rebels who were able to, traveled as fast as they could into the backcountry to escape capture. Governor Houstoun's executive council assumed the responsibility for removing the seat of government from Savannah to Augusta, although without officially holding office. Assembly representatives had been elected for 1779, but at the moment of invasion the state government lacked a governor and executive council and many of the representatives were caught in the fighting. The last entry in the executive council minutes stated, "The Town of Savannah being taken by the British Troops, on the twenty eighth of December put a final end to public business of a civil nature."

Poor participation by both the South Carolina and the Georgia militia and little assistance from the Continental Congress would continue for many years to come. Joseph Clay complained to the firm of Bright and Pechin on March 23, 1779, that Georgia had not received any support, and, in addition, Georgians themselves "do not seem to possess that Spirit of Enterprise and Patriotism I expected and of which they boasted." Support from South Carolina was slim because men had to remain at home to prevent their slaves from rebelling or deserting to the British. The Continental Congress would not detach additional Continental forces in 1779. From the relative safety of Pocotaligo, South Carolina, General Benjamin Lincoln wrote hopefully to Henry Laurens on the last day of 1778 that, despite "the want of men, artillery and stores," he would attempt to block the British supply lines and thus convince them "that though they are in possession of a town, yet they have not conquered [a] State."[58]

CHAPTER FOUR

Stalemate

British and Continental Forces

in Georgia, 1779–1780

The loss of Savannah was not the only misfortune we met
with in General Howe's defeat, we lost the aid of almost all the
citizens of that state, as the British immediately encamped
the troops along Savannah river up to Augusta, and it also
damped the ardor of the well effected in our state [South
Carolina] for a time, and I believe continued the war one year
longer.—General William Moultrie of South Carolina

Highly trained and experienced troops and officers formed the British
invasion force of approximately three thousand men. They served in the
Seventy-first Scottish Regiment of Foot and a detachment of royal artillery
and in two battalions of highly trained Hessians, the Wollworth or Trum-
bach and the Wissenbach, later called Knoblauch regiments. Three provincial battalions, Delancy's, Skinner's, and the New York Volunteers, were
also included. Lieutenant Colonel Archibald Campbell, commanding officer of the Seventy-first Scottish Regiment, commanded the expedition, and
Commodore Hyde Parker directed the naval force. Lieutenant Colonel
John Maitland commanded the Seventy-First Foot and the regiment of
Highlanders and also served as the deputy adjutant general of the expedition. Sir James Baird commanded the Highland light infantry.[1]

Campbell posted soldiers throughout Savannah and by the end of the
first day had surrounded the town with other troops. British seamen took
possession of the shipping that lay in the river, which included the prize
vessel *Hichenbrook.* Wary that the town might be set on fire by rebels,

Campbell took "Every possible Care . . . to secure the Town of Savannah from Plunder and Conflagration." He reported 83 rebels killed and 38 officers and 415 noncommissioned officers and privates taken prisoner. In addition, the British captured 106 rebel seamen over the next three weeks. British losses included 2 officers and 5 privates killed and 1 officer, 1 drummer, and 17 privates wounded. Losses for the British naval forces were low as well, and included 1 seaman killed and 5 wounded during the first three weeks in Georgia.[2]

Major General Augustine Prevost arrived in Savannah on January 15 and took over command from Colonel Campbell. His troops from East Florida arrived over the next few days and consisted of 38 officers and 905 men of the Sixteenth and Sixtieth Regiments, as well as various loyalist companies from the New Jersey or Skinner's volunteers, the South Carolina Royalists, the East Florida Volunteers, and the East Florida Rangers. Campbell had totaled the number of effective soldiers at 3,420 on January 16, so it is likely that Prevost's troops brought the number of soldiers in Savannah to well over 4,000.[3]

The Return of British Authority

When the British army reoccupied Savannah and various parts of Georgia, it discovered a land with no money medium in operation, an agricultural system beginning to break down, and few loyalists in sight. The effects of several years of depredations, mutinous rebel soldiers, uncooperative militiamen, and weak civil authority forced many to take a cautious attitude toward this latest military event. Loyalists in Georgia at the time of the invasion had been living under rebel government since 1776 and either were tolerated or had not let their opinions show. Predictions that loyalists would join the British effort did not take into account the ambiguous nature of Georgia's military action and political climate. Inhabitants ran away from Savannah as they had done when British warships came upriver in January 1776.

Elizabeth Lightenstone Johnston, who came into Savannah from the countryside soon after the invasion, reported that the British soldiers "committed much outrage, ripped open feather beds, destroyed the public papers and records, and scattered everything about the streets." John Houstoun, hiding at his brother George's place on a creek off the Vernon River, wrote to the president of the Continental Congress on January 2 that "Most

People in and about the town have lost their all" and that the "Rapine Insolence and Brutality" of the soldiers exceeded description. Houstoun noted, however, that people who had left Savannah after the invasion reported that both Campbell and Parker "possess great Humanity, and totally disavow many horrid Acts committed by their People."[4]

Campbell had issued orders regarding depredation and plunder to his officers on December 22, while the convoy was off Charleston. He made clear his opinion that the former would ruin the country and the latter would reduce discipline. All property that fell into the hands of the invasion force would be turned over to agents who would distribute it as needed among the units. Officers were commanded to "examine the Baggage of the Troops at Discretion; and bring to Disgrace and Punishment, such who shall dare to act in Opposition to these Orders." Additionally, Campbell warned the troops that by looking for plunder they became ready targets for "an Enemy whose Practice it is, by every Species of Allurement to tempt and ensnare the unguarded."[5]

Not only had his strict orders against plundering been disregarded by many, but Campbell had to stem the flow of refugees into the countryside. Thousands of women, children, and slaves, "traveling to they knew not where," crossed into South Carolina. He hoped for a population of peaceable settlers who had pledged their allegiance to the king and would fight when asked. One of Campbell's officers thought this attitude most generous: "The Government here established is to the greatest Degree lenient, so that I conclude it is imagined they will be sooth'd into a Change of Sentiments and receive Money and Property as Greater Goods than Rebellion and Poverty." Campbell proceeded to reestablish royal civil government, an effort acknowledged by the rebels.[6]

While the arrival of the British invasion force brought renewed civil authority, it also placed Georgians in the unenviable position of once again considering where their allegiance lay. Commodore Parker and Lieutenant Colonel Campbell issued a proclamation on January 3, 1779, announcing the presence of British troops in Georgia and ordered it posted along the road from Savannah to Ebenezer. The proclamation offered protection to all citizens and their property "on the Condition that they shall immediately return to the Class of peaceable Citizens, acknowledge their first Allegiance to the Crown, and with their Arms support it." Deserters were pardoned if they returned within three months. The oath of allegiance to the king included a renunciation of the Continental Congress, and the proclamation ordered all citizens to take it. "War would be waged" against those opposed to the reestablishment of civil government.[7]

By January 16 civilians who had fled in late December began to return to Savannah and its environs and seek the protection of the British. Across the Savannah River in Purrysburg, South Carolina, Colonel William Moultrie wrote to Colonel Charles Pinckney, a fellow Continental officer, that at least the Georgians had not gone so far as to rise up against the rebel forces. He noted that "most of them have delivered up their arms, and have submitted quietly to the British government." He suspected that Georgians would remain neutral until such time as a significant rebel force convinced them that they might win a battle against the British, at which time "perhaps they may join us."[8]

Campbell issued a proclamation on January 8 offering a reward of ten guineas for any member of a rebel committee or the assembly brought to a military post. He also offered a reward of two guineas for any other rebel.[9] Those who had wielded the power of the rebel oaths were now in a position to be hunted down and turned in by the very people they had harassed. Nor can the desire for British specie as a reward be discounted in motivating citizens to turn in known rebels.

While the British encouraged people to turn in rebels, rebel civil and military officials safe in the backcountry attempted to punish those taking the British oath of allegiance. Meeting in Augusta at the house of Mathew Hobson on January 8, 1779, representatives from Wilkes, Richmond, and Burke Counties formed themselves into a convention and elected a committee to serve until such time as a formal executive council could be established. The committee proceeded to garrison private forts and note disloyalty among the citizens of Augusta.[10] Lieutenant Colonel James Ingram, adjutant to General Benjamin Lincoln, commander of the Southern Department, and twenty-six other militia officers established a camp at the Burke County jail.

In an attempt to reclaim those inhabitants in the lower counties who had already pledged allegiance to the British, on January 14, 1779, rebel military leaders issued a proclamation naming nine individuals to be taken prisoner or, if absent, their estates to be confiscated for the use of the state. All others who had taken the oath of allegiance to the king were to come in within three days or be considered enemies and dealt with accordingly.[11] The rebels wanted a quick turnaround in allegiance by people in the backcountry, as would the British.

Along the coast, civilians had been maneuvering in a complex political environment since 1775. Colonel Campbell had no choice but to take this situation into account when selecting local men for temporary royal government posts. Among them was Lewis Johnston, who had remained in Savannah during the rebel government, had refused all oaths, and considered himself a prisoner of the rebel government. William Telfair, in England since 1772, had returned to Savannah just before Campbell's invasion to collect business debts and, although he took no oaths, had been forced to fight against the British. On December 31 Campbell formed the Board of Police, appointing Lewis Johnston superintendent of police at Savannah and William Telfair his assistant. "By this means, the Town and its Environs will acquire some good Order; and Regularity will be introduced from distracted Confusion."[12]

The jurisdiction of the Board of Police included all disputes concerning private property and the recovery of debt; breaches of the peace and all personal injury; the granting of tavern, public house, and liquor licenses; and the redress of grievances arising from extortion regarding the price of goods. The board also organized companies of male inhabitants aged fifteen to sixty from Savannah and its suburbs to mount guard at night and patrol the streets and bring in all disorderly people.

The Board of Police met through March 10 and dealt primarily with property; Campbell joined them on occasion to allocate specific property to certain individuals. The board's responsibility included determining the number of plantations abandoned by loyal subjects as well as known rebels, assessing their condition, and determining if anyone had legitimate claim to them. It appointed men to assist in this survey. General Augustine Prevost provided support for the task of sorting out property by proclaiming that people who had lost their lawful property must report the information to army headquarters. He also threatened all those who were presently under the protection of the king and simultaneously stealing property from abandoned estates with losing their protection and being punished.[13]

The board placed all slaves, crops, stock, buildings, equipment, and household furnishings under the care of authorized attorneys, appointed overseers, and tenants. Campbell allowed certain people to take into their possession the property of those who owed them money with the stipulation that the authorized men would protect and maintain it, work with the Board of Police to make inventories, and accommodate the needs of the army as necessary.

The board notified all agents or attorneys acting for "Absentees" with Georgia estates to show them their authority to do so. John Hume presented himself to the board as one of Sir James Wright's attorneys, with permission to assume the management of the governor's numerous estates. Anxious to protect the property of other wealthy absentee government officials, the board appointed overseers to the plantation of Governor Wright's son Alexander, the plantation of William Knox (former agent to Georgia and now under secretary of state in the American Department with the British government in London), and Anthony Stokes's former plantation, which may have been confiscated by rebels. They also appointed overseers for various wealthy rebel plantations, including those of Noble Wimberly Jones, Joseph Clay, and John Habersham.[14]

In consideration of their service, Campbell gave various people permission to reside on specific plantations and carefully stipulated their residence as temporary, "till such time as his Majesty's pleasure is known with respect to rebel property." Campbell hoped in this way to protect valuable property from plundering and destruction and enable the civilian government, once reestablished, to benefit from the regularization of plantation production.[15] The board functioned under the power of the military, and while Lieutenant Colonel Campbell was in charge it had his assistance.

Anxious to establish effective government in that area of Georgia controlled by British forces, Campbell recommended to Lord George Germain in January that a governor be sent out immediately. He appointed Lieutenant Colonel James Mark Prevost as lieutenant governor with the hope that General Augustine Prevost would support his brother's civil role. The ministry accepted Campbell's recommendation and Prevost was appointed lieutenant governor pro tempore in early March 1779 and the members of the Board of Police became members of his council. Campbell sailed for England on March 13, 1779.[16]

Lieutenant Governor Prevost did not want people forced off their land as a result of lawsuits now made possible by the British reoccupation of the province. In April, he initiated legal action to postpone litigation to recover debts until those indebted could have the opportunity to raise the money. He wanted to prevent the sale of estates owned by absentees or those currently unable to pay their debts because of "the present situation of affairs and where specie is so scarce." He directed the magistrates to encourage people to employ impartial arbitrators rather than the courts. Prevost believed that in time specie would circulate in the community again, and he did not want citizens to lose their property unnecessarily. In this way he supported the limited civil authority's attempt to regularize and encourage agricultural production.

"With a provincial treasury entirely exhausted," Mark Prevost sought permission from Lord George Germain to spend money from a contingent fund. He wanted to repair "the ruinous state of public buildings" and assist "loyal and distressed inhabitants" who were arriving daily from South Carolina.[17] Besides loyal citizens, deserters and slaves came into the British lines from South Carolina.[18] It is probable that they swelled the population of Ebenezer and Savannah and sought sustenance from the British authorities.

Despite Campbell's expectations, the military and civilian authorities clashed, particularly over control of rebel and loyalist property. Lieutenant Governor Mark Prevost, firmly aligned with the military, limited the commissioners of claims' jurisdiction to that of the property of loyalist absentees. The commissioners, Martin Jollie and R. Kelsall, carried on the work of the Board of Police under this new charge.

They administered the property as carefully as they could, requiring an inventory from all those residing on the absentee plantations or possessing any goods belonging to them. Those interested in renting absentee houses, plantations, or slaves under the board's jurisdiction applied to it. The army prevented loyalist Georgians who had fled to East Florida when the rebels took power from retrieving their Georgia property in the form of slaves and cattle. Governor Tonyn had hoped to call a House of Assembly to establish legal procedures for handling property claims, particularly in the form of claims to retrieve slaves, but the East Florida Assembly did not meet until 1781.[19] The army took what it needed, as determined by Lieutenant Governor Prevost and his brother Major General Augustine Prevost.

Before his departure, Campbell had attempted to secure Savannah and bring the rest of the province under British protection. He marched to Augusta in late January 1779 to lay claim to the upper part of Georgia. By this time, the rebels had formed an executive council, elected a president, and received four thousand Continental dollars from General Benjamin Lincoln. While the executive council purchased salt, paid back its debts, commissioned officers, and relocated cannon and ammunition, troops began to gather at Purrysburg, South Carolina. When Campbell, on his way north, drove Colonel Elbert and three hundred men into South Carolina, Lincoln gathered as many troops as possible at Augusta in the hope of defeating

Campbell there. Whoever controlled the backcountry also controlled significant food supplies, a population wavering in its loyalty, and communication and trade with the Indians.[20]

Arriving in Augusta on January 31, the British army found "but a few families, and some of these had but the female part at home." After several days the local men returned to the area, surrendered their weapons, and took the British oath of allegiance. They agreed to form militia companies in the different districts and to keep guard at various stations. A British army engineer commented that although these settlers elected their own officers, no one expected dependable service from them because "they were mostly *Crackers*, whose promises are often like their Boasts."

While at Augusta, Campbell received a communication from the inhabitants of Wilkes County (St. Paul Parish) to the north, saying they would surrender their forts to the British. The settlers had built the forts for protection against the Indians. Campbell sent officers and men to receive the forts and sent the inhabitants a letter in which he urged them to remain on their land and grow food for the British army.[21] He could offer them little protection from the Indians, or later, as it turned out, from rebel forces.

The British found limited support. The engineer noted that settlers from the Wrightsborough area, to the west, supplied flour, provided for the distillation of whiskey, and built a magazine and ovens for the commissary. Evidently these people responded seriously to the British intent of having "a well-regulated, and well-supplied Garrison established here." Campbell sent emissaries into South Carolina as well as an Indian chief, who came to the British "to receive and give a *Talk*, [and] was loaded with presents and sent back satisfied." Although the British had hoped for Creek assistance during the initial stages of the reoccupation of the backcountry, this support did not arrive in a timely way because communication was poor. By February 10, Campbell noted that eleven hundred men in the Augusta area had taken the oath of allegiance and formed into twenty militia companies "and a proper Rendezvous established in each District, convenient for their respective Plantations."[22] He did not receive enough reliable support to remain in the area very long, however.

A force of approximately two thousand rebels gathered across the Savannah River from the British encampment at Augusta during the first two weeks of February. These included General Andrew Williamson of the South Carolina militia and Colonel Elbert with his Georgians, totaling approximately eight hundred men. General John Ashe of South Carolina had approximately nine hundred men. Georgia militia colonel William Few "collected a few men, and crossed the Savannah River" to join them. He stated that approximately fifteen hundred men camped along the river in full view of the British. General Moultrie wrote from Purrysburg that "the back people [are] waiting to see the event between the two armies."[23] They would pledge allegiance, presumably, to whichever side won.

No battle occurred to sway the undecided settlers. Colonel Campbell and his officers conferred on February 12 and agreed that they should return to Savannah because there appeared to be "scarcely a hope" of loyalists from the backcountry joining them, the area around Augusta lacked both supplies and rum to support the army any longer, they could not expect reinforcements of either supplies or men from General Prevost, the militia "could not be much depended upon in a general Action," and the topography of the land made them vulnerable to attack. Campbell and his approximately seventeen hundred men marched out of Augusta on February 14 at four in the morning, leaving twelve beef killed and skinned on the ground. By seven that morning General Williamson's rebel forces crossed the river and reoccupied Augusta without plunder or bloodshed.[24]

That same day, militia under Colonels Andrew Pickens, John Dooly, and Elijah Clarke defeated a group of loyalists at Kettle Creek, about forty-five miles northwest of Augusta. Colonel James Boyd and his group of between six hundred and seven hundred loyalists were within six miles of their appointed rendezvous with British troops from Augusta when they were attacked. Had Boyd's loyalist force made its planned connection with a group of five hundred loyalists already in Georgia, fighting in the backcountry might have been severe and prolonged. But, the coordinated efforts of the rebel militia and Continental troops eliminated any strong military opposition to the rebels in the backcountry at this time.

Lincoln continued to try to push the British out of Georgia. By early March his combined force of militia and regular troops included between 7,000 and 8,800 men. He stationed them along the Savannah River at Augusta, Briar Creek, Black Swamp, and Purrysburg. Colonel Campbell, aware of the rebel troop movements in Georgia, again hoped for a decisive battle "because in that Event we might see peace soon established in Georgia upon honourabale Terms." He suggested a plan of attack on rebel forces stationed at Briar Creek to Colonel James Mark Prevost, who carried it out on March 3.[25]

The British caught the rebel forces, numbering between 1,700 and 2,300, completely by surprise. They captured 170, including Colonel Elbert and 22 officers, and killed or wounded 100. The defeat altered Lincoln's plans for he lost a considerable number of weapons that could not be replaced and a considerable number of men, many of whom ran away. Lincoln retreated to Purrysburg and there united what troops remained, leaving a small detachment at Augusta.[26] Because this battle did not destroy the rebel forces, many settlers remained ambiguous in their allegiance.

According to Continental general William Moultrie, the British victory at Briar Creek on March 3, 1779, prolonged the war by at least one year and brought it into South Carolina. Had the rebels defeated the British, "all the disaffected would have immediately joined us."[27] Instead, the combined rebel forces slowly disintegrated over the next few months. Although the evaporation of British strength in the upper counties enabled the rebels to keep a grip on that area, the British occupied much of the Georgia seacoast and approximately twenty-five to forty miles around Savannah.

The rebels had difficulty maintaining their hold on the backcountry, however. On August 18, 1779, the Georgia state government acknowledged that its difficulties in trying to keep backcountry settlers on their land centered upon lack of military support. In a letter to General Benjamin Lincoln of the Continental army, the state government wrote that these settlers considered moving out of Georgia to the north because of raiding parties. Additionally, should the British return, "the greatest part of the inhabitants, worn out with fruitless opposition, and actuated by the fear of loosing their all, would make terms for themselves." Without military support, rebel leaders predicted that the settlers would make up their own minds about how best to survive, and their decisions would not be based on political ideals.

Back in Savannah, commerce and trade began to revive under British rule. There apparently was plenty of food, and Campbell and Prevost encouraged the establishment of markets so the army could purchase produce and livestock. Campbell established price regulations for wine and other commodities. Local merchants had permission to trade with anyone who had taken the oath of allegiance to the king. Governor Tonyn of East Florida proclaimed free trade between the two provinces among those who had pledged their allegiance to the king. Legal trade commenced between Georgia and Britain, full trade was established early in 1780, and commerce between Georgia, New York, and the West Indies was active by the summer of 1779.[28] Although trade picked up enough to bring in money from duties, the British army proved to be the primary source of goods and specie coming into Georgia.

There were numerous troops in and about Savannah, particularly between late December 1778 and the spring of 1780. Convoys from Britain brought in supplies and army pay, as well as new troops and officers. The French captured several British supply ships heading for Savannah during September 1779, and their contents give a glimpse at the amount and variety of goods entering Georgia. The biggest prize was the ship *Experiment,* of between fifty and fifty-four guns. It carried wine, beer, rum, cloth, seven hundred thousand pounds of army rations, £30,000 sterling to pay the army, and General Augustine Prevost's replacement, Major General George Garth. Two ships, separated from the *Experiment* by a gale, were captured carrying provisions, anchors, and cables. The *Victory,* of eighteen guns, carried public stores, clothing, and shoes. The French also captured the *Ariel* of twenty guns, the *Myrtle,* a victualer, the *Champion,* a storeship, the *Fame,* the frigate *Rose,* and various merchant vessels, sloops, and three schooners, laden with rice, flour, and timber for masts.[29] Many citizens no doubt welcomed the return of the British army, for it might revive the economy of Georgia.

The province's dilapidated plantation system could not be repaired in time to provide the army with sufficient food, however. The herds of cattle remaining in Georgia during the spring of 1779, although described as very numerous, were either slaughtered or run off within a year. Major General Augustine Prevost requested permission from Sir Henry Clinton to search for provisions in South Carolina, possibly as a motive for remaining as long as he did in the neighboring province. He explained that there was a shortage because of the loss of a supply convoy and "the approaching scarcity of every article of provisions in a country so much exhausted on all sides." By early July royal governor Patrick Tonyn of East Florida described Georgia as pillaged and desolate.[30] The British hope that Georgia's agricultural system would supply the army with food over a prolonged period had been dashed.

Prevost's search for provisions in South Carolina distracted Continental general Benjamin Lincoln from his plan to attack the British and confine them to Savannah. In April he left General Moultrie at Purrysburg with a small force and entered Georgia at Augusta with approximately five thousand troops. As Lincoln made his way south toward Savannah, British colonel Augustine Prevost gathered his forces and moved toward Purrysburg and Charleston. Rather than lose Charleston, Lincoln led his troops back across the Savannah River to its defense.

No vital movement existed in lower Georgia to crush the British occupation. Citizens along the coast settled down under the limited civil authority established by Campbell and Mark Prevost and enjoyed the benefits of economic ties to Great Britain. Although the British army itself plundered, many property owners probably felt better protected from marauders and unaligned plundering bands by its presence. If the imminent return of Governor Wright and other respected royal officials to reestablish full civil government made citizens hopeful that conflict with the military would decrease, they were soon to be disappointed.

Wright resumed the governorship of Georgia upon his arrival in Savannah on July 14, 1779, and he remained until the evacuation in July 1782. He, Lieutenant Governor John Graham, and Chief Justice Anthony Stokes made the voyage from England together.[31] Wright did not find the province in the state of military security he had anticipated. When he discovered that the inhabitants were under the erroneous impression that they had been restored to the king's peace under the civil government established by Colonel Campbell in March, he immediately confirmed this status of public peace, for the maintenance of which the sovereign bore responsibility.[32]

Before Governor Wright's return to Georgia, Lord George Germain informed him that the British government would require no tax revenue except that accrued by trade regulations, and this would be put into the colony's account. Germain ordered Wright, upon his arrival in Georgia, to give gratuitous allotments of land to those refugees he and the council thought merited the help in order to become settlers. Parliament followed Germain's recommendation and allotted Georgia £5,000 in January 1780 for defraying the costs of reestablishing order and civil government.[33]

The presence of the army in Georgia, particularly with its headquarters in Savannah, required Governor Wright to accommodate its authority. The basic conflict between military and civil authorities involved property, particularly in how slaves were viewed: Wright saw them as the property of either their owner or the province; General Augustine Prevost saw them as a labor pool and as booty and reward for army personnel. Considering that the army brought back approximately three thousand slaves from its South Carolina expedition, it had a considerable number of slaves under its jurisdiction and thus unavailable to the civil government to work on rehabilitating the plantation system.

In an effort to find a way out of the tangle, Wright and his council agreed not to interfere with any of the slaves captured by the army. The office of commissioners of claims took charge of all abandoned estates and all fugitive slaves and rented both out to raise money. The civil government agreed to build a workhouse to retain fugitive slaves, and some of the slaves under civil authority produced barrel staves and naval stores for the use of the military.[34]

Wright noted in a letter to Lord George Germain in late July that Prevost's military expedition into South Carolina had alienated many loyalists who had subsequently withdrawn their support from the British reoccupation effort because of the plundering. He delayed issuing writs of election as a result, even though this forestalled the return of representational government.[35] As Wright labored to reestablish civil authority in and around Savannah, so too, the rebels hoped to legitimize their government in the backcountry.

A supreme executive council replaced the executive council of the rebel government, which had been operating sporadically since January 1779, on July 24, 1779.[36] It met in Augusta and appointed John Wereat president. Over the next two months the council accomplished a variety of tasks. It received the signed support of nearly five hundred "free citizens" from Burke, Richmond, and Wilkes Counties during August. The council ordered the courts to be held in the counties of Wilkes and Richmond and appointed commissioners of claims in an attempt to sort out plundered property. It requested that accounts and public money left in the hands of the state treasurer be presented. In the event that no council was in session, it gave President Wereat the power to order the militia as he saw fit. The council elected delegates to attend the Continental Congress and declared that citizens entering the enemy lines without leave were guilty of treason. In a display of bravado, it wrote a letter to Governor James Wright declaring him its prisoner because he had never been discharged from the parole he broke when he escaped from Savannah in January 1776.

In the late summer General Lachlan McIntosh returned to Augusta after serving in the Western Department of the Continental army. He assumed command of the Continental and militia forces in the state and gave hope that the Continental Congress would send more troops to Georgia. McIntosh encouraged the council to allow citizens who wished to return to their former allegiance to the rebel cause to do so.[37] Unfortunately, McIntosh's return to Georgia and the support he received from the Wereat government stirred up old resentments.

Colonel George Wells had bitterly opposed General McIntosh for years. Wells was Button Gwinnett's second in his duel with McIntosh in May 1777, and, as Gwinnett's doctor, he failed to prevent the spread of gangrene, which resulted in Gwinnett's death. The return of his foe may have spurred Wells's attack on the Wereat government: not only did the council support McIntosh's suggestion to allow citizens to return to their former rebel allegiance, a sore point with Wells, but McIntosh had replaced Wells as head of the Richmond County militia battalion.

Wells took it upon himself to call for elections in late August, which the council countered by sending John Dooly to inform the citizens of Wilkes County that there would be no August election.[38] On August 6 the council members acknowledged the "jealousies" among some citizens regarding the powers the council might exercise. They stated that they had no intention of contravening or destroying the radical state constitution of 1777 by assuming any legislative or judicial functions and hoped for the resumption of a constitutional government whenever possible.

In addition to trying to curb destructive factionalism, the council sought money to pay its militia and meet its supply needs. In an August 16 letter to General Lincoln, the council pointed out that the British army needed the grain supplies and herds of cattle found in the backcountry, and to defend the area from their incursions the state needed help from the Continental Congress to fund its defense. It needed money to pay debts to private citizens who had loaned the state supplies, to pay for militia expeditions, and to augment the pay of the Georgia militia from six to thirty dollars so it would equal that of South Carolina. The Continental Congress sent $500,000 to Deputy Paymaster Clay to give to the government of Georgia, if it met the requisites of a constitutional body. Although the money arrived in Charleston in mid-September, Clay and General Benjamin Lincoln would not release it to the Wereat council.[39]

Although the Wereat council had elected delegates to the Continental Congress during the summer, their failure to attend hampered Georgia's ability to obtain financial support. William Glascock wrote to the Continental Congress in July 1779 to explain that the British reoccupation of the state created adverse conditions that prevented the delegates from traveling any distance. Some had been driven from their homes and had lost their property, which no doubt was why they remained in the South to try to recover their fortunes and take care of their families rather than assuming their responsibilities in Philadelphia. Glascock further explained that the state had no money to pay their way to Congress, should the delegates be able to attend.[40] With no delegate in Philadelphia to keep the Congress informed of its needs, the Wereat council functioning without an assembly, and no constitutional government yet in operation, Georgia's presence remained weak.

Well aware of the situation in the South, rebel governor John Rutledge of South Carolina had asked Count d'Estaing, commander of the French fleet and troops in America, to recapture Savannah. Much to everyone's surprise, the French fleet arrived off the coast of Georgia on September 1, 1779, on its way home to France, catching not only the British but the rebels off guard. The Continental army and militia units from Georgia and South Carolina under the command of General Lincoln joined Count d'Estaing only on September 16.

Colonel Maitland, in Beaufort, South Carolina, with eight hundred Highland Scots troops, left the hospital, artillery, baggage, and stores behind so he could reach Savannah before the enemy encircled the town. Several slaves fishing near Dawfuskie on September 16 showed him how he and his troops could cross the Savannah River by way of Wall's Cut and through Scull Creek without encountering the French and rebel forces.[41]

The Siege of Savannah

British civil and military authorities cooperated fully to prepare Savannah for a siege. Supplies of food and water were plentiful. Governor Wright and his council ordered four hundred to five hundred slaves to work on repairing the fortifications under the direction of the chief engineer, Captain James Moncrief. Governor Wright and Lieutenant Governor Graham joined a council of war held on September 16 to determine if Savannah should surrender to the French, as d'Estaing demanded. Several years later, during testimony to the Royal Commission, the former Captain Moncrief, now a colonel, related that Governor Wright stated during this meeting that "he had rather see his whole Property torn to pieces than so shameful a thing should be done as to surrender the Town without fighting."[42] Moncrief testified that Wright's conduct was of material importance in saving Savannah.

Chief Justice Anthony Stokes fled his country home in early September when the French forces came ashore and moved into the outlying area. Once in Savannah, he observed that the French "entrenched themselves up to the chin, about two hundred yards from our lines." Many thought the enemy would retreat and were surprised when the bombardment began in the middle of the night of October 3.[43]

The French tried to set the town on fire by bombarding it with approximately one thousand shells and twenty carcasses over the course of the siege. A carcass consisted of a hollowed-out cannonball filled with turpentine which ignited upon impact. A French artillery officer wrote that the bombs "caused much disorder" and twice set fire to Savannah. The wide and sandy streets protected the town from complete destruction, however, for cannonballs caused little damage when they hit the sand, which often put out the fuse. Elizabeth Lightenstone Johnston wrote that slave children would "pick up the spent balls and get for them seven-pence apiece" from the military, who were happy to obtain scarce twelve-pound shot courtesy of the French. Banks of earth and strategically placed barrels of sand served to protect the exteriors of many houses while featherbeds lined the cellars and timbers shored up their ceilings. As women and children huddled in the cellars, men outside acted as firemen and "wet blankets and other means were taken to guard the opposite house from taking fire; the streets were broad."[44]

Stokes noted that the troops were much safer from the bombardment than the civilians. Women not only sought refuge in the British line, they also went over to the French line. Other women, children, and the elderly went to Hutchinson Island; Elizabeth Lightenstone Johnston lived there in a barn with fifty-eight women and children. Although French guns and boats attacked both the island and the British ships in the river, Cherokees and armed slaves protected the island, at least, from French gunboats. Although a French naval officer reported that the British evacuated Hutchinson Island, Elizabeth Lightenstone Johnston and others apparently remained there until the siege ended.[45]

Women and children were pawns during the siege, for neither side allowed them to leave Savannah in the hope of maneuvering the other into giving up. In late September, before the bombardment began, General Lachlan McIntosh of the Continental Army requested Major General Prevost to allow Mrs. McIntosh and their children, as well as any other women and children who so desired, to leave Savannah. Prevost denied this request, possibly hoping the rebels would not use their artillery on the town because of the women and children. By October 6, after several days of bombardment, General Prevost changed his mind. He wrote to Count d'Estaing requesting permission to send the women and children downriver "under the protection of a French ship of war until the business should be decided" and was refused. After the siege, the French apologized to Prevost, blaming the refusal "on the scoundrel Lincoln and the Americans."[46]

On October 9 the Franco-American forces attacked Savannah directly, sustaining heavy casualties. Only Bunker Hill proved to be more costly to a single side than this battle at Savannah was to the French and rebel armies. Fighting continued until the eighteenth, and there are reports of the British using units of armed slaves to defend the town. The lack of supplies, poor weather, and eventual defeat of the combined French and American forces undermined the discipline of the siege troops. The French soldiers began to desert once the siege commenced and continued to do so right up until the departure of the fleet. The black troops from the West Indies became insubordinant. A British naval officer determined that although uncertain, French losses outnumbered those of the rebels because the French "fought like soldiers, and were killed and wounded, but the Rebels' loss is from desertion immediately after the defeat."[47]

While the French fleet sailed away, French and rebel deserters, militia and their families, and the rebel army made their way from Savannah over bad roads and across swamps and creeks whose bridges had been destroyed by the British before the siege. The Georgia forces diminished to the point of containing only one company and most of the officers for four regiments, who had no men to lead. Either the enlistment period had come to an end by early December and the men had gone home, or they had died. The defeat undermined the morale of the rebel population of Georgia and South Carolina. General Moultrie wrote: "This disappointment depressed our spirits very much, and we began to be apprehensive for the safety of these two southern states."[48]

The *London Gazette Extraordinary* first published the news of the repulse of the French and American forces on December 20, 1779, which many greeted enthusiastically as a British victory against the French. King George III ordered the artillery pieces in St. James's Park and at the Tower of London fired in honor of the occasion. Other newspapers treated it as more of a prevention of a French victory than a clearly British one. Scotland celebrated the victory with an illumination of the city and suburbs of Edinburgh and the Scots papers emphasized Colonel Maitland's contribution to the defense of Savannah and mourned his death in battle. A variety of poems were published about the victory, and current plays added specially written prologues and scenes referring to Savannah and various military leaders, which apparently delighted the audiences.

The *Royal Gazette* of New York published numerous poems, eyewitness accounts, and verse tributes to the victory beginning in early November. Unlike the papers in Great Britain, the New York paper acknowledged that the rebel army had been defeated along with the French. Anthony Stokes was to comment that "the siege has rendered famous a sickly hole." [49]

The siege had not only disrupted the reestablishment of civil government in Georgia but severely damaged the capital. Many houses in Savannah had been damaged beyond repair by cannonballs, and the army barracks lay in pieces, having been deliberately dismantled to form a defense work during the siege. Major Prevost appropriated fit rebel houses as winter quarters for the troops despite the fact that the commissioners of claims had hoped to rent rebel property to raise money to run the government. Governor Wright, despite his frustration, could only acquiesce for fear of "an open Rupture with the Army." [50]

Nearly one year after the British invasion, Chief Justice Anthony Stokes called the first court of oyer and terminer and general gaol delivery for mid-December 1779 and appointed a grand jury. The grand jury published in the newspaper a list of grievances regarding the ruinous state of much of the city of Savannah and the surrounding countryside that had resulted from the siege. Presumably selected because of their respectability as leading citizens, this group of jurors wished to get civil government functioning again so that civic order could be restored. It is interesting that among the list of fourteen individuals whose names were published as members of this grand jury, at least three (John Henderson, Thomas Tollemash, and James Butler) had taken oaths to the rebel government before the return of royal government, and one (John Murray) had questionable dealings with it. [51] The way men had contributed to the defense of Savannah during the siege began to form the basis for all future loyalty considerations.

The siege offered the royal governor a means of observing the loyalty of his people. If a man picked up a gun and defended the town of Savannah or otherwise participated in its defense, Wright judged him loyal. From this time on, Wright appeared to dismiss past rebel oath taking or temporizing as insignificant in comparison. Instead, he found the act of defending Savannah a more reliable means of determining loyalty than any written or spoken proof.

Governor Wright initiated interrogations of citizens who absented themselves during the siege. For those not found materially culpable, fines, taking the oath of allegiance, and signing the test resulted. Jail and a trial awaited citizens suspected of rebellion. Wright reported to Lord Germain on January 20, 1780, that the court of sessions had found three people guilty of misdemeanors for treasonable practices and had acquitted one for high treason. Two had confessed to misdemeanors for treasonable practices. Three additional indictments for misdemeanors and one for high treason remained to be heard at the June court session. Wright hoped that these legal proceedings would strengthen and support the government, "which I assure your Lordship at Present Stands in Great Need of it."

The rebel government also struggled to function in the backcountry after the siege. George Walton, a signer of the Declaration of Independence and militia leader, returned to Georgia's political scene upon his exchange by the British in October 1779. General Lincoln wrote to him on October 17 suggesting that "it would be for the interest of the State if the Assembly were convened as soon as possible, your Government organized and Members sent to Congress." When he arrived in Augusta ahead of John Wereat and Lachlan McIntosh, who were probably still traveling north from Savannah, Walton joined a radical faction opposed to the Wereat council. Members included Richard Howley and George Wells, and now, joined by Walton, they called for a new government.[52]

On November 23 Walton convened an assembly in Augusta which elected him governor and William Glascock speaker. The executive council met for one week, apparently much of the time at George Wells's rooms, and attended to business regarding the protection of the frontier. It also drafted a lengthy dispatch to the Continental Congress asking for money and for the transfer of General Lachlan McIntosh out of Georgia. Some months later George Walton described how the members of this government "were obliged to sit in Council at day, and scout against the Enemy by night."[53]

When John Wereat arrived in Augusta and found the competing council established, he and his council set December 1 as the date for the election of a new House of Assembly, to convene in Augusta on the first Tuesday in January 1780. Wereat's supporters suggested that Walton and his group had formed a government so as to gain control of the $500,000 stored in Charleston for Georgia's next constitutional government. Walton's council applied for but did not receive the requested Continental funding. When General McIntosh arrived in Augusta, Colonel Richard Parker refused to give him back his command of the regular and militia troops.[54] McIntosh sought advice from General Lincoln regarding which council to work with, Wereat's or Walton's, and reported that his officers had become politically polarized. Wereat and his council, having forged a moderate coalition, refused to give way to Walton's radical one, and neither held sufficient authority to govern effectively.

As a result, two hostile temporary state governments operated in the same small town on the edge of a nearly defenseless frontier during late November 1779, shortly after a major rebel defeat. Unable to create a constitutional civil government despite the fact that tantalizing operating funds were stored in Charleston, these councils succeeded only in further factionalizing civilian and military personnel at a time of increased British strength in the South. Former governor John Houstoun viewed Augusta at this time as the epitome of what the state used to be: the residence of both worthy men and pests to society who had crept into power.[55] Fortunately, Walton and his faction did not impede the election called by Wereat's council. On December 1 the voters, primarily backcountry settlers, elected many members of the radical faction to the state assembly.

The Beginning of the End of Rebel Authority, 1780

The assembly convened in Augusta in January 1780 and elected Richard Howley governor, George Wells president of the executive council, and George Walton as a delegate to the Continental Congress. On February 5, the government decided to send Governor Howley with George Walton as a delegate to the Continental Congress, and George Wells, president of the council, assumed the executive power. Soon afterward, Brigade Major James Jackson of the Georgia militia killed Wells in a duel. As a protégé of John Wereat and from the same town in England, Jackson may have dueled with Wells for political or personal reasons.

After Wells's death, the council appointed Stephen Heard as president. George Walton and Stephen Glascock, while serving as governor and speaker, respectively, had written to the Continental Congress that Lachlan McIntosh did not enjoy the confidence of Georgians. On February 14, the Congress removed Brigadier General McIntosh from his command, without giving him a hearing or consulting either General Lincoln or George Washington. Lachlan McIntosh learned of his removal from command while serving at the siege of Charleston in May. The Continental Congress recognized the government as constitutional and released $597,000 in long-awaited funds.[56]

With the defense of the frontier area precarious and the civilian population increasingly polarized, civil government weakened. Citizens made their opinions about the conditions in Richmond County known in March 1780, when a "Respectable" grand jury met in Augusta and presented grievances to Chief Justice William Stephens. In addition to its concern for the many threats to daily life, including a smallpox outbreak, rambling slaves, and impassable roads, the grand jury expressed concern about the extravagant civil government. The grand jury, with conservative John Wereat as foreman, noted that not only did the high number of representatives and the salaries they earned make a seat in the legislature "a place of profit" but the treasury had insufficient money to pay them.[57]

General Lachlan McIntosh supported the grand jury statement. He calculated that with only two upper counties held by the state and approximately five hundred men supporting the rebel cause living there, the need for government spending did not appear great. The new governor, Richard Howley, received an estimated salary of $30,000, however, while the six Continental Congress delegates received a total of $75,000 and the assembly and council members a total of $160,000 per year. McIntosh figured the state paid 260 men in either a civil or military capacity, and 240 received pay as soldiers. This brought the state expenditure to a total of $1,081,000.[58] These fiscal arrangements apparently evolved as a result of the monetary support provided by the Continental Congress, for no circulating medium existed in Georgia other than what came from out of state.

The state government did its best to govern the backcountry through May 1780. Acknowledging its distress, the Continental Congress did not require Georgia to meet a supply quota for the Continental army, unlike other states. The government issued a proclamation on March 3, 1780, declaring it a felony "for any person or persons, under any pretence whatever, to plunder or take away from any of the inhabitants of this State within the said line, any property." This line extended from Hudson's Ferry to the Ogeechee, and within it resided, for their own protection, persons loyal to the cause of the United States. The government determined that an oath be administered to the inhabitants of Wilkes, Richmond, and Burke Counties to affirm their allegiance. Rough stockades or blockhouses built by the settlers served to protect the sparse population of these three northwesterly counties from Indian raids.[59] The rebels hoped that these people would remain on the land rather than leave the area or go over to the British.

The assembly wanted to attract settlers and voted to open a land office. The office would grant lands to any citizen of any state who would take the oath of allegiance, bring in his entire family, and settle within nine months. Heads of families received two hundred acres and fifty acres for each additional member, whether white or black. The government requested people who had located lands but not settled on them and those who claimed to have titles or rights to lands desired by new settlers to submit their cases to the state. On May 22 and every Tuesday thereafter, the traditional land day in colonial Georgia, petitions for uncontested land grants would be signed. As the government apparently stopped functioning three days later, people had to wait until August 1781, if not later, to claim their land officially. It is probable that families squatted, a practice common in colonial Georgia.[60] Not willing to give up what was so nearly theirs, they waited for government to return, thereby increasing the population of the frontier.

Georgia state government came to an end as a result of the surrender of the Continental army at Charleston. Council president Stephen Heard and a small group of men formed a council and remained in Wilkes County with Colonel Elijah Clarke and three hundred militia for as long as they could. According to Colonel James Jackson, Heard, Myrick Davies, and other members of the council "animated the militia with their presence[,] underwent every difficulty with the troops & were in most of the severe actions which the Georgia Militia were engaged in." Clarke and his men finally abandoned their property and families in Georgia and established themselves in South Carolina near Berwick's Iron Works, possibly after first going to North Carolina. Colonels John Twiggs and Benjamin Few and their men evidently fled first to North Carolina, eventually returning to South Carolina. Myrick Davies became council president when Heard and the militia went to South Carolina, and he may have moved the council from place to place in Wilkes County and South Carolina before abandoning the effort.

Governor Richard Howley left Georgia sometime after May 12 with a group of Continental and state officers, among them Major James Jackson, and narrowly escaped capture by a detachment of soldiers sent after him by Lord Charles Cornwallis. This group apparently transported money and state archives to New Bern, North Carolina. This retreat and Howley's subsequent trip to Philadelphia evidently cost the state half a million dollars, probably taken from the treasury as they fled the British forces.[61]

Rebels in Royal Georgia

In March 1780, commander in chief Sir Henry Clinton had offered a proclamation of amnesty as he gathered his invasion force outside Charleston. Rebels who surrendered to the British as prisoners of war and gave up their arms would be allowed to return to their homes on parole if they promised not again to take up arms against the Crown. When Governor James Wright received a copy of Clinton's proclamation, he viewed the offer as far too generous. It would encourage any and all rebels who had fled Georgia to return, claiming protection of the military amnesty Clinton issued. Unfortunately for Wright, Georgia was under Clinton's military jurisdiction, and he could do nothing to alter the terms.[62]

The British captured between 2,500 and 5,700 men when they took Charleston in May and quickly paroled most of the militia and civilians. These men, not formally exchanged, continued as prisoners and pledged not to bear arms against the British. Many accepted Clinton's offer "in hopes they would have been suffered to remain peaceably and quietly at home with their families, and to have gone on with their business undisturbed."[63]

During the year between their release on parole and potential formal exchange, the men on parole could not rejoin the rebel army and have the hope, at least, of receiving pay. In order to survive, many of them probably made their way back to their property in Georgia, took to plundering, or joined the rogue rebel bands operating along the Savannah River. Wright informed Germain on July 19, 1780, that "all our most Violent Rebels . . . are Preparing to Return here, indeed Several are come already."

He was concerned about the return of rebels to Georgia, in part because there was no strong military force to control them. Approximately 2,350 troops had defended Savannah during the siege in the fall of 1779, but Clinton ordered most of them to South Carolina and they never returned. Loyalist troops made up of approximately 600 men fit for duty were garrisoned in Savannah for the rest of the war.

In addition, Wright was concerned that returning rebels might infiltrate his government. He had hoped to issue writs of election in February but postponed doing so when troops were not available to deliver the writs to the backcountry. On March 24 Wright proposed to the council that the writs be issued immediately in reaction to Clinton's general pardon. The council supported the governor, anticipating that rebels would come into Georgia and have the opportunity to be elected to the assembly, "which Event might totally destroy the Ends proposed of establishing the King's Government here, and render it of little or no Effect."

The council issued the writs the following day and received all of the returns by May 5, except for the town of Augusta and St. Paul Parish. Abimelech Hawkins, who was appointed to execute these writs, reported to the council on May 4 that he had been warned "by universal Report" not to proceed north beyond Abercorn "without the Utmost Risque to His Person, and the Writ[s] he carried" because rebels controlled the backcountry. He prudently returned to Savannah. Wright had been correct in his assessment in February that the army's presence in the backcountry would have assisted in the election of representatives to the assembly, for without a show of force, the writs had not been executed.

The first session of the assembly met on May 9, in Savannah, and adjourned on July 1. With only eighteen members, including the speaker, the assembly established a quorum of ten members to do business. The assembly determined that any member who left the province without permission from the assembly, if sitting, or the speaker, if not, would be expelled or receive an appropriate censure. It also decided on a three pence per minute fine for lateness. With so few representatives, strict control of their attendance became important, for without a quorum the assembly could not meet. Conceivably, a boycott by a handful of rebel-influenced representatives could bring royal civil government to a standstill.

The assembly acknowledged that rebels were returning and worked to formulate a legal response to their presence. At the meeting of the assembly on May 31, 1780, the Commons House resolved that those rebels active in state government and the rebellion who might return to Georgia should not be pardoned or allowed to enter Savannah or to come within twenty-five miles of it until the assembly determined what actions to take.

This delaying tactic was passed on to the governor, who brought it up in council on June 9. After citing the example of John Glen, rebel chief justice of Georgia, who had expressed his intention of sailing to Savannah, Governor Wright suggested that the government's response to Glen might very well set a precedent "for as many as may come into this Province under the like Circumstances of having borne Offices under the Rebel Government, or otherwise favored it." The arrival of rebel physician James Houstoun, on parole from Charleston, brought the issue to a head.

Captured at Charleston along with General Benjamin Lincoln's army in May, James Houstoun had previously served the rebel army as physician at the siege of Savannah. He received permission from Sir Henry Clinton and General Alexander Leslie to travel to Savannah, having given his parole under the terms of the capitulation. Although the British military authorities in Charleston apparently assumed that under the protection of his parole neither Houstoun nor any one else would be answerable to civil law, Chief Justice Anthony Stokes ordered him arrested upon his arrival in Savannah.

Accused of treason for his participation in the siege and held in custody without bail, Houstoun wrote to Colonel Alured Clarke protesting his treatment by British civil authorities. Eventually Governor Wright, Lord Cornwallis, Attorney General James Simpson of South Carolina, and Attorney General Robertson of Georgia became involved themselves with Houstoun's case. Simpson wrote that Lord Cornwallis and Brigadier General James Patterson believed Houstoun could not be charged with an act of treason that antedated his being under the terms of capitulation. Robertson answered that Governor Wright could not discharge a man accused of treason. Civil authorities released Dr. Houstoun from custody and placed him on bail when he agreed to take the oath of allegiance.[64] Governor Wright had much to contend with when the leaders of the British army in the South operated under the assumption that military law overrode civil law in Georgia.

Dr. Houstoun and others like him may have been motivated to return to Georgia because of the effect Sir Henry Clinton's next proclamation had on the population of South Carolina. Still considered a prisoner on parole because he had been captured at the surrender of Charleston, Houstoun remained unaffected by this new proclamation. But all those who had not been captured now lost their status as neutral parolees. The British military required them either to take the oath of allegiance and "resume the characters of British subjects" or be considered in rebellion.[65] The civilian population of South Carolina became polarized, and civil war soon erupted.

The attorney general reported his opinion regarding a legal response to the return of rebels on September 8. By this time John Houstoun, former state governor of Georgia, was expected in Savannah. After months of discussion it was determined that no legal action could be taken to prevent the return of rebels. The assembly directed the attorney general to take due notice of the arrival of such persons and to proceed against them legally, if he could.

The case of John Houstoun, James's brother, further illustrates the difficulty posed by the Clinton amnesty on the loyalists in Georgia. Even though Houstoun had been a state governor of Georgia and participated in attacking Savannah during the siege, he claimed that he had been induced to join the rebellion. The hands of the attorney general were tied: he determined that the king's pardon alone provided Houstoun with legal protection.[66]

In the meantime, the assembly struggled with the issue of treason. It could not agree to attaint 112 prominent rebels for high treason and confiscate their property. Beginning on June 1, a bill proposing this action traveled from the upper house to the Commons and back again but was never passed. Although elected before many rebels had returned to Georgia and presumably loyal, the assembly members could not pass a treason bill. The distinction between loyalist and rebel was too blurred, perhaps, to be firmly determined by these men, who themselves might possibly be questioned for past actions should such a bill become law.

The assembly did, however, pass the Disqualifying Act on July 1, which targeted many of the rebels named in the unpassed treason bill. The act listed a total of 151 prominent rebels by name and occupation and included all civil and military officeholders under state government. These people no longer could hold or exercise any office of trust, honor, or profit in the province of Georgia. Essentially, they could not be a part of the government, but they could live on their property. They would have to prove to the governor and council that they were loyal subjects before the disqualifications could be removed.

To prove their loyalty, they had to give up all of their weapons to the nearest justice of the peace, or pay a fine of £25 sterling, and £10 if found with a weapon. Their houses could be searched for weapons, though upon application, they could receive permission to retain one. Those who had not proven themselves loyal since November 1, 1779, must go before a justice of the peace upon entering Georgia and provide a bond of £100 for twelve months of good behavior and take the oath of allegiance to King George and renounce allegiance to the state government. An additional option was to serve in the army as a private soldier for the rest of the war. A certificate would be given to all who did these things. Anyone who did not cooperate could be put in jail for three months without bail. If, after spending three months in jail, the individual still refused to cooperate in any way, he was to be impressed into the navy and denied the right to become a resident of Georgia. This bill favored persons who had resided in Georgia before or during the siege of Savannah, allowing them to own weapons and go about their business. Those who came in after the siege were the target group of the act, for they had not proven their loyalty by defending Georgia.

Wright, as head of the civil government, could go only so far with threatened consequences against those who did not pledge allegiance. He never succeeded in putting in place a tougher law than the Disqualifying Act. Wright reported to Lord Germain on January 26, 1781, that the act did not go far enough, particularly when "we still have many thorough Rebels and Villainous Incendiaries amongst us even in the Town of Savannah." He proposed a stronger bill, which passed in April 1781, to attaint for high treason twenty-four persons named and all others who held military or civil positions in the state government who had not yet conformed to the Disqualifying Act. They were to stand trial for treason on or before October 9, 1781, and their property would be forfeited. There is no evidence that Wright put this bill into practice, for it never received the royal approval it needed to become law.

Governor Wright found Sir Henry Clinton's proclamation establishing a lenient attitude toward rebels who pledged their allegiance to the Crown grossly unfair when compared to the plight of many returning loyalist refugees. In his address of May 9 to the first royal assembly to meet "after an Interruption of five Years," Wright stressed the significance of reestablishing legal property ownership after the confiscations that occurred under rebel government. He blamed the revolution in Georgia on "a few Individuals of little or no property" who wished to become "Men of Power, Leaders and Governors, and accumulate Fortunes to themselves by Rapine from the General Wreck of the Property of Honest men." He stated that the inhabitants must receive "Aid and Relief with respect to the Destruction and Loss of their Title Deeds." On June 1 the assembly passed a bill begun in the council to amend and improve an attachment bill from 1761 to enable citizens to put a lien on the land and property of absent debtors. An act directed at loyal subjects with real or personal property in Georgia whose proof of ownership had been either lost, destroyed, or carried off during the last five years passed the assembly on June 10. For many returning loyalists, the recovery of their property proved to be difficult, if not impossible.

In contrast, the rebels who renewed their allegiance to the Crown and returned to Georgia reclaimed their property with little or no consequence. Wright told Germain on July 19 that, rather than having lost everything, as many returning loyalists had, returning rebels experienced "no sufferings or losses, as to Property [taken] by the Rebels, but a kind of Small Temporary loss, and now sitting down again with all their Property Lands and Negroes." They regained their property at a time when rebel military fortunes were particularly low in the South and the possibility existed that the British might win the war. Taking up their lives again within a somewhat revived economic environment based on specie enabled them to regain at least some of the financial security they had lost when the British reoccupied Georgia, if not earlier, and might have provided their motivation for changing sides. Wright did not like to see them successfully reestablish themselves while many returning loyalists struggled to recover their property.

With the return of royal government, the people of Georgia had a currency based on specie, or as Wright put it, "Money of *Real* and not merely nominal Value." In his speech to the assembly on May 9, Wright contrasted the lack of commerce and high amount of debt endured by the inhabitants under the rebel government with the advantages of trade and commerce with the "Mother Country." To straighten out old debts to the government, he directed the assembly to determine the amount of loan office paper currency, £7,410 sterling of which had been issued before 1776, still in the possession of the citizens, and a committee was established to do so. Citizens did not have to pay any arrears in quitrent, and the civil government could use any money generated by future quitrents and fines owed to the king for the good of the province.

According to Chief Justice Anthony Stokes, the assembly passed several bills to bring representative government and civil law to all parts of Georgia over the next two years, some of which were not enacted before the evacuation in July 1782. The legislature combined the criminal and civil courts into a general court, which met four times a year, with four grand juries called to serve them. The criminal court had previously met only twice a year, and it "was considered as not sufficient in a warm, unwholesome climate, where men suffered much from the length of confinement in close gaol." The civil government also passed a law to divide the ceded lands into parishes that would select representatives to the assembly, but this bill was not acted on. Nor did the legislature establish a circuit court to serve this area twice yearly, as had been planned.[67]

Anxious to reclaim upper Georgia, Sir Henry Clinton ordered loyalist troops under Colonel Thomas Brown to subdue the backcountry once resistance to the British forces in the South had dissipated following the surrender of Charleston.[68] They gained control of Augusta peaceably in June 1780, after receiving the surrender of a number of rebel militia units while making their way north along the Savannah River. Colonel John Dooly and four hundred of his men surrendered to Brown, who discharged them under easy terms. The rebel militiamen were allowed to return to their homes on parole on the condition that they would not again fight against the British.

Evidently authorities made little effort to take weapons from the paroled men or compel them to declare their allegiance or enforce the Disqualifying Act in any way. Governor Wright had observed the polarization of the paroled population of South Carolina as a result of Sir Henry Clinton's second proclamation of June, in which he required them to give up their neutral status and pledge allegiance to the king. Many of those paroled under the March proclamation responded by taking up arms once more against the British in South Carolina. Wright disagreed with sending troops to the ceded lands to ensure peace, perhaps hoping the population would remain neutral while on parole without any enforcement or fearing a military presence might polarize them. At the request of Augusta citizens, Governor Wright declared the king's peace in effect in the backcountry on July 10.[69]

Rebel colonel Dooly and others on parole and named in the Disqualifying Act found their lives problematic now that they resided on their land under British civil government. Not only were they restricted by the act, but they were responsible for old debts to returning loyalists. Additionally, their previous raids against the British made them unpopular with the loyalist population and vulnerable to plundering. Dooly had served as attorney for the weak rebel state government during 1779 and in that capacity prosecuted captured loyalists in Wilkes County. A group of loyalists led by Captain William Corker assassinated him during the summer of 1780. For the loyalists, however, the presence of an estimated five or six hundred rebels armed and on parole in the Augusta area generated concern for their potential to arouse the population to rebellion.[70]

Their fears were realized when rebel colonel Elijah Clarke, attracted by the storehouse of Indian supplies at Augusta, gathered approximately five hundred men in the ceded lands and launched an unsuccessful four-day attack on the loyalist garrison there in mid-September. Unlike John Dooly,

Clarke had not surrendered to the British in June 1780 but fled to North Carolina, leaving his family to suffer the consequences. Clarke pressured parolees to take up arms under the threat of death, and his troops apparently committed atrocities. Rebel colonel William Moultrie described Clarke's attempt on Augusta as "ill-timed" and "of very great injury to the inhabitants." The repercussions they faced from the loyalist troops forced many to take up their weapons again "for their own security, and join the Americans."[71]

In retaliation for Clarke's attack on Augusta, Lieutenant Colonel John Harris Cruger, commander of the loyalist post at Ninety-Six, sent raiding parties into the ceded lands. They failed to capture Colonel Clarke and his men, who led between four hundred and seven hundred people northward to escape the loyalist troops. Cruger's troops destroyed nearly one hundred plantations and settlements belonging to those allegedly involved with the attack on Augusta, however. They brought in sixty-eight rebels; more than half took the oath of allegiance and posted bond, and Cruger had the rest taken prisoner and sent to Charleston.[72]

Lieutenant Governor Graham traveled to the ceded lands to assist Cruger in enforcing the Disqualifying Act; he estimated that 255 of the 723 male inhabitants of the area were loyal, 57 neutral, and the rest rebel. Increased activity of partisan bands, especially after the defeat of the British at King's Mountain in October, extinguished Governor Wright's hope for a neutral population in the ceded lands and the parishes of St. Paul and St. George.[73]

Polarization of the population, long feared by the governor, began in the backcountry as a result of the violence. According to rebel colonel James Jackson, strong feeling rose up among the population of the backcountry as a result of the treatment of the families of the men who had attacked Augusta. Giving as a reason that they had held correspondence with rebels, loyalist colonel Thomas Brown ordered these families out of Georgia to North Carolina, a journey of approximately two hundred miles. The families, many consisting of mothers with small children and aged parents, had no alternative but to obey, for their neighbors could not assist them without breaking the law. The refugees, including the wives of General Clarke, Colonel Williamson, and General Twiggs, arrived in North Carolina "almost famished with hunger and some never recovered."[74] The rebel victory at Augusta the following June brought reprisals for this behavior upon Brown, who required a heavily armed guard to get him safely out of the backcountry.

Lieutenant Colonel Henry Lee, who led the Continental troops at the siege of Augusta in June 1781, remarked that the Georgia militia under Elijah Clarke wanted to kill every prisoner taken and were prevented from doing so with great difficulty. The "cruelties mutually inflicted in the course of the war in this state" motivated their retaliatory behavior. Lee remarked: "In no part of the South was the war conducted with such asperity as in this quarter. It often sunk into barbarity." Evidently the loyalist and rebel militias in the backcountry, under Brown and Clarke respectively, had ceased making terms with each other during 1780 – 81 and instead "a war of extermination became the order of the day." Later, Colonel Moultrie remarked about Georgia: "That country had been entirely laid waste by the desolations of war: the rage between Whig and Tory ran so high, that what was called a Georgia parole, and to be shot down, were synonymous."[75]

It is probable that some of the inhabitants of this area of Georgia experienced pressure to change their allegiance seven times between January 1779 and October 1780. After having sworn allegiance to the king when the invasion forces first arrived in Georgia, those fleeing to the backcountry swore allegiance to the rebel government in January 1779. They then swore allegiance to the king at the urging of Lieutenant Colonel Campbell in February 1779, with the result that the rebel militia then prodded them to resume allegiance to the state once the British troops returned south. With the return of the British in 1780, they either resumed their allegiance to the king or were placed on parole. Rebel colonel Elijah Clarke, however, urged these people to take up their arms for the rebel cause or they would die.[76] Although Lieutenant Governor Graham enforced the Disqualifying Act and required allegiance to the king be sworn yet again, the backcountry inhabitants understood all too well the limitations of royal military commitment to the area and that the rebels would be back, no doubt with another request for their allegiance.

On September 20, after hearing of the attack on royal forces in Augusta, the council in Savannah decided that the assembly should be recalled and asked to determine what might be done to strengthen defenses in this emergency. Two days before, Wright had approached Lieutenant Colonel Alured Clarke, the commanding officer in the province, to discuss the chances of sending reinforcements to Augusta. Clarke, too sick to discuss these matters, told Wright to "consult with the Gentlemen of the Council" and he would support whatever they decided to do in the emergency. Wright sent a rider to Augusta to gather further information and dispatched an express to Colonel Nisbit Balfour in Charleston detailing the facts of the attack and the current status of the garrison at Savannah and the provincial militia. The troops that reinforced Brown at Augusta came from Fort Ninety-Six in South Carolina, led by Lieutenant Colonel John Harris Cruger.[77]

The assembly met on September 27, and Wright asked its members to formulate two bills, one to fortify and defend the towns of Augusta and Savannah through slave labor and possible embodiment, the second to strengthen the militia laws by empowering the civil government to impose fines, imprisonment, and corporal punishment for nonparticipation. The assembly combined the charges into one bill and limited Wright's power to call out and arm the slaves and exercise additional power over the militia to "only in time of *Alarms actually fired.*" Wright made the bill law on October 30.[78]

On November 6 the council advised Wright to put into effect that part of the new militia law that enabled him to call out a sufficient number of slaves to begin work on the new fortifications and to impress the necessary equipment and building materials. The council ordered that the works built by both the British and attacking French and rebel forces in September 1779 be leveled, for "the Lines around Savannah should be Contracted now that His Majesty's Forces here are greatly diminished both by death & Removal, from what they were at the late Siege." Wright ordered the commanding militia officers in Christ Church, St. Philip, and St. Matthew Parishes to fill out lists or "returns" of all male slaves from age sixteen to sixty on the plantations in their areas.

On the first of December Wright reported to Germain that extensive progress had been made on the fortifications of Savannah. He had called out approximately four hundred slaves and expected the fortifications to be completed by January. He acknowledged that requiring one-fourth of all the male slaves in the area to work for nearly three months had proved to be a heavy tax and inconvenience on their owners. Wright's statistics imply that a pool of sixteen hundred male slaves existed in the general area. It is likely that additional slaves living further away from Savannah had not been summoned.

Wright and the assembly dealt with other issues of defense. On November 15, the governor suggested that the assembly establish a "Troop of Thirty Horsemen" to pursue plunderers, particularly "one M'Kay, a notoriuous Rebel," and establish a reward for his capture. The assembly adjourned on November 15, but Wright recalled it on December 11 for the defenseless state of the seacoast was by then of grave concern. Wright had requested a galley from Admiral Marriat Arbuthnot but received no answer.[79] The assembly determined on December 18 to build and arm a rowing galley of seventy-five- to eighty-foot keel, capable of carrying fifty white men and ten slaves.

Struggling to make pragmatic defense plans, Wright also had to deal with a crumbling infrastructure. By December the governor understood that the plan to furnish loyalists with property from the confiscated estates and to aid refugees with funds accrued from the estates' produce and rental had failed. The commissioners had reported to Governor Wright and the council in early February that despite their care in placing overseers on the deserted plantations to protect and manage the slaves, produce, stock, and other property, "such Plantations have been plundered, and a vast personal Property hath, from time to time, been carried away." Public notices urging citizens to respect the commissioners' jurisdiction did little good.

Georgia's plantation system had been reduced to near ruin by the time Governor Wright had returned to Georgia, and the siege as well as continual depredations and civil-military conflict had reduced the province's land assets even further. The governor wrote to Lord George Germain in December 1780 that, with no income from the deserted estates and other estates now in possession of their owners, he did not "know what the Assembly can do to put it in my power to make any compensation to the loyal refugees for their losses."[80]

Land and Allegiance

Royal and Rebel Governments Compete

for Citizens' Support, 1781–1782

> Though I am not yet sued, the debts I owe with Interest
> accumulating for these five years past, amounts to a sum I
> shall never be able to pay and my property is so greatly re-
> duced that I can hardly support my Family in any decent
> manner, this cursed War has ruin'd us all.—Robert Baillie,
> Georgia loyalist and resident of East Florida

Troop movements in the South eventually led to a resurgence of rebel activity in South Carolina and Georgia. Lord Charles Cornwallis moved his
troops out of South Carolina during the fall of 1780 into North Carolina
and eventually to Virginia. Lord Francis Rawdon commanded the remaining British forces in South Carolina, and General Nathanael Greene, appointed to head the Southern Department in October 1780, moved his
Continental troops toward that area in March 1781. Regular state troops
began to be raised in South Carolina, and these, in combination with the
Continental forces, enabled the war to be "renewed in South Carolina with
great vigor and spirit, and more regularity."[1] This buildup of forces allowed
many Georgia rebels to return home from North and South Carolina and
begin fighting and raiding in their own state.

Although it would be some time before Greene came into the lower
South with his Continental troops, he began to search for ways to improve
conditions for soldiers and civilians alike. He wanted to improve supply
lines as well as encourage loyalists to switch their allegiance "before the door
of mercy is totally shut against them." He promoted prisoner exchange and

the granting of paroles "to lessen the sufferings of the unfortunate on either side." Greene insisted that partisan leaders behave as much like regular army as possible by preventing plundering activities, conserving forage and provisions, and issuing receipts for impressed materials. He hoped partisan leaders would hold an important place in retaking the South.[2]

Renewal of Rebel Support, 1781

In March 1781 rebels returning to Georgia began to rendezvous along the Little River in hope of recapturing Augusta. As the rebel military presence increased, raiders of all kinds operated in the backcountry. Distracted and lean in number, neither the British troops at Augusta nor at Savannah offered much deterrent to those determined to plunder and assassinate Georgia loyalists. Governor Wright, in a letter to Lord Cornwallis in April, expressed his dismay that loyal subjects "should be suffered to be thus murdered for want of a few troops to support and protect them."[3]

Wright had to turn to the legislature to provide the means to defend the province because his superiors did not respond to his requests for support. He had recently written to Lord Cornwallis about a troop of horse and to Admiral Arbuthnot for a galley to protect the sea coast, to no avail. Wright had pressured Lord George Germain for nearly two years to fund a troop of horse, and Lieutenant-Colonel James Mark Prevost had recommended the same defensive measure to Germain in early 1779.[4] Upon the unanimous advice of the council, sixty men, with their own horses and weapons and providing their own provisions, left the militia and formed into three companies to be sent to the backcountry. Wright began to use the parliamentary stipend to fund the defense of the province and support for the refugees. He showed a remarkable ability to improvise under increasingly oppressive conditions.[5]

By late April, Wright understood that Augusta would likely fall under attack and he could do nothing to assist the garrison there. The Savannah garrison could spare no men because Brigadier General Alured Clarke and part of the troops had gone to St. Augustine in April to confront a potential Spanish attack. Wright declared that the assembly had done everything it could to protect the province through legislation and its actions were insufficient without armed forces backing the government. Although Brigadier General Clarke brought a detachment from St. Augustine to Savannah and Lord Rawdon sent one hundred men from Charleston, they arrived too late to assist Lieutenant Colonel Thomas Brown in holding Augusta against the rebels. The council attempted to protect Savannah and ordered the gates of the defensive works surrounding the town shut at nine o'clock and a guard kept to question people out at night.[6]

During the spring of 1781 rebel raiders killed approximately one hundred loyalists, both officials and settlers, and this had its effect on the civilian population. Governor Wright had great compassion for the people and explained in a letter to Lord Germain on May 1, 1781, how militia members "are now Fatigued and worn out by continual Alarms" and becoming afraid to "stand Forth" because so many good men had been assassinated. Additionally, Wright stated that loyalists joined rebel bands out of fear of being murdered. Despite the terrorism, Wright believed loyal subjects were still willing to fight to protect Georgia. Lack of pay and provisions as well as little if any military support from the British army severely tested their loyalty.[7]

The Georgia rebel bands that raided and plundered the backcountry did not win the support of the settlers there. Continental lieutenant colonel Henry Lee cautioned General Nathanael Greene in February 1781 that the citizens of Georgia would welcome only regular troops, for militia would force them to take an active part in the fighting. Lee feared that "instead of a general insurrection in our favour, we shall strengthen the enemy." The settlers preferred to remain on their land to protect it from plundering bands rather than join the militia and become plunderers themselves; in addition, they probably did not believe the militia could overcome the British forces. In Colonel Lee's opinion, "The minds of the people are wavering; their general inclination favours us, but they cannot, they will not, declare, when they understand our effort is confined to the exertions of their own militia."[8]

Apparently the Continental officers held little regard for militia bands. After they fought together at the siege of Augusta in June, Colonel Lee expressed a low opinion of the Georgia militia leaders, apparently based on their interest in plunder and murder.[9] It seems possible that Continental general Greene grew determined to reestablish civil government in Georgia as expediently as possible after learning of the unrestrained behavior of the militia officers and their men.

In June 1781 British troops withdrew from Augusta after a two-week siege and the British also abandoned the South Carolina post of Ninety-Six. The exodus of loyalists from the backcountry before and after the fall of Augusta swelled the population of Savannah with refugees and additional military. Wright estimated about 1,400 people, including women and children, had run to Savannah. The census in June 1780 indicated 742 nonmilitary white inhabitants of Savannah, thus the white population possibly nearly doubled at this time. Wright purchased rice, flour, beef, and pork at the cost of £2,652 to the British treasury. He armed and placed the male refugees on duty with regular militia to hold the redoubts at Ebenezer and defend Savannah. In June Wright reported that rebels controlled "the whole Country between Ebenezer and Augusta" and the inhabitants hid in the swamps "or come here for Protection."[10] Over the next year, Governor Wright became the administrator of a town rather than the governor of a province.

Despite their increasingly vulnerable position, or perhaps because of it, many of the inhabitants in and around Savannah were motivated to rebuild their former holdings or accrue additional property. The return of royal civil government enabled the legal processes of property attachment for debt, of marshal's sales of court-confiscated property, and of private sales and debt settlement to occur once again. Returning loyalist and rebel refugees as well as people who had remained in Georgia participated in these property transactions, whose announcements took up a great deal of space in the *Royal Georgia Gazette*.

The legal process to establish an attachment on property began with the filing of a declaration of the debt owed in the general court followed by the repeated advertising of the case in the paper. While the initial ad named only the two parties, as time elapsed the provost marshal announced the legal attachment of specific property of the absent debtor and listed the name or names of those prosecuting for the payment of debt by its sale. The potential property to be legally attached included the lands and tenements, dwelling houses and buildings, goods and chattels, monies, debts, and books of account belonging to the absent debtors and their heirs. This legal process proved very popular, and the paper published long lists of these cases, beginning in 1781, of forty or fifty at a time, sometimes more. The advertisements warned anyone claiming ownership of any of the attached property to contact the general court immediately and prove ownership. Attached property was sold a year and a day after the writ had been established.

Approximately one month in advance of each sale, the civil government advertised the sales of attached property in groups of cases. The property was "to be sold to the highest bidder, for cash." To his dismay, Governor

Wright learned that some "notorious rebels" were so indebted that selling their property under attachment would not cover the debts they owed.[11] It appears that the attachment of property for debt occurred continuously under the restored civil government of James Wright. The lengthy legal process, including the wait of a year and a day, resulted in much attached property becoming available for sale in 1782, leaving the new owners little time to enjoy their property before evacuating, while other sales never occurred because of the return of the rebel government.

The provost marshal began to advertise the sale of property confiscated by the court beginning in the fall of 1780 and continued to do so on a regular basis into June of 1782. The advertisements described the tracts of land, town lots, dwellings, and slaves available for sale but did not necessarily name the owner. The property had been seized "by virtue of executions" and not as a result of writs of attachment. For example, Levi Sheftall brought a case against Joseph Wood to the general court, which found in late April that Wood owed Sheftall "Forty two pounds lawful money of our province" plus court costs. Anthony Stokes ordered the money made available to Sheftall at the court session held the first Tuesday in June, but Provost Marshal Donald Fraser informed the court that since Wood "hath no Lands or tenements[,] Goods or Chattals in my Bailiwick" no property could be seized by the court to sell.[12]

These sales advertised that the property would go to the highest bidder, "for cash, in gold and silver at the current exchange." The governor ordered Donald Fraser, whose name appeared on all the provost marshal's sales advertisements in the newspaper, and other acting provost marshals to keep good account books and file the information with the prothonotary within one week of any sale. They needed to keep track of the names of the creditors and how much money they had received from the sale of the property and how much money remained to be paid them.

Private sales occurred as well. For example, Sabine Fields, the plantation of Edward Telfair, which eventually had writs of attachment placed against it, was first advertised for private sale on March 1. The ad described the plantation as containing 580 acres, including 130 acres of cleared swamp ready to plant and another 120 acres of cleared and fenced high land, and 4 acres of garden to supply the public market at Savannah, only three miles away. Various people wishing to clean up more current debts placed announcements in the newspaper notifying the public of their intent to collect or to pay. Richard Wylly, a rebel, advertised his departure from Georgia and asked "all persons having demands against him to send in their accounts to him at Rae's Hall." He already had a writ of attachment placed against his mill in St. Matthew Parish, which became available for sale on December 1, 1781. Executors of estates asked that those indebted to the estate make immediate payment and that those who had accounts against the estate send in the attested bill for payment. Firms called in debts when they dissolved their partnership, as did the firm of Cowper and Telfair. If there had been unsatisfactory response to the first ad, executors, firms, and others seeking payment of current debt next advertised that they had placed the unsettled bonds, accounts, and notes in the hands of an attorney and were prepared to litigate.

The *Royal Georgia Gazette* also printed descriptions of property claimed by individuals who had lost their legal proof of ownership. Lieutenant Governor John Graham was such an individual, and lengthy descriptions of his extensive property ran in the *Gazette* for four months. During this time anyone could go to the prothonotary's office in Savannah and review his claim. The provost marshal's notices requested those who felt their property had been wrongfully advertised as attached to notify the court immediately.

The payment of debts incurred before they left Georgia proved to be very complicated for returning loyalists. These old debts had been incurred when business transactions were carried out with the old provincial currency, which depreciated on a regular basis, with various forms of specie, or, beginning in 1776, with the new state script or "rebel" money. Loyalists leaving Georgia in 1776–77 paid their debts with whatever form of money proved acceptable at the time. Subsequently, those remaining in Georgia under the rebel government transacted business with state or Continental script, which depreciated dramatically, various forms of specie, barter, and possibly old provincial script. Now, in 1781, returning loyalists and those who had not left Georgia differed over the actual monetary value of prewar debts in the current legal tender and how to collect or pay them.

Several individuals spoke their minds on the subject of depreciation in the *Royal Georgia Gazette* during the fall of 1781. While Chief Justice Anthony Stokes recommended arbitration, others thought it a waste of time, for those who had remained in Georgia under rebel government had a financial advantage. A letter in the October 11, 1781, paper, signed "A Loyalist," explained how those who took the rebel oath of abjuration made money by planting and other means, "which the times afforded an ample choice of," and maintained their solvency despite the depreciation of rebel currency. Exiled loyalists, in contrast, had been forced to receive rebel money when they sold their property or received payment of debts before leaving Georgia and had used the rebel money to pay their own debts. Now, many returning loyalists had only the depreciated rebel currency, if any of that, to show for the property they had once owned in Georgia. They could not force a refiguring of payment of debts owed to them by those continuously residing in Georgia and now once again loyal to the king. As far as recovering the depreciation of debts paid by absentees, the writer considered them "already beggared with attachments, and judgments" and probably unable to survive financially should they reclaim their property.

At present, the author continued, loyalist refugees were fleeing to Savannah "stript to the skin by the Rebels in the back country, and sent down here to be clothed and fed upon Charity." These backcountry loyalists, facing a situation similar to that of the exiled loyalists in 1776–77, threatened by increasing violence, abandoned their property and thus their economic base to save their lives. The writer cautioned that these very refugees could be further "sheared for depreciation" within the year, "by the very men, if they become subjects, who have made them so miserable." Because of easy amnesty, rebels could become loyal subjects once again and sue refugee loyalists for old debts they could no longer pay because they had lost their property.

The Commons House appointed a committee in March 1781 to establish a table of depreciation of the "Rebel or Congress" paper currency in circulation before the return of the British. The table might have been used in arbitration for the committee thought it "may be of the utmost importance to publick justice as well as to the interest of individuals." To establish statistics, they asked, in the March 22 newspaper, for anyone who had either bought or sold lands, slaves, goods, or any other property, including gold and silver coin or bullion, for the paper currency "in time of the rebellion" to inform them within two months of the terms of these transactions. The year before, the grand jury had recommended that the old paper currency be called in and the colony's monetary system be reorganized, certainly a complex task considering the variety of currency available and the change of governments and hence monetary systems many had witnessed.

The British probably issued new paper currency or government bills in Georgia sometime after Governor Wright returned. A June 7 advertisement for twenty-three bay lots in Savannah stipulated that payment be divided between the legal currency of Georgia and gold and silver "at the present rates." In October an ad appeared offering £350 "Old Lawful Paper Currency of this Province," as well as £175 of bills of exchange on England, for cash on reasonable terms. In November an ad offered £190 of "the lawful current money of this province, which is a tender in law in all cases whatever" on easy terms. In December Governor Wright offered to pay the going rate for clean rice at 17 shillings the hundredweight in government bills or cash. Apparently, by the end of 1781 government bills, lawful current money, and cash were acceptable means of payment, as well as specie, and pre-1776 provincial paper money might have been.

With many account books and money certificates lost or destroyed as a result of the tumultuous times, debt proved hard to establish or clear up. In March 1781 the Georgia Assembly passed a law that made the recovered account book of the commissioners of the general loan office or land bank evidence in all courts. The ledger supplied information regarding loans made by that office between February 17, 1769, and September 17, 1775. Although the loans had amounted to not more than £80 sterling per person, the government wanted to get the money back and bring the general loan office books as up to date as possible. Those who owed money quite naturally refused to pay it back until the loan office returned to them the bonds and mortgages they had left as security. Some of this paperwork had been lost, stolen, or destroyed in the ensuing years of rebel civil government.[13] Wright hoped the general loan office ledger book might untangle debts to the government and facilitate the return of mortgages and bonds to their rightful owners and thus help them prove their legal ownership of various property. Overall, however, the debt situation remained extremely knotted.

Annoyed merchants in London sent a memorial to the Board of Trade in July 1781 stating their grievances regarding the recovery of debt in Georgia as well as in South Carolina. The merchants noted that normal trade relations again operated between the two southern colonies and London and that since extending credit to the colonists, "They ought to be in respect to their Property, upon an equal footing with the Inhabitants thereof, in every Act of the respective Legislatures." Essentially, the merchants felt at a disadvantage because of their distance from the debtors. The colonists were given the benefit of the doubt in regard to paying back debts under several provincial legislative acts, and the London merchants felt that this leniency only served to deny them their due.[14] Perhaps a commission would have been set up to handle transatlantic debt had the British held on to Georgia.

Basil Cowper and the Telfair brothers William and Edward had been in business together before the Revolutionary War, and their legal entanglements as a result of separate loyalties exemplify the complexity of debt in Georgia during and after the war. Edward Telfair and Basil Cowper remained in Savannah once Governor Wright left, Edward as a firm rebel and Basil as a rebel who eventually returned to loyalty. William had been in London since 1772, running the merchant house from there, and was a loyalist. The business partnership had apparently lasted until December 28, 1775, with Edward Telfair continuing to run it "'until the late revolution put a stop to all intercourse between Great Britain and America.'"[15]

The partners came and went depending on which side was in power in Georgia. Basil Cowper remained in Savannah, playing a role in the rebel government for a time, and then he went to the West Indies. William's creditors in London asked him to return to Savannah, despite the fact that it was under rebel rule, and secure his property as a £7,000 credit was due them and no money had been received since 1776. He did so in 1778, just before Campbell's invasion, and he remained until the British evacuation in 1782. Basil Cowper returned to Savannah in 1779 and later claimed he was in partnership with Mr. Telfair (probably Edward) between 1774 and 1779 and said he was worth £30,000 in 1774. Meanwhile, Edward fled Georgia when the British returned in 1778 and lost a good deal of his business property through actual destruction or legal attachments and confiscation. According to the *Royal Georgia Gazette,* William Telfair and Basil Cowper dissolved their business partnership in late August 1781.[16] They both left when the British evacuated.

In 1784, now back in Savannah, Edward Telfair received a letter from the English creditors of the firm he, his brother, and Basil Cowper had jointly owned before the war. From it he learned that the creditors had absolved his brother and Basil Cowper from debt and assigned it all to him, apparently without taking any legal action to do so. He did not respond to the request for debt payment and apparently no further action was taken until 1792, when William Telfair returned to Savannah. He asked his brother Edward to determine how to liquidate his holdings and pay the debt. Edward offered to surrender half of his "real and personal" property to William, but William wanted all of it. Edward then offered to go to court either in England or in the United States to resolve their difficulty, which William refused to do. The debt was legally erased in England in 1798 and in the United States in 1800.[17]

Another instance shows how old friends, despite their political differ-
ences, commiserated with each other about their business difficulties. Robert Baillie, formerly a Georgian, now a member of the East Florida Assembly and living in St. Augustine, wrote to Lachlan McIntosh in July 1781.
McIntosh was on his way to Philadelphia at this time, having been recently
released on parole after being held prisoner by the British at Charleston
since May 1780. Baillie offered his help in tending to McIntosh's business
affairs in Georgia, as well as those of their mutual friend rebel John Wereat.
McIntosh referred to himself after the war as "under the most embarrassing
circumstances, incredibly poor after a long and necessary absence from his
country, [and] plundered of almost everything he possessed." Baillie related
how he would never be able to pay off his interest, and "my property is so
greatly reduced that I can hardly support my Family in any decent Manner." [18] He ended his letter asking McIntosh to remember him to all their
old acquaintances.

Although royal government provided a structure for financial and property transactions, it could only struggle against the steady erosion of customary daily life in Savannah. The *Royal Georgia Gazette* published regulations for cleaning the town in June 1781, and these may well have helped
to prevent the spread of disease as Savannah became crowded with refugees.
In January the newspaper had reported the church and marketplace in ruinous condition and the roads and bridges down the coast, despite the appointing of roads commissioners, in such bad shape that communication
and travel were almost impossible except by boat. The civilian groups called
upon to repair the heavy damage and rebuild had not succeeded in doing
so, possibly because so many slaves had been summoned to work on the
fortifications of Savannah or had run away. The government gave rice to
petitioners who were unable to feed their slaves, in the hope that the slaves
would not be forced to rob or run away in order to survive. [19]

Armed and unsupervised slaves had roamed in bands or taken up habitation in and around Savannah ever since the siege in October 1779. Other
slaves, no doubt including those abandoned by the British army when it
went to South Carolina in the spring of 1780, had joined them. Beyond the
reach of civil authority, armed slaves proved a threat to the inhabitants of
Savannah, and attempts had been made to restrain them. Apparently these
efforts had been unsuccessful, for the grand jurors of the general court reported in the January 18 and April 11 issues of the *Royal Georgia Gazette* that
numbers of unsupervised slaves had erected and were inhabiting houses in

and about the town of Savannah and had established a settlement of huts called Durnford Village between Savannah and a place called the Citadel.

The grand jurors accused the slaves of behaving insolently, robbing, trading without limitation, skulking about in the woods, and plundering.[20] In addition, the armed slaves prevented owners from retrieving runaway slaves from among them. By arming themselves and banding together, slaves not only protected themselves from plunderers, the military, and their owners; they established a reputation as ungovernable and unpredictable.

In an attempt to gain control over the slave population, the assembly, sometime between March and April 1781, appointed several commissioners for each parish to take into their care and under their management all idle and runaway slaves as well as deserted property. Apparently these measures were not successful, for in late October the Christ Church Parish commissioners voiced their concern in the newspaper for the "many idle, disorderly, and runaway negroes, wandering about town and country, committing acts of theft and plunder." The commissioners called for the public to help establish the names and habitations of these slaves, so they might "be fetered and properly disposed of," probably either placed in the Savannah workhouse or returned to their owners or confiscated plantations.

Armed slave bands survived well into peacetime. At least two bands plundered from their camps along the Savannah River in 1786. Georgia militia destroyed one camp along Bear Creek, consisting of a fortification protecting twenty-one houses and crops and either killed, scattered, or captured the inhabitants on May 6, 1786. Militia attacked a second encampment on Belleisle Island in late October 1786, scattering the estimated one hundred inhabitants, destroying their rice fields, and burning their houses.[21]

Despite the erosion of normal urban life in Savannah, the governor and assembly continued to meet and maintain a political structure. Wright, well aware of the "singular mark of attention" the Lords of Treasury had paid him and the province of Georgia by assuming financial support of the troop of horse and aid to the refugees, hoped they would continue their generosity by assuming the cost of the additional provision bills. He confided to Lord Germain on June 14, 1781, that, although the assembly had drafted a tax bill, the Lords of Treasury could not count on recouping any money in this way because "the People are *Ruined* and can pay no Taxes."

Even though at this time unaligned bands combed Georgia for plunder, rebel raiders harassed loyalists from bases across the Savannah River in

South Carolina, and acts of retaliation occurred among the population, civil authority was in place and the population did not sink into anarchy.

The withdrawal of British troops from Augusta and Ninety-Six in June 1781 freed rebel Georgia's upper counties from the threat of enemy forces; with General Greene's assistance, state government began to revive. The Georgia delegates to the Continental Congress sought Greene's approval and protection when they proposed that Dr. Nathan Brownson, former Georgia delegate and newly appointed deputy purveyor for hospitals for the southern army, return to Georgia to unite the armed forces as a brigadier general. Additionally, rebel justice of the peace John Wilkinson wrote Greene a letter in early June requesting the reestablishment of civil government in the backcountry, now that Augusta had been taken from the British.[22]

Greene ordered General Andrew Pickens to the Augusta area to prevent rebels from murdering loyalists and to encourage loyalists to join the Continental army. Newly appointed lieutenant colonel James Jackson promptly enlisted loyalists taken at the surrender of Augusta into his infantry. Hoping to form a temporary council as a first step toward reestablishing government, Greene sent Joseph Clay to Augusta in June to organize one.[23] Greene wanted people to remain in Georgia and understood that they might not do so without a functioning civil government to offer some measure of control over the plunderers and murderers operating in the backcountry.

The Georgia delegates to the Continental Congress also pressed for the reestablishment of civil government because the emperor of Austria and the empress of Russia had offered to mediate peace proceedings between Britain and the United States; the possibility of peace being established according to *uti possidetis* now definitely existed. In international law *uti possidetis* formed the basis of a treaty that left belligerent parties in possession of what they had acquired by their arms during the war. The Georgia delegates published the pamphlet *Observations* so that the general public could learn of their concerns regarding Georgia's potential status at the end of the war.[24]

They also sent fellow delegate William Few to Augusta in mid-July to "advise the citizens to convene and elect Members of the Legislature and organize Government." The Georgians in Philadelphia anticipated that the people gathering in Augusta might try to draft a new constitution, thus delaying the formation of civil government. They wanted Few to encourage them to form a government quickly and assume authority over as much territory as possible before peace proceedings began.[25]

Greene did not want factions to inhibit the development of a state government and, as the delegates did, anticipated difficulties. He thought conflict might develop between partisan leaders John Twiggs, Elijah Clarke, Benjamin Few, and Dr. Nathan Brownson should Brownson receive the proposed military appointment of brigadier general. Greene also expressed concern that Joseph Clay might attempt to gain support to write a new and more conservative constitution once in Augusta. He cautioned Clay that such a move would throw efforts to build a government into paralyzing confusion.[26] Additionally, he urged citizens who had sought refuge elsewhere to return to Georgia and vote in the upcoming election. The old patterns of conservative against radical and civil against military authority did not grow into factions at this crucial time in Georgia entirely because of General Greene's leadership.

Citizens elected an assembly in August, which included representatives from all but the southernmost county of Camden. The assembly convened on August 17 at Augusta and selected Dr. Brownson governor. It had a moderate leadership: Noble Wimberly Jones and Samuel Stirk replaced George Walton and Richard Howley as delegates to the Continental Congress and John Wereat became chief justice. (Despite giving them power in the temporary rebel government of 1779–80, evidently Georgians now viewed Howley and Walton "as very abandoned characters.") The assembly retained William Few and Edward Telfair as delegates. Militia colonel John Twiggs became the new brigadier general and Greene ignored Twiggs's quarrels with Governor Brownson over authority.[27]

Through a series of laws during August 1781, the rebel government began the process of determining who could remain in the backcountry, who must be forced out, and what property should be confiscated to defray the expenses of government. The assembly appointed commissioners from each county to collect and manage the property of those who had either joined the British, been ordered into the enemy lines, or been killed while fighting for the king. Applying more pressure on those known to be or generally considered to be loyalists still in the backcountry, on August 22 the assembly passed a bill to prevent internal conspiracies. County committees examined suspicious people and ordered them out of the backcountry, if necessary. The boundary separating rebel from British consisted of an imaginary line drawn from Hudson's Ferry on the Savannah River to the mouth of the Little Ogeechee River, to Beards Bluff on the Altamaha River, to "the Cow ford" on St. Marys River.[28]

While clearly interested in obtaining the property of loyalists, the assembly at the same time encouraged people who had at one time pledged allegiance to the king to become citizens. The act, passed on August 22, required that individuals, excluding murderers and plunderers, join either the state or Continental forces. Those who had already done so on or before the British surrender of Augusta on June 5, 1781, would gain the status of citizen immediately. Those who joined up by October 1, were not accused of any crimes, and took an oath, would gain citizenship. The assembly set in motion legislation that, while it found a means to establish greater control over the backcountry and run the government, also drove many useful settlers away.

The assembly, in an attempt to attract enlistments, on August 20, 1781, increased the land bounty for joining the state militia from 100 to 250 acres with a tax exemption for ten years.[29] This legislation implies that militia members had only to remain on their land and do their duty in their district by not plundering or causing distress in order to receive the 250-acre land bounty at war's end. The governor issued a proclamation urging citizens to return from South and North Carolina, Virginia, and points northward to help defend their state or have their Georgia property treble taxed.

Colonel James Jackson served as commandant of the Augusta post while the legislature convened and formed the new state government. Following the recommendation of General Greene, who had unaccountably taken a liking to Jackson during the campaign in North Carolina earlier in the year, the assembly appointed Jackson head of the new Georgia State Legion on August 21. It consisted of two cavalry companies and one infantry.

The *Royal Georgia Gazette* reported that in mid-September loyalist militia in the Brier Creek area formed a plan with twenty members of Jackson's infantry, noncommissioned officers formerly in the British service, to bayonet Jackson in bed, murder the principal officers of the corps, and carry the governor, "the virtuous Nathan Brouson," to Savannah. A detachment of forty-five men sent by Lieutenant Colonel Alured Clarke had reached the vicinity of Augusta to support the insurgents when Jackson's servant, David Davis, uncovered the plot and warned Jackson. The British detachment returned to Savannah as soon as it learned the plot had been discovered. After a general court-martial, the army hanged the three ringleaders and pardoned and restored the seventeen others to their places in the ranks. For his part, the assembly awarded David Davis several hundred acres, a horse with saddle and bridle, a slave, and a new suit of clothes.

Despite the betrayal of several of his loyalist recruits, Jackson decided to place his complete confidence in his infantry. In September he and his men established a post with Twiggs and the militia halfway between Augusta and Savannah and skirmished repeatedly with the British. Jackson captured Ebenezer and made it his headquarters sometime before December.[30]

The state legislature worked to provide food and supplies for the state military as well as citizens between August and December by using confiscated property. The state sequestered property abandoned by loyalists fleeing the up-country for Savannah or East Florida. The executive council directed that the commissioners for sequestered estates postpone sales and supply slaves and other items to commissaries and military personnel. The state could not afford to pay cash for horses, and it bartered cattle from the sequestered estates to acquire horses for the army.

Militia general John Twiggs ordered drivers to collect nonbreeding cattle from the south side of the Ogeechee River while the governor requested that purchasing commissaries carry out this work in such a fashion that the inhabitants would not be alarmed. The government noted that the practice of officers foraging for their own food abused property owners and ordered the quartermaster's department to take charge of collection and distribution of all forage and provisions. The state requested that Colonel Elijah Clarke have the army distribute corn rations to those distressed persons with a certificate from the commanding officer of their district stating the number of members and situation of their family. Those holding public office had ration allowances. The government and the military cooperated with each other and with the settlers to provide food for everyone.

The rebel government reinstated the judiciary system of the state, setting the stage for the first constitutionally legal election in years. The legislature appointed justices for the state counties in August and on November 12 opened the Richmond County court to try criminals. The election day was set for the first Tuesday in December. Carrying out the election proved difficult because loyalist, Cherokee, and Creek parties continued to oppose rebel control in the backcountry. In November, militia general Andrew Pickens waged war against the Cherokees, who had been marauding in the Ninety-Six region, and General Twiggs drove Creek bands across the Oconee River. With much of the backcountry in alarm, first Augusta and later

Brownsborough, approximately twenty miles to the northwest, became the "safe" site for electors to meet to select representatives.[31]

Captain Benjamin Brantley and his loyalist militia made a second attempt to disrupt rebel civil government in mid-December, according to the *Royal Georgia Gazette.* Brantley and his riflemen surprised a group of rebels, evidently part of a larger party led by General Twiggs. One of the men they killed, Myrick Davis, described as "an old miller from Briarcreek," was president of the rebel council. Davis's assassination, in addition to the unsettled condition in the backcountry, affected rebel leaders. Lieutenant Colonel Jackson described both Governor Brownson and John Martin, who replaced Brownson as governor in January 1782, as accepting their positions of leadership "with halters as it were around their necks." He also noted that members of the assembly were "compelled to carry their arms with them to the Senate House to prevent surprise."[32]

General Greene kept Congress apprised of conditions in the South and informed the delegates of his need for additional troops to recover and defend the area. Delegate William Sharpe wrote to Greene on June 21, 1781, stating that despite the logic of his request, those states not in danger from the British army "look with too much indifference upon those which are suffering and unable to make a vigorous opposition." Congress passed an act on July 23 providing a loan of $30,000 for the distressed citizens of South Carolina and Georgia and soliciting charitable donations for the further relief of the population. Greene had probably hoped for more. By July, without clothing, pay, and provisions, Greene's army "began to be sickly, discontented and mutinous."[33]

As the Continental army came into the South, it supplied itself generally through impressment because the credit of the Continental Congress had all but disappeared by 1781. Continental currency was depreciating and quartermaster and commissary certificates were not accepted for purchasing supplies for the army. Greene discovered that rather than money, some southern militia units would accept only slaves or plunder in payment for their services. Slaves enabled many settlers to place their fields in cultivation once again, and Greene encouraged the production of food. Plunder, however, was not a means of payment Greene supported. He wrote that "no Army can act with vigor where the Men and Officers are in pursuit of wealth instead of glory and the public good."[34] Continental general Anthony Wayne, whom Greene sent into Georgia in January 1782, had no choice but to go along with these arrangements because Continental money had no value.

Royal Government Comes to an End, 1782

Georgia had very little money with which to operate, and in January 1782 the state assembly set about to get the finances of the state in order. A thorough examination of the monies drawn from Georgia's Continental funding brought former government and military officials such as John Houstoun, George Walton, and Seth John Cuthbert to account, as well as deputy quartermasters, commissaries, and commanding officers of the state. The assembly agreed to serve gratis with militia officers receiving subsistance pay. The books and records kept by the commissioners of the forfeited estates came under close scrutiny. The governor and council decided to appoint agents for each county to create an inventory of all the land and confiscated property in each and assumed the authority to dispose of the remainder of the confiscated estates jointly with the commissioners. Not only did the assembly members want to account for past fiscal dealings and establish methods of good record keeping, they needed to manage the confiscated estates with care because this property provided the primary means by which the government functioned.

This assembly passed the Confiscation Act that allowed the government to issue certificates on the credit of the confiscated estates to the amount of £22,100 in specie. To be used immediately to supply the army, support the executive council and secret service, and equip the Georgia Legion, these certificates assumed the character of a certified debt to be collected some time in the future by those who accepted them in payment. The act also defined more narrowly which backcountry inhabitants the government wanted out.

The August 1781 assembly had defined the category of property owners whose land could be confiscated by the state as those already behind enemy lines, those who had fought or died in the service of the king, or both, and it had also set up committees to prevent internal conspiracies. The January 1782 assembly went further. Anyone named in the 1778 Confiscation Act, anyone who had ever been within the British lines, anyone who had not joined the militia by October 1, 1781, or those "who are not at this time looked on and respected as Citizens of this State" could expect to have their property confiscated. Loyalists who had fled the backcountry at the height of the partisan fighting before passage of this legislation certainly had no hope of returning to claim their property.

The legislature also passed various requisition acts to use the confiscated property as a means of payment for a variety of debts: to pay for war materials, provide special bounties and bonuses to soldiers, pay the salaries and expenses of government officials, and pay for public service. These requisitions took the form of certificates of indebtedness or special scrip to be cashed in confiscated property or out of the receipts therefrom, orders against particular property, and requests for special sales. The Georgia rebel government offered what it had in abundance, confiscated property and public domain land, and people took it in payment for goods and services.

The state offered confiscated loyalist property in the form of slaves and plantations as payment for services. Officers of the Georgia line received certificates for one hundred guineas each, payable in confiscated property. Colonel James Jackson received a house in Savannah and his dragoons one slave each. Colonel Elijah Clarke received a plantation and his troops one slave to each three men or a certificate of twenty guineas each. The state later acknowledged these certificates, known as "Gratuitous Certificates," as a part of the state debt if they had not been exchanged. The state awarded a plantation and a five thousand-guinea certificate to General Nathanael Greene and a plantation and a four thousand-guinea certificate to General Anthony Wayne in gratitude for their services to the state.[35]

Between January and April the government accomplished a variety of tasks. The legislature appointed county agents to take an inventory of the property on the sequestered estates and later allowed these agents to employ people to assist them in collecting cattle and other property stolen from the estates. The executive council reviewed the renting of a variety of confiscated items, including millstones. The council appointed Andrew Shields to gather up those slaves belonging to the sequestered estates that had not been hired out. It asked magistrates to rent out all the remaining plantations belonging to sequestered estates, resolve disputes over the possession of those already rented, and report back to the council. In late April, in an effort to keep close watch on confiscated property, the legislature requested that a full report of the expenditures on, sales, and monies (rents) received from these estates be presented, along with an account of exactly what property the state held in this manner and to whom it was rented.

After debate, the Georgia legislature resorted to the bartering of slaves from the sequestered loyalist estates to obtain needed supplies locally, for people now preferred a visible commodity in exchange for goods rather than government certificates redeemable by the future sale of sequestered property. "Public negroes," used initially to purchase horses for Colonel James Jackson's troops, soon were used by the government to obtain a variety of items, including whiskey.

The legislation passed by the restored rebel government secured the neutrality, if not allegiance, of the backcountry population. While the last of the targeted loyalists fled to Savannah, those who remained kept their land by joining the rebel militia and thus received easy amnesty and land bounties. In essence, the rebel civil and military authorities offered land and citizenship in exchange for passive support. This support (or promised lack of aggression) allowed the rebel forces to move out of the backcountry toward Savannah between January and June 1782.

In contrast, British civil government offered no bounties to those who pledged their allegiance. Had Governor Wright been able to offer land in return for militia duty, more men, particularly poor settlers, may have joined the loyalist units. Unable to rely on the support of the British military and perfectly aware of the deteriorating situation of the civilians, Wright understood their choice in accepting rebel amnesty and bounties in order to retain their land and plant their crops.

Many Georgians responded to the exigencies of war in such a way as to keep their families alive and their land and possessions safe. British and rebel civil and military authorities vied simultaneously for the loyalty of Georgians between 1779 and 1782 and eventually were compelled to modify the ancient concept of allegiance as a formal bond between themselves and the civilian population. Neither the rebels nor the British could protect the civilian population, yet both needed the peoples' support; without settlers to farm and join the militia, famine and anarchy would overcome all civil claim to Georgia held by either country. While the traditional taking of an oath or declaration of allegiance remained a requirement of citizenship, the continual pattern of oath taking, oath breaking, and renewal of allegiance broke down the symbolic authority of the oath. The loyalty oath had once been a political tool wielded by civil and military authorities to control the civilian population; by the end of the Revolutionary War in Georgia the loyalty oath had become a pliant tool of survival manipulated by the settlers to remain on their land.

By early 1782 rebels and loyalists alike faced famine, for there had been little chance to plant and tend crops the year before and both armies had destroyed food and forage. In February British brigadier general Alured Clarke ordered the provisions and forage in the outlying posts destroyed so Wayne's troops could not use them. Jackson's Legion, part of the Georgia militia under Wayne, in turn destroyed the forage at Governor Wright's plantation at Yamacraw and at Hutchinson Island so the garrison at Savannah could not use them. The resultant lack of provisions in the greater Savannah area made the rebel troops dependent on rice and corn from South Carolina. Wright did not blame the starving civilian loyalists for making "the best Terms they can" with the enemy so they could remain on their land and put in a crop.[36] Instead, he blamed the British government and the military for placing its loyal citizens in the position of going over to the enemy in order to eat.

While Governor Wright did his best to feed the refugee population gathering in Savannah by using the parliamentary stipend, Governor Martin struggled to keep farmers on the land in the backcountry. Few crops had been planted the year before and famine loomed as a distinct possibility: he did not want to see the population starve or be forced to leave Georgia.

During its first session of 1782, the rebel legislature addressed the near famine conditions when it passed the Act to Relieve Distressed Citizens of the State. Widows and children of deceased republican soldiers and individuals who applied to the executive council for aid received food rations. The military commissary distributed these rations, which consisted chiefly of cornmeal. The executive council, informed that some people drew rations to which they were not entitled, appointed a committee to investigate them.

Caught between the state's need for crops to be planted and the need to supply militiamen, Governor Martin did all he could to mollify General Anthony Wayne's complaints about the slowness with which the state responded to the Continental army's call for military support. Wayne came into Georgia in January with a force of approximately five hundred Continental soldiers and militia. Martin wrote to the general on March 14, 1782, stating, "I'm confident the reason why the people have been so tardy in turning out is the present distress of their families and their preparing for a future crop." The previous June, when the state militia recaptured the upcountry, it was not only too late to plant a crop, but the men needed to remain in the militia so as to hold on to the territory.[37] As a result, there had been little to eat for the past year and no surplus was available now. A grain crop needed to be planted in 1782, or families would either perish or be forced to leave the state.

As the April 1782 planting commenced, Governor Martin took it upon himself to raise a rifle corps to take the place of the militia farmers for two months in a pragmatic attempt to meet Wayne's call for troops. To induce men to join the rifle corps, Martin authorized a bounty of one cow and one calf to each one who enrolled. He wrote to Brigadier General Wayne that although he knew he had exceeded his authority under the state constitution in this matter, he wanted to support the military operations as best he could. During this same month, or "season of distress" as the assembly called it, Martin asked Major Greene for two to three hundred pounds of powder and lead until the expected supplies from Philadelphia arrived. With no stored food supply available, Martin explained that "one cause of the great consumption of ammunition is, that our back inhabitants are obliged to support their families almost entirely with gunning."[38]

Civil government officials also suffered from lack of food. In May 1782, just before the assembly adjourned for want of provisions, Governor Martin made it clear to the representatives that he was greatly annoyed at having to live in poverty while governor. He had not sufficient money to employ a private secretary out of his own salary, nor could he purchase "the most trifling necessaries." He supplied his family with provisions from the commissary and gave permission to various members of the assembly and the guard to obtain grain on his private credit. He could only hope that the assembly did not intend to have him become "a butt, a laughing stock, to the Continent [Continental Congress]; it would be a disgrace, a scandal."[39]

As the rebel forces pushed down from Augusta and Continental brigadier general Wayne established a post at Ebenezer, refugees continued to come to Savannah. In early January the assembly set up a lottery to raise money for the distressed refugee families and established a committee to assist refugees and destitute people. Many of these loyalists, respectable landholders in the backcountry, brought an undetermined number of slaves with them, whom they could not feed. Chief Justice Stokes wrote that Wayne's troops came within two or three miles of Savannah, making it dangerous to go out of town. As a result, many refugees from the healthier backcountry, unused to the "putrid air from the swamp, and bad water and provisions" in Savannah, died.[40]

Wright continued to improve the defense of Savannah by employing slaves from the surrounding plantations as pioneers and using refugees to supply manpower. Lieutenant Colonel James Moncrief, appointed commanding engineer in the Southern Department by Sir Henry Clinton in 1780 and stationed in Charleston, visited Savannah in mid-January 1782,

apparently to give advice on improvements to the fortifications. The newspaper referred to his visit as a welcome one "in the present critical situation
of affairs" and hoped Moncrief's assistance would frustrate the enemy's de-
signs on Savannah as it had during the 1779 siege. The garrison at this time
contained thirteen hundred troops, and Wright thought "at least 500 loyal
militia might have been added to them." The assembly wrote a letter to
General Alexander Leslie in June, stating, "The Town of Savannah has
been put into a good posture of Defence at an immense expence to the
Inhabitants."[41]

Governor Wright continued to maintain civil authority in and about Savannah even as he shipped government documents to England from 1780
through 1781. He administered the colony and attempted to get a quitrent
law passed in the assembly to generate money within the province. He
wrote to Under Secretary Knox that it had been a mistake to reestablish
royal government in Georgia without supporting it with military force.[42]
Governor Wright used what remaining power he had and at his own discretion spent the operating funds of the province to feed the loyalist population in Savannah.

Wright and his civil government operated the militia and probably contributed to the third attempt to throw the rebel civil government into disarray by kidnapping its leaders. The *Royal Georgia Gazette* reported the attempt in early March to kidnap rebel governor John Martin. Seven men
from the Volunteers of Augusta, a loyalist militia unit stationed in Savannah, led by Cornet Weatherford, traveled to Augusta with at least one slave.
They arrived at dusk and the slave ran away, possibly to give the alarm of
their attempt to kidnap the governor. As a result, the men immediately
went to William Glascock's house, where they captured Glascock, a Continental officer, and David Douglas, who had recently deserted the loyalists
in Savannah. Unable to proceed with their plan to capture the governor at
his home nearby, they took the prisoners with them and, after several miles,
released them on parole.

While traveling back to Savannah they succeeded in capturing various
rebel militia parties. They placed them on parole, after taking their horses
and weapons. Weatherford made it clear that these paroles were not the
"Georgia Parole, or Coup de Grace, [which] he reserved for Col. Dunn,
Capt. Paddy Carr, and the rest of the *Virtuous Few*," all known rebel militia
leaders and plunderers. Had their bold attempt succeeded, it very well could
have precipitated a crisis within the fragile rebel state government as well as

strained the limited combined military resources of the state militia and the Continental troops under Brigadier General Anthony Wayne.

Wayne, hoping to damage British morale and augment his forces, urged the rebel assembly to encourage desertion from the British army. A proclamation was issued on February 19, and Governor Wright had the details by early March. Three announcements had been issued, one to the king's troops, one to the Hessians, and another to the militia, inviting them to join the rebel troops. The proclamation stated that the situation of the soldiers at the garrison would "shortly be such as scarcely to be envied by the damned," for Parliament had passed an order to send the troops to the West Indies to fight the French. The soldiers had the chance to "become wealthy and happy Citizens of a free Country, by seizing the first opportunity to come out and accept of the bounty offered by Governor Martin's proclamation": two hundred acres of land, a milch cow, and two breeding swine for every noncommissioned officer and private who became a citizen of Georgia. They also had the option to leave Georgia. General Wayne wanted to add to the number of men in his service, for his army kept evaporating and he could get no reinforcements from General Greene.[43]

Although some responded to the proclamation by deserting, Wayne did not gain the number of fighting men he had hoped for. The proclamation was issued in German and evidently distributed by "slatternly" women from Ebenezer. Nineteen Hessians deserted in March, and more did so over the next few months. Many of these men had been impressed for military service and came from other areas of Europe, making their desertion less of a moral issue than for soldiers actually from Hesse. Fewer than one hundred Hessian soldiers deserted, possibly discouraged by the mounted patrols of blacks and at least one German-speaking Creek posted along the routes out of Savannah to capture them. Militia members and loyalists deserted, as many as fifty a month. Governor Wright felt personally betrayed when men such as Sir Patrick Houstoun and his brother William fled to the rebels outside Savannah.[44]

Desertions occurred in the rebel army as well. The March 21, 1782, edition of the *Royal Georgia Gazette* reported that three more deserters from Wayne's camp at Ebenezer had come in, telling of lack of provisions and forage. The deserters' lot within British lines was apparently easy, for the article stated that a deserter could sell his horse to the highest bidder rather than have it requisitioned by the British army. After obtaining the commandant's certificate stating that they had come into the British lines for protection, they received public assistance, were not required to join a fighting unit, and were allowed to go where they wished. State governor Martin, when informed of desertions among the rebel forces, ordered the deserters apprehended and military law enforced.[45] Each side needed troops and offered easy terms to deserters.

Despite Savannah's increasingly isolated and vulnerable position, advertisements in the newspaper show that regular business regarding property and town life continued. Francis Lewis declared the opening of his tavern, and merchants offered a variety of wares, including "superfine" flour, muscovado sugar in barrels, tea, treble distilled lavender water, china, paint, and boots. Various notices appeared in the newspaper from the provost marshal, advertising the sale of property through late June and early July and proclaiming that those who had yet to pay the provost marshal's office for property received at a sale would be held in contempt of court.

Along with the opportunity to acquire land through the provost marshal's sales and writs of attachment, loyalists had the opportunity to obtain slaves. Many slaves had been lost between 1776 and 1778 through confiscation by the rebel state government, plundering raids, natural causes, and flight. Returning loyalists needed slaves to restore their property and reestablish themselves financially. Those who remained on their property in rebel Georgia certainly had the opportunity to purchase slaves confiscated by the rebel government between 1776 and 1778. After the return of the British in late 1778, the opportunity to purchase slaves probably increased because of the influx of slaves into Georgia through their own volition or as army plunder as well as through legal channels for the settlement of debt. It appears as though many loyalists retained possession of their slaves at the time of evacuation, considering the large number leaving with their owners in July.

The probable end of British rule motivated some to announce their plans to leave Georgia, call in their debts, and advertise property they wished to sell before departure. Levi Sheftall advertised his houses in Savannah, a 445-acre plantation five miles from Savannah, and other tracts of land and a share in a tanyard in Savannah in exchange for slaves or any property permitted to be carried from the province. James Herriott stated that he planned to leave for Great Britain immediately and wanted to sell his plantation above Ebenezer called "Fryingpan" and his bay lots in Savannah for cash or government bills. John Henderson stated that he planned to leave the colony the middle of June and wanted his debts paid, and in the meantime he offered madeira wine at a cheap price.

In an address to Sir Guy Carleton on May 31, the assembly made it clear that it hoped its members' property might be protected in the increasingly precarious position they found themselves. Begging for his attention, they pleaded "at this Important Period, *that the property and interest,* of His Majestys faithful Subjects will not be neglected, nor our Peculiar sufferings and Loyalty forgot." Among their peculiar sufferings was the rebel state government's recent initiation of the sale of loyalist property, which they declared confiscated. At the very time many loyalist writs of attachment came due and the prospect of the repayment of rebel debts and the purchase of rebel property became a reality, the rebel state government began to sell loyalist property under the Confiscation and Banishment Act of 1782.[46] Rebels were just as interested as loyalists in obtaining property.

The state assembly passed the Confiscation and Banishment Act on May 4, 1782. The act declared 277 people guilty of treason, banished them from the state forever, and confiscated their property and debts due as of April 1775. Others, accused of aiding and abetting treason, could receive the same punishment, if convicted in a court of law. The act also confiscated the property of Georgia loyalists no longer in residence. The act directed the board of thirteen commissioners appointed as administrators to advertise and supervise the sales of confiscated property and directed the assembly to check their records. Governor Martin wrote regarding the act that "in many respects the terms there held out are hard."[47]

This act included the names of 61 individuals listed in the 1778 Act of Attainder. The additional 216 people named were presumably Georgians who had gone over to the British once they returned and reestablished civil government. The 56 names listed on the 1778 Act of Attainder but missing from the 1782 list were probably individuals now living outside North America with no property left in Georgia to confiscate, living in Georgia but too elderly or too poor to bother with, or dead.[48]

Several examples can be found among those named in the act that illustrate the category of Georgian who had supported, at least initially, the rebel/republican government and then had gone over to the British. James Butler, who had been born in South Carolina in 1738 and counted himself among the most wealthy planters of Georgia, had temporized with the rebels and joined their assembly in 1778. He then fought for the British under Campbell and supported civil government under Wright. He maneuvered as best he could for seven years but in the end lost everything through banishment. Basil Cowper, business partner with the Telfair brothers, served in the rebel assembly until 1776. He fled to the West Indies, returned to

Georgia and took the oath of abjuration, and was placed on parole. After being named in the Act of Attainder in 1778, he fled to South Carolina and returned with the British army. The state banished him. Sir Patrick Houstoun, brother of onetime state governor John Houstoun, went over to the rebels, asked Governor Wright to restore him to full royal citizenship in 1780, then went back to the rebels.[49] The apparent ease with which he transferred his loyalty did not put him in good standing with the state government, and his name appeared on the list of those banished from Georgia in 1782.

While the act lacked the generosity General Greene had encouraged, during the following decade the Georgia Assembly showed remarkable willingness to grant requests to remove individuals from this act and restore them to citizenship. According to one source, approximately one-third of those named in the Act of Confiscation and Banishment eventually returned to Georgia, one-third remained abroad, and the final third could not be traced.[50]

Despite the grim situation, or maybe because of it, James Wright celebrated the king's birthday on June 4, perhaps aware that this would be the last time he would do so as governor of Georgia. The cannon at Fort Prevost and the batteries at the garrison, as well as on board his majesty's ship *Otter* and other vessels in the Savannah River, were fired at noon. In the afternoon Wright hosted a dinner, attended by Brigadier General Alured Clarke, the lieutenant governor, council and assembly members, officers of the royal army and navy, and officers of the militia. That evening the town was illuminated and, according to the *Royal Georgia Gazette,* "every mark of respect shewn that is due from subjects to the best of Kings."

By this date Sir Guy Carleton had received orders to evacuate New York, Charleston, and Savannah. He ordered General Alexander Leslie to evacuate troops from Savannah and Charleston, with no destruction permitted. This news reached Savannah on June 14, "which reduced many of the loyalists almost to distraction." People in the North learned of the evacuation weeks before those in Georgia. A spy in New York informed George Washington that one fleet had sailed "and another much larger is now preparing and falling down, consisting of all the square rigged Vessels in New York harbour which are fit for service." The informant reported that the British intended the ships "for the removal of the Army and Stores from South Carolina and Georgia" and that they had impressed a great number of men, even in daylight, to serve aboard the fleet.[51]

The assembly wrote a letter to General Leslie on the sixteenth, presenting the idea that East Florida would be an appropriate asylum for the Savannah loyalists and their slaves because the increase in population would enable East Florida to defend itself more successfully. The upper house also wrote to General Leslie, stressing Savannah's defenses, the weakness of the enemy, and the loyalty of the inhabitants. The council determined on June 21 that it would not be wise for the Crown officers and other loyal subjects to remain in Savannah once military support had been removed.[52]

The evacuation of Georgia lasted three weeks. The army built fortifications on Tybee Island to protect the thousands of loyalists and their slaves from rebel forces and French naval squadrons as they gathered on the "barren island." Governor Wright protested the brief amount of time that the loyalist inhabitants had been allowed "to quit the province with such of our moveable property as we could collect almost *instantly*." Many people died from bad water and heat exhaustion while waiting to board the ships.[53]

Sir Guy Carleton, General Leslie, and Admiral Robert Digby managed to obtain between thirty-four and thirty-six transports and victualers. These ships brought loyalist refugees, their slaves, effects, and limited provisions to St. Augustine and Jamaica. Other refugees sailed to New York, Nova Scotia, and England. While the troop ships sailed to Charleston and New York, a shortage of vessels forced many civilians to find their own way out.[54]

The end of the British occupation of Georgia placed the confirmed loyalists in the position of yet again having to choose their allegiance. While the British provided transportation to East Florida or Jamaica for many, rebel general Wayne granted protection to those remaining in Savannah. Anyone who wished to serve in the Georgia Continentals for two years or for the duration of the war would regain full American citizenship. Two hundred individuals joined by July 12. They were formed into a corps under the pay of the Continentals and commanded by Major John Habersham.[55]

The British army evacuated Savannah at noon on July 11, leaving the town and garrison in perfect shape. Wayne noted in a letter to Greene that for this "the Inhabitants are much obligated to that worthy and humane Officer Brigadier General [Alured] Clarke." The assembly met in Savannah on July 14 and Wayne turned the town over to the civil authorities at that time. He posted sentries at the town gates for the time being and ordered his soldiers not to commit insults or depredations on people or property and to leave it to civilian officials to deal with crime or questions of property. Wayne kept tight control of the valuable goods in Savannah, however, ordering the merchants and traders to compile invoices of "all goods[,] wares and merchandizes of every species, dry wet and hard respectively belonging to them or in their possession" and bring them with the original invoices to an army official. These goods remained under careful watch until the public and the army had a chance to purchase them at a reasonable price.[56]

General Wayne and Governor Martin had made an agreement with the merchants of Savannah on June 19 that allowed them to remain to sell their goods after the British evacuated. Because little if any merchandise was available in Georgia except from these merchants, Wayne and Martin no doubt thought it expedient to encourage them to stay and make their goods available to the army and general public. Wayne commented in a letter to Greene that the "honorable Congress have been totally silent on *that* and every other transaction of mine whilst in command in Georgia." The Congress did not respond to this arrangement until December 1782, at which time it reluctantly confirmed Wayne's contract with the British merchants.[57]

General Greene and the Georgia delegates to the Continental Congress understood the need to keep an active military force in operation, for the state remained vulnerable. The last skirmish between the British and rebels occurred on July 25 at Delegal's Point on Skidaway Island, where the British succeeded in destroying a plantation. The delegates recommended that the assembly seek aid from Congress and request a force of 150 men: this number would enable the militia to go home and "provide for their families" and perhaps also grow enough provisions to help support the military. General Greene wrote to the president of Congress in mid-August that both South Carolina and Georgia continued to require protection not only from sudden invasions but from the disaffected, the Indians, and the refugees in East Florida. He stressed the importance of keeping the people on their land: "Georgia is nearly depopulated and unless the people can be secured against the enemy they will be in a wretched situation."[58] Nonetheless, Greene ordered all the Continental troops to the Charleston area and left Jackson's brigade and the newly formed battalion of former loyalists to protect the state.

CHAPTER SIX

Pillaged, Plundered, and Carried Off

The Laying Waste of Georgia, 1779–1782

The practice of plundering which I am told has been too much indulged with you, is very destructive to the morals & manners of people; habits & dispositions founded on this practice soon grow obstinate & are difficult to restrain. Indeed it is the most direct way of undermining all Government, & never fails to bring the laws into contempt, for people will not stop at the barriers which were first intended to bound them after having tasted the sweets of possessing property by the easy modes of plunder.—General Nathanael Greene

Georgia was extremely vulnerable to raiding parties, including Indian parties from the west, rebel parties from the northwest, and irregulars and unaligned marauders from the seacoast, East Florida, and the Indian Territory. The ceded lands and the upper part of St. Paul Parish (or Wilkes County and the upper part of Richmond County) were generally under rebel control. They, as well as the parishes below them, St. George (Burke County), St. Matthew and the upper part of St. Philip (Effingham County), Christ Church and the lower part of St. Philip (Chatham County), St. John and St. Andrew (Liberty County) all bordered Creek Indian territory. St. John, St. Andrew, St. David, and St. Patrick (Glynn County) and St. Thomas and St. Mary (Camden County) were in close proximity to East Florida. All of Georgia but the ceded lands and St. Paul, St. George, and St. Matthew Parishes had a seacoast, and these had numerous rivers, including the Savannah, Little, Ogeechee, and Altamaha. Plunderers roamed throughout the countryside, along the seacoast, and up and down the rivers.

Many Georgians stayed on their land rather than flee the wartime conditions because they did not want to forfeit the status that land ownership brought them or lose their slaves. Plunderers could not steal land, but they could destroy the fields, crops, fences, and buildings and run off the livestock. They could capture the slaves and steal the tools, furnishings, means of transportation, and personal items. They could kill or injure the people trying to protect their property and in general make the land uninhabitable. The courts and militia did their best to support property rights, but they could not protect private property from partisan and unaligned plundering bands.

The civil and military authorities further failed citizens by disagreeing with each other over the use of the private property that remained intact. Military units viewed enemy property as a resource with which to feed, clothe, reward, arm, and transport troops; civil government viewed enemy property as a means to raise needed cash to support militia units and meet operating costs. The commissions established by civil government to sort out the abandoned property and reestablish and maintain plantations had little authority to prevent stealing or destruction, whether done by unaligned plunderers or the military. The resultant conflict further weakened civil authority, and numerous civilians assumed a neutral stance.

Military Depredations, 1779

The social fabric of Georgia unraveled as violence steadily eroded civil and military authority. People took the law into their own hands for various reasons: to protect their property and persons from marauders, to gain property though plunder, and to kill enemies. Even as the large British invasion force camped at Savannah in late February 1779, the *Royal Georgia Gazette* reported plundering activities and "horrible murders" in the vicinity.

One involved the death of Joseph Weatherly, manager of Governor James Wright's Ogeechee plantation. The other involved the murder of Mrs. Hearn, her one-year-old child, and her brother Sylvanus Bird and the wounding of her husband. All the victims were shot, Weatherly and Mrs. Hearn scalped, and Weatherly's body further mutilated. Although both crimes happened on the same day, they were committed by different people. Two slaves belonging to Governor Wright, Sandy and Charles, may have murdered Weatherly, and their case came before the Board of Police in February.[1] Plunderers murdered Mrs. Hearn and members of her family and carried off three horse loads of valuable effects after setting fire to the house and barn. These crimes call attention to the brutal frontier conditions under which settlers lived and the inability of any authority, be it civil or military, rebel or British, to prevent them.

Although the return of the British did not inhibit plunderers, the army had a profound effect on the slave population of Georgia. It has been stated that approximately five thousand slaves escaped their bondage before, during, and after troops arrived in late 1778. Probably in December 1778, shortly before hearing that the British had taken Savannah, Henry Laurens estimated from Philadelphia that not fewer than five thousand slaves would be plundered in Georgia by the invading British forces. How many slaves were forced through capture to exchange their condition of bondage under a Georgia master for one under the British military or permanently escaped bondage during the invasion and fled to the woods and swamps is not known.[2]

Many slaves had run to the British ships anchored off Tybee Island in early 1776, believing the army would free them. Governor James Wright, who had witnessed that phenomenon firsthand, grew concerned for the fate of his slave property while in London in 1778. Joined by other prominent Georgians residing there, including John Graham, Anthony Stokes, and Josiah Tatnall, Wright presented a memorial to Lord George Germain stating their hopes that their property, "especially negroes, may not be damaged by British forces in Georgia."[3] The long-held fear that the British would form an alliance with the slave population and establish black troops in Georgia proved groundless, however.

Neither Colonel Archibald Campbell nor General Augustine Prevost wished to alienate slave-owning Georgians by changing the status of their slaves, nor did they wish to destroy the plantation system by removing the labor force. The British army needed the support of slave owners so they would keep their plantations producing food to feed the army. Additionally, the British needed the cooperation of slave owners to use slaves as pioneers and servants as well as for fatigue duty on land and aboard ship.

The Continental Congress considered raising black troops after the British returned to Georgia. Thomas Burke's draft committee report, published before March 25, 1779, presented the reasoning behind this idea: Continental troops could not be spared to go to South Carolina and Georgia; the troops already there could not adequately defend the area; and citizens in

South Carolina could not join the militia because they had to remain at home "to prevent Insurrections among the Negroes, and to prevent the desertion of them to the Enemy." Numerous troops could be formed out of the slave population and easily disciplined. Additionally, the "most Enterprising and vigorous Men from amongst the Negroes" would be put into the army and not cause difficulty at home.

The idea found support among delegates from South Carolina (Georgia had no delegates at this time) as well as the Congress in general. A resolution passed to raise three thousand black troops out of the states of Georgia and South Carolina at a cost of one thousand dollars per slave. Colonel John Laurens, appointed to lead these troops, found it impossible to purchase slaves from their owners for this purpose and sought his father's advice. Henry Laurens responded that "it is certainly a great task effectually to persuade Rich Men to part willingly with the very source of their wealth and, as they suppose, tranquility." Georgia's temporary government did not resolve this act and the South Carolina government refused to adopt it. The Continental Congress put forward the same act on December 8, 1780, but no action was taken.[4]

Once in Georgia, the British military forces acquired and attracted numerous slaves, as anticipated. In mid-January 1779 Rawdon Lowndes reported to Continental Congress president Henry Laurens that the British sent "Flying Parties" across the Savannah River into South Carolina which "carried off many slaves." On February 12, 1779, deserters from a British warship coming into the rebel camp at Port Royal, South Carolina, reported that "they have carried off above 300 negroes belonging to different people." Lieutenant Colonel Archibald Campbell reported that ninety of George Galphin's slaves joined his army on January 30 as they marched to Augusta, and four slaves on horseback rode through rebel lines to join them on February 11. In early April Continental general Moultrie reported that the British, positioned as they were with a galley and sloop at Yamassee bluff on the Savannah River, "received all our deserters before we could overtake them, whilst a great number of negroes in this part of the country got over to them in spite of our care."[5]

While the regular British army sought to preserve property in Georgia, according to one eyewitness both rebel and loyalist forces plundered and destroyed property. As the British army marched to Augusta in January 1779, most of the settlements it passed between Ebenezer and Augusta were found to be "in a ruinous, neglected State." The population was divided in its loyalty with the result that loyalist and rebel were "both revenge-fully destroying the property of each other."[6]

At Abercorn, Campbell and his troops found "a very elegant Mansion built and furnished in the modern Taste, belonging to Mr. Martin, a Gentleman of considerable Fortune, and of great Respect in the Country." Although Mr. Martin had been killed while fighting against the British forces, Campbell reported that the rebels had plundered the family and de-molished "the furniture, Wainscotting, Paper Hangings, Looking Glasses, Doors and Windows etc. etc. to a Degree beyond what the most wanton Barbarians had perhaps ever attempted."[7] The rebels blamed the destruc-tion of this house on the British troops.

While Campbell noted on January 26 that thirty rebels crossed the Sa-vannah River "for the purpose of plundering the Inhabitants of Georgia," he recognized that not all plunderers were rebels. He referred to the Florida Scout traveling with his army as "a mere Rabble of undisciplined Freeboot-ers." On January 30 two of them fell into enemy hands while they "had [been] as usual in quest of Plunder." Of the backcountry militia units Campbell established in the Augusta area, he described the men as "*crackers*, a race of men whose motions were too voluntary to be under restraint" and whose "scouting disposition in quest of pillage," although remarkable, in-terfered with the plan of attack.[8]

Even with the British encamped at Augusta in early February, rebel par-ties continued to cross the Savannah on plundering raids. At this time they apparently met with resistance because of the presence of the British troops. The *Royal Georgia Gazette* printed an extract of a letter from Augusta written on February 6, 1779, stating that "a villaenous tribe of plunderers, under the celebrated horse thief, Captain Few" had ravaged the country for thirty miles above Augusta and claiming that the citizens rose up to drive them away. While the British army remained in the Augusta area the newly formed militia reported rebel movement and the army checked their "predatory Incursions." Rebel militia colonel John Dooly wrote to Colonel Samuel Elbert of the Continental army in February that the rebel plunder-ing raids inhibited recruitment for they turned the backcountry settlers from the rebel cause toward the British.[9]

Continental general William Moultrie also questioned the wisdom of rebel raids into Georgia. He did not approve of South Carolina governor John Rutledge's orders directing rebel forces to go into Georgia "to destroy all the cattle, horses, provisions, and carriages they meet with." Although this would certainly bother the enemy, the indiscriminate plundering would devastate "those unhappy ones who could not possibly get off with their little property" and flee into South Carolina. Moultrie had told these settlers "to remain quiet at home until we should be able to cross the river and give them protection."[10] Civilians became equally wary of rebel and British forces.

Although the British plan to use Cherokees and Creeks to supplement British troops in the backcountry failed, enough Indians arrived after Campbell's departure in mid-February to alarm settlers. Colonel William Few of the Georgia militia recounted in his autobiography that during the early months of 1779 he and his men kept constant guard along the frontier of Richmond County (St. Paul Parish) against "Indians and predatory parties of Tories." British lieutenant colonel James Mark Prevost wrote Lord Germain that two or three hundred Indians came into the backcountry after Campbell left the area, divided into parties, and drove off cattle. After rebels defeated one party on March 21, most Indians returned to their villages. Although the rebel government entered into a peace treaty with the Creeks and Cherokees, the Indians changed their minds, according to Few, and began "cruelly murdering many families of women and children, and in destroying and carrying off much property." Both Creeks and Cherokees suffered famine during 1777–78 as a result of destructive rebel attacks and eventually became dependent on British supplies to survive.[11]

During the early months of 1779 the British army maintained an active presence in much of Georgia, pushing the rebel forces into the backcountry and South Carolina and securing part of the coastline. A steady stream of runaway slaves and rebel deserters came into the British army; few deserters and apparently very few if any slaves went to the rebels. Raiding parties from South Carolina plundered the backcountry, jeopardizing rebel support in the area, and Indians raided along the border. The British damaged little property in Georgia for they depended on its agriculture for food. Abandoned property soon became the center of discord, for it represented booty to the army and economic security to the civil government.

Lieutenant Colonel Campbell set up a civilian Board of Police in January 1779 to manage the abandoned estates of loyalists and rebels alike. The board initiated an inventory of the abandoned estates under its authority and submitted a report for the plantations between the Savannah and the Ogeechee Rivers between January and March. It listed what remained on the abandoned plantations in this area: 925 slaves; 1,337 head of stock of all kinds; 1,178 barrels of clean rice, 14,489 bushels of rough rice, and 105 stacks of rice in straw; and 5,730 bushels of corn and potatoes.[12] Campbell wanted this valuable property protected from plundering so it could be used by the civilian government to generate money to rebuild the colony.

General Augustine Prevost took over from Campbell on January 15, 1779. While the Board of Police and the commissioners of claims that replaced it received numerous complaints regarding plundering, neither General Prevost nor his brother Lieutenant Colonel James Mark Prevost had any interest in addressing civilian concerns regarding the plundering activities of the military.[13] Unfortunately for the Board of Police, James Mark Prevost was the quartermaster general and in early March 1779 was appointed lieutenant governor pro tempore. Unlike Campbell, the Prevost brothers had little interest in cooperating with the civil government.

Reports frequently mentioned one man, Benjamin Springer. He had authority from the quartermaster general, Lieutenant Colonel Mark Prevost, to gather provisions for the army but gave no receipts for items he took. Springer and his associates had "Pillaged, Plunder'd and Carried off" rice, cattle, slaves, silver plate, and household furniture all under the "Cloak and Pretext of furnishing supplies for the Army," according to citizen complaints. In addition, "a number of loose disorderly People were employed by the Commissary to hunt up Cattle." They drove off all cattle that came their way, regardless of who owned the stock, and received five shillings a head from the army. The board claimed that Springer, his subordinates, and the cattle rustlers carried great quantities of stock, provisions, and slaves into East Florida and sold them.[14]

Apparently members of the board and commissioners of claims suspected that Lieutenant Colonel James Mark Prevost knew of this activity and profited by it. While both Prevosts had been stationed in East Florida they may have observed how food was obtained: on one occasion the rangers drove nearly two thousand head of Georgia cattle into East Florida and Governor Tonyn sold them to dealers at twenty-five shillings a head.[15]

James Mark Prevost had a history of acquiring booty in Georgia before becoming the lieutenant governor pro tempore. He led a foraging expedition as far north as Midway in November 1778, with the support of Colonel Lewis Fuser, who traveled north with a small fleet along the inland passage to draw attention away from Prevost's activities. Prevost cut the expedition short when he gained all the booty his army could transport and traveled south rather than joining Fuser at Sunbury. When he reached the St. Marys he held a public sale of his plunder and took in £8,000.[16]

The commissioners of claims continued to try to oppose British army plundering, but to no avail. They called Benjamin Springer before them and cautioned him that they now controlled all the property of the province belonging to rebels and absentee loyalists and he should watch his step. This action by the civilian group was apparently unacceptable to the Prevosts, for James Mark Prevost appeared before the commissioners and "in a very unusual manner" read a letter from his brother Augustine which viciously opposed their operation and called them malicious and a hindrance to the army. The brothers reduced the commissioners' jurisdiction to only absentee loyalist property and threatened to establish martial law if they persisted in interfering with the army.[17]

The commissioners eventually reported to Governor Wright that their lack of authority and the attitude of the military created an environment of devastation and immense waste in Georgia. Great numbers of plunderers felt free "to enter Houses and Plantations at their discretion, to live at free quarter wherever they pleased and carry off Negroes, Cattle, Horses and Property of all kinds under the Idea that *all* was free Plunder."[18] Wright, unable to take any action, could only include the commissioners' report in his correspondence to Lord George Germain.

In the spring of 1779, Major General Augustine Prevost brought an army of twenty-four hundred troops, including regular, loyalist, and Indian units, into South Carolina. Although the original intention was to lure Continental troops down from Georgia's backcountry and to seek food, once in South Carolina the army plundered indiscriminately for several months before returning to Savannah. The army carried off stock, household items, and an estimated three thousand slaves but did not engage the enemy in battle. Prevost's incursion wiped out any chance of loyalist support from South Carolina and provoked retaliatory plundering raids against Georgia until the end of the war.[19]

Rebel general Moultrie described the British entrance into South Carolina on May 3: "The enemy with parties of horse and Indians, are ravaging the country in a barbarous manner, killing people and burning a number of houses as they go on."

Evidently hundreds of slaves willingly followed the army, carrying their masters' property with them. Many of these slaves died of camp fever, and in July, the British segregated the remaining slaves on Otter Island, where hundreds more died of the fever. When leaving South Carolina, the British did not have enough vessels "to carry off all their own troops at once; (much less the negroes, and plunder they have taken)" and so abandoned many slaves. Once back in Savannah, the British did not share the plunder with the Hessians participating in the expedition, as protocol dictated. The British army transported approximately three thousand slaves out of South Carolina, and their eventual destinations included Georgia, East Florida, and the West Indies.[20]

The Indians who accompanied Prevost apparently "behaved extremely well, preferable to the Georgia Volunteers who committed shocking Outrages," according to Deputy Superintendent of Indian Affairs David Taitt. Exposure to the plundering practices of Prevost's troops in South Carolina changed their point of view regarding slaves; for the first time they considered slaves as valuable plunder, along with horses and cattle. Approximately seventy Upper and Lower Creeks traveling with Prevost brought slaves back with them to Savannah.[21]

Governor Wright arrived in Savannah soon after the army's return. He described himself in a letter to Lord George Germain on July 31, 1779, as "Continually haz'd and Perplexd with Complaints and Claims for Negroes." Although Wright reported to Lord Germain that a great number of the slaves had been captured or come into Georgia by their own volition, he did not estimate the numbers. He used "vast" and "some or several Thousands" to describe the number of slaves in the Savannah area in mid-July and placed them into categories. "A great number" had been captured by the army, the Indians had captured 140 slaves in South Carolina, and a "vast Many" had come in on their own. Volunteer intelligence scouts employed by the army, or as Wright referred to them, "Volunteer Plundering Partys," had "taken up great Numbers" of slaves as plunder. Wright and his council quickly agreed not to interfere with the slaves captured by the army but to leave the matter of their export or retention to Major General Prevost.[22] The complexities regarding rightful civilian ownership of slaves never ceased to be a problem for him.

Although Wright did not interfere with the army's slaves, he tried unsuccessfully to convince the Creeks to exchange the slaves they had captured for horses or to sell them to whites. He did not succeed in persuading them, for many slaves followed their new masters into Indian territory and slave traders followed the Creeks to sell them more slaves. It is thought that the slaves the traders brought into Indian country came primarily from Georgia and may have been linked to the plundering activities unofficially sanctioned by Colonel James Mark Prevost.[23] Ownership of slaves for whites was a risky business during wartime because they might run away or be taken by plunderers. Thus traders exchanged slaves with the Creeks for cattle.

Plundered slaves participated in the defense of Savannah. During the siege in the fall of 1779, the army embodied 250 slaves brought from South Carolina into a pioneer corps while the civil government ordered between 400 and 500 slaves, presumably under the commissioners' jurisdiction, to assist in the fortification of the town. Two companies of black volunteers served in combat, presumably coming from both the commissioners' group and the army's pioneers. Some of these slaves escaped and began living in the Savannah area, armed and unsupervised. The commissioners of claims reported in May 1780 that the greatest part of the slaves that had fled to or were brought into Georgia, as well as those belonging to rebels, were now pioneers for the army or employed on the public works. Many others were in the possession of the "Commissaries, Quarter Master General, their Deputies and other Military Departments as also many Officers and even Soldiers of the [British] Army." [24]

The siege brought destruction to much of Georgia through the plundering activities of the rebel and French soldiers. According to rebel Joseph Clay, who participated in the siege, French and rebel seamen and soldiers and bands from South Carolina plundered the seacoast and the backcountry indiscriminately. He noted how the coastal inhabitants had been "plundered of every kind of Property in some instances even the Cloaths on their backs." Inland, "property of every kind has been taken from its Inhabitants, their Negros, Horses and Cattle drove and carried away," chiefly into South Carolina. They also plundered great quantities of the movable property just outside the British lines for the commissioners of claims reported that much of what they were charged with managing had been carried off. [25]

A method of sorts apparently existed among some rebel military units whereby plunder became somewhat respectable. General Lincoln of the Continental army recommended this method to Colonel John Dooly and his militia: any prize taken would be shared by the entire detachment following a ten-day waiting period. During this time any items thought to belong to someone other than the one from whom they were taken would be advertised in the main camp. If they should belong to a friend of the state, this friend could retrieve his property upon paying one-sixth part of the value thereof. [26] Although Lincoln's "method" acknowledged that plunderers might mistakenly take the property of citizens on their side, it fully recognized plunder as one of the major components of both the army's and the militia's activities. With the rebel militia in Georgia operating primarily on the personal inclination of the men and their leaders, this method may or may not have been put into action.

The raids continued after the siege. Governor Wright reported to the council on November 23, 1779, the "almost daily Complaints" of "Small Parties of Rebells, or others who may come to, or be in the Province, distressing the Loyal Inhabitants, and plundering them." He viewed the rebel raids as retaliatory, a direct result of the plundering expedition General Prevost had led into South Carolina during the spring of 1779. In a letter to Lord George Germain on April 14, 1780, Wright expressed his opinion that the plans for raising revenue for the government through the management of the refugee slaves and deserted property had been thwarted "by the Conduct of the Army, Invasion, and Siege."

Partisan Bands, 1780

Beginning in the spring of 1780, circumstances conspired to make Georgia more vulnerable to plunderers than ever before. The removal of British troops from Savannah to Charleston and the subsequent capture of Continental general Benjamin Lincoln's entire army there in May significantly reduced the number of regular army soldiers in Georgia. The rebel civil government ceased to operate, leaving backcountry settlers to seek civil authority from Governor Wright in Savannah.

Nineteen inhabitants of Queensborough and the nearby settlement on Ogeechee River, in St. George Parish, wrote in March 1780 describing how they were unable to protect themselves from the Creek Indians because of fear of offending the "other Partie" (rebels). Nor could they move their families away because "all our Horses are Carrued [*sic*] off Either By Sculking People from Below or Plundering Parties from above." They asked Wright to influence the Creeks to cease attacking them and to send a small supply of ammunition. They requested that he view them "A Neutral People . . . to [order] your Scouting Parties Not to Molest us or our Remaining fiew Horses that yet remain amongst us."[27] Although loyalist units held Augusta and nearby Fort Ninety-Six and British regulars and Hessians remained stationed in Savannah, this military presence did not deter the formation of partisan bands.

It is not surprising that partisan bands made up of former southern rebel militiamen rose up in Georgia and South Carolina during 1780. These men in general had an independent nature, and even when a part of the Continental army, they suffered only minor consequences for not obeying orders. General Moultrie noted that militiamen quickly tired of camp life, got homesick, and then "off they go, without giving the least notice, or obtaining leave, because they know that the fine for their disobedience is so trifling that they care not about it."[28] Once the British captured the Continental army in Charleston in June 1780, what little control that organization had over local militiamen all but disappeared, as did the money to pay them.

Both the Continental army and the Georgia state government found it almost impossible to supply and pay the troops as the Continental dollar continued to depreciate. Joseph Clay, deputy paymaster general, wrote to the Board of War and Ordnance in March 1779 of his concern regarding sufficient cash to purchase supplies and in June of his inability to pay the troops. Georgia's troops and military department received money from the "Carolina Chest," and Clay predicted that the paying of Georgia troops, in particular, would become increasingly difficult as more of them returned to their state to fight while military headquarters remained in South Carolina. General Lincoln wrote to General Moultrie at Charleston in July: "We have at present neither men, stores or money." Lincoln discussed the depreciation of money with Moultrie and concluded that unless some means could be found to increase its value, it would not meet the needs of carrying on the war, and then "our only resource is the VIRTUE of the people; how far that will avail us at this day, I leave you to judge."[29]

Militiamen were motivated to join partisan bands for yet another reason after the British occupation of Charleston: Sir Henry Clinton's June 3, 1780, proclamation required men with the status of prisoners on parole to declare allegiance to the Crown by June 20, 1780, or be considered in rebellion, with the exception of soldiers captured in the garrison at the surrender of Charleston. General Moultrie held the opinion that had Clinton let the militiamen remain on parole and essentially neutral, "many of them would have been very well pleased to have staid at home quietly." Instead, the proclamation forced them to choose sides. Those who did not align themselves with the British at this time, and Moultrie estimated half the partisan fighters in South Carolina were in this category, "were then obliged to keep the field as a place of security."[30] If they returned home, they might be captured and executed, so they remained partisan fighters. This motivation to fight, not necessarily out of strong support for the rebel cause but rather as a means to stay alive, could very well have been shared by Georgia militiamen fighting as partisans.

Because no decisive military victory brought dominant control of Georgia to either rebel or British forces, and neither the state government nor the Continental Congress had the means to support troops there, those Georgians interested in fighting formed partisan bands under the leadership of respected local men. In July 1780, while a delegate in Philadelphia, Richard Howley wrote to General Horatio Gates, head of the Southern Department, describing some of the partisan leaders of Georgia. He listed Colonels John Twiggs, Benjamin Few, John Dooly, and Elijah Clarke and the Captains Inman as "all tried and brave men." These men, as well as James Jackson and William Few, operated on both military and political levels, attracting volunteers to ride with them without pay, supplies, or specified term of service. Jackson noted that his men "rejoiced in an opportunity of revenge for the many injuries their unfortunate relatives & friends had suffered." He estimated that approximately 750 militia saw constant service from 1779 to 1782 inclusive, during which time state government had little if any power and limited external support.[31]

The British retook Augusta in late May 1780 and held it for one year, despite a fierce attack by Elijah Clarke in September. While some partisan bands surrendered to the British after the defeat, others continued to function in the backcountry of Georgia or joined larger groups of partisans in South and North Carolina. As Clarke and his men retreated deep into South Carolina, after the failed attack on Augusta, British major Patrick Ferguson and his loyalist troops attempted to intercept them. Instead, backcountry rebels rose up and defeated Ferguson on October 7, 1780, at King's Mountain, along the South Carolina border. This victory strengthened rebel support in the South.[32]

Clarke sent a militia group led by Captains Stephen Johnson and John Hampton back into Georgia after the King's Mountain victory to alert settlers in South Carolina and Georgia that he would be back. His planned return did not occur, however, because the rebels were defeated at the Long Cane settlement near Ninety-Six on December 11, 1780, and he was wounded. The militia group remained near the Savannah River, however, harassing Thomas Brown's supply line to Augusta and capturing £20,000 sterling worth of goods. Colonel William Harden and his men joined this group, and Brown defeated them in late January 1781.[33]

With only 500 troops at Savannah and 240 in Augusta, the approximately 140 miles between the two British military posts remained vulnerable to unaligned and rebel raiders on horseback. Although still hoping that the military might respond to his requests for reinforcements, on May 9, 1780,

Governor Wright suggested to the first meeting of the assembly that its members consider how the civil government and militia might protect the settlers from plunderers who had "murdered several of the Inhabitants in cold Blood, also some Negroes, and who have Committed Great Devastation, and carried off a great Number of Negroes."

Governor Wright reported to Lord George Germain on August 20, 1780, that a man named McKay led a band of between twelve and twenty "with which he Robs on the Highway between this [Savannah] and Augusta and goes Frequently to the Banks of Savannah River and has Stop't Robbed and Plundered Several Boats." This was Captain James McKay of the rebel militia, who with his men roved the swamps along the Savannah River and plundered supply boats headed for the garrison at Augusta. In November the civil government offered a reward of £500 sterling, an enormous sum, for his capture or death. Wright described another band of over twenty, led by Daniel McGirth, who stole over one thousand head of cattle and drove them to East Florida. McGirth availed himself of every opportunity to plunder and went from rebel to loyalist to unaligned plunderer during the course of the war. When affairs became even more desperate for the British in August 1781, Governor Wright gave McGirth a commission, but he remained uncontrollable.[34]

Wright described plunderers to Lord Germain on August 20, 1780, as active during the middle of the day, unstoppable by either the "poor inhabitants" or civil authority, "for what can the Provost Marshall and a few Constables do against upwards of Twenty Horse men well Mounted and Armed." Warrants taken out against known plunderers proved useless, for these men "Stand in Contempt and Defiance of that and all Law and Government." In late August it came to the attention of the council that "Masters of Vessels" transported presumably stolen or plundered slaves out of Georgia on their ships; all the council could do was publish the law prohibiting this behavior in the newspaper. Civil authority needed the backing of the military to bring some order out of this chaos, and it got none.

Thirty-one merchants in Savannah petitioned the governor in early December 1780 for better protection for the "trade and Property" they transported by sea. Frenchmen, possibly deserters from D'Estaing's siege army, and rebels in galleys and armed boats "infested" the coast, rivers, and inlets of Georgia and plundered the cargoes of merchant vessels. In addition, they plundered the plantations on the sea islands "of Negroes and other Effects." As no armed provincial vessel existed, the petitioners offered to assist in paying to have one built. They also requested that the governor bring this situation to the attention of the assembly, as well as write to the commander at Charleston, Sir Henry Clinton, and Admiral Arbuthnot.[35]

The governor called a special session of the assembly on December 13 to address the merchants' petition. The assembly decided to build and arm a vessel and man it with "fifty white men and Ten Refugee Negroes, whose Masters are now in Actual Rebellion" at a cost of £741. The assembly also agreed to offer a reward of £100 for the apprehension and conviction of the individual or individuals who set fire to Governor Wright's barn on December 14. Civil government responded as best it could to provide protection.

Daniel McGirth and Others, 1781

As the rebel military presence increased in the Augusta area beginning in March 1781, raiders of all kinds plundered the backcountry. Governor Wright, in a letter to Lord George Germain on April 24, 1781, explained that because of the weak British military presence, it was now possible for the "disaffected to Collect and Murder, Plunder etc. in a most cruel and shocking manner." He estimated to Germain on May 5 that five hundred rebels camped about seven miles from Augusta, waiting for reinforcements, and two hundred men on horseback were "Murdering[,] Plundering, Laying Waste and doing all the Mischief they Possibly can particularly to the Wheat Fields and Provisions." At this time, the Savannah garrison contained 500 troops and approximately 350 militia nearby and Colonel Friedrich von Porbeck, who commanded these troops, refused to send any of them to the backcountry.[36]

Raiders hit the settlement of Wrightsborough, located near the Little River in March, murdered eleven loyal citizens, ran off or slaughtered nearly two thousand head of the settlement's communal herd of cattle, and destroyed much of the leading Quaker's property, including a plantation, gristmill, and fields. Many Quakers eventually sought asylum in Savannah. In April the Anglican priest for St. Paul Parish, James Seymour, reported that a band of "Rebel Banditti" rode into the Augusta area and "murdered thirty five innocent Loyalists in their Houses and committed various Outrages." The *Royal Georgia Gazette* reported these activities, among others in the Augusta area, as having been committed by between 200 and 250 "barbarous wretches."[37] Any or all of these plunderers could have been part of the militia groups gathering to attack Augusta or part of unaligned bands.

With no state government yet in existence, citizens in the backcountry had only royal Governor Wright to ask for help. Twelve petitioners from the upper part of St. Philip Parish, who may have lived along the Ogeechee River, requested that Wright appoint three nominated men magistrates in March 1781. Without additional civil authority, "The inhabitants sufers grately by Reason these parts is Cheafly settled with ill Desposed persons that Dont want Law nor Civell government to take place." Seven petitioners from St. George Parish described in an August 1781 memorial how McGirth, "with many others (some of whom have even left our stations here)," stole rebel and loyalist cattle from the upper settlements. They could not afford the cost of initiating legal action against these plunderers in the form of depositions and prosecution and asked Wright to pay the expenses of those who wished to appear "before Magistrates in publick Courts or bound by solemn obligations."[38]

Wright received a lengthy petition in September 1781 from two men representing the inhabitants of St. Philip, St. John, and St. Andrew Parishes detailing the activities of McGirth and his gang. The petitioners wrote to the governor that "they now go about disquised in the night time, breaking into Houses, beating, abusing, shooting at the Inhabitants, and Plundering them in many Cases of their all." They threatened the lives of magistrates and constables and tried to prevent the militia from forming: "Several attempts being made by them to ride over the men in the Ranks—others were severely beat in the Presence of both Militia Officers and the Civil Majistrate."[39] Not only were inhabitants fleeing, but those drafted into the local militia probably would not march far from home because they feared for the safety of their families.

McGirth's claim that he had a commission from the British army intimidated people and made them fearful to testify against him, "their safety Purchs'd only by their Silence." Most recently, the memorialists reported that McGirth and his gang had destroyed fields of corn and driven approximately three hundred head of cattle from the backcountry. Many of these cattle were owned by loyalists now seeking protection within the British lines and fearful of claiming them. They ended their testimony with the statement that unless speedy steps were taken to stop McGirth, militia officers and civil magistrates would be forced to resign and the honest and loyal inhabitants would be forced to leave the area or be "strip'd of the little which they have hitherto found means to Preserved [*sic*]."[40]

McGirth's reputation served the rebel militia, at least on one occasion. Colonel James Jackson of the Georgia rebel militia related an incident of mistaken identity that gave a Lieutenant Hawkins the advantage over three noted loyalists. General Samuel Elbert ordered Hawkins to follow the loyalists as they headed for the British camp near Augusta. The three loyalists discovered him "so near as to preclude a possibility of escape. Hawkins therefore resolutely advanced and demanded who they were. They answered him they were going to join Col. Daniel McGirt the famous plundering partizan in British pay." Hawkins, who wore an old British uniform coat, "told them he believed they lied, that they were Rebels, that his party was near and he would put them to death, that he was McGirt himself." When they swore their loyalty to the British cause, he told them "to ground their rifles and hold up their hands, the Presbyterian mode of attesting and swearing to it." They obeyed, and he took them prisoner and marched them back to General Elbert. "This officer from this and other actions of a similar nature was afterwards called Mad Hawkins."[41]

Although Daniel McGirth's name figures in many accounts, other people also wreaked havoc as plunderers, murderers, irregulars, and pirates. Rebel governor John Martin labeled Captain Sam Moore of St. George Parish (Burke County) a loyalist irregular. James McGirth was listed as a member of his brother Daniel's gang. Rebel militia leaders Elijah Clarke, John Twiggs, Benjamin and William Few, James Jackson, and John Dooly operated without orders from a superior for periods of time. Many labeled rebels Patrick Carr, George Dooly, Josiah Dunn, and Samuel Alexander as plunderers and murderers. Pirates plundered the coastline and rivers, among them George Osborne, who was captured and murdered in October 1781, probably by rebel militia. According to the *Royal Georgia Gazette,* in June a pirate named "the noted Anthony" apparently commanded a fleet of galleys from which he sent boats upriver to plunder slaves and property.[42]

Many robberies occurred that probably had nothing to do with organized gang activity. The *Royal Georgia Gazette* reported firewood stolen and trees cut on property in the vicinity of Savannah by black and white plunderers in March 1781. In late April David Zubly reported that he had been robbed at noon twenty-three miles from Purrysburg of his horse, saddle, bridle, spurs, saddle bag containing clothing, and various gold buckles and buttons.

Sarah Gibbons reported her house, located five miles from Savannah, broken into in late July and cloaks, shoes, a pair of silver buckles, table and bed linen, and a variety of women's wearing apparel stolen. Several men probably worked together to rob the Orphan House in July of slaves, furniture, and valuable possessions and the Indian Gift Storehouse in November of blankets, clothing, cloth, and silk handkerchiefs. Absalom Hoper reported that he had rescued a slave man and girl, who spoke little English and could not name their owners, from a small party of white men on August third. While Hoper advertised for the owner of the slaves, the other accounts of robbery offered a reward for information leading to the capture of the criminals and the retrieval of the property; those too poor to advertise a reward in the newspaper suffered their loss in silence.

The *Royal Georgia Gazette* reported occurrences of soldiers engaged in plundering and murder. In April the paper named four men under the protection of the royal government or on parole and a rebel officer as having killed Captain Richard Pendarvis ninety yards from his house on the River May, as well as William Patterson. The murderers then went to the house, insulted Mrs. Pendarvis, and took three horses and the dead captain's gun. In late July seven rebel plunderers took the horses and goods from Captain Buhler's wagon while he traveled from Savannah to Ebenezer. This rebel party got only to the vicinity of Hudson's Ferry before a group of Georgia loyalists and a Hessian soldier attacked them, killing one, capturing another, and recovering nine horses and a good deal of plunder. Lachlan McGillivray, a well-known merchant planter, accused soldiers from the British garrison of killing stock and damaging property on his plantation in mid-August. After a battle along the Great Ogeechee River, rebels retreated to James Butler's plantation, where they dragged Captain Howell from his sickbed and murdered him in the yard, "inhumanely butchered" Captain Goldsmith, and killed four other men as well. In late November a group of about seventy-five mounted rebel militia, possibly led by Lieutenant Colonel James Jackson, came down from Augusta and killed and plundered among the settlements between Ebenezer and Savannah.

Irregular Rebel Troops

In January 1782, Continental general Nathanael Greene sent General Anthony Wayne into Georgia. Governor John Martin understood that the attention now given to the state's strategic importance by the Continental army required the rebel militia and fledgling civil government to function effectively and cooperate with Wayne and Greene. He wrote to both men, pledging his support.[43]

Martin's pledge to get militia into the field was not easily met, however, for he had to consider near famine conditions and the absolute necessity of the planting of crops. In addition, the militia system continued to depend on the presence of known and respected local leaders, and without them enlistment was slow. Martin thought that if General John Twiggs had been present, "his influence, by having been always on duty with the militia, would have induced them cheerfully to turn out when drafted." With the additional absence of Colonel Elijah Clarke, Martin now had "no officer to enforce my orders generally, nor the militia any one to look up to in camp as their chief. These little circumstances are of great importance among them."[44]

Plundering and murder committed in the backcountry also inhibited recruitment, for potential militiamen felt trepidation at leaving their families and farms unprotected and open to the violence of marauding gangs and individuals. Martin expressed his determination to stop plundering and killing, practices that had been frequent and, in his opinion, somewhat justifiable in the past. In a letter to General Greene, Martin referred to plundering as "a diabolical practice, and one that I am determined to crush." The governor responded immediately when Burke County inhabitants complained that inhabitants of Wilkes County had driven off "several gangs of cattle" and that a party of forty men were "daily expected there on the same horrid business" by ordering Colonel Elijah Clarke to prevent further cattle rustling. Unable to guarantee the safety of loyalist turned rebel David Douglass from probable assassination, and commenting on the recent assassination of another loyalist in broad daylight, Martin wrote to Wayne: "If every man [is] to be a judge in his own cause, there will shortly be no safety in this country."[45]

Martin also had to try to meet the needs of frontier communities beset by raids from "Indians or others," no doubt unaligned plunderers. A group of twenty-three men wrote to the governor from Burke County, on the Ogeechee and Rocky Comfort Rivers, in early March 1782 asking for militia, scouts, and spies to assist them in remaining on their land. If they could not get assistance, they would have to move closer to the Savannah River. The result of moving, the men explained, would be twofold. First, they could no longer feed and house themselves on their own farms. Second, since their farms lay on the frontier border, if they moved, that border would move closer to more settled areas. Martin found it necessary to send militia into the back settlements to protect them from "the many daily murders committed, in which women and children are not excluded."[46]

Not only did Martin have to be persuasive at recruiting and timely in his delivery of troops to Wayne, he had to see that the requisitioning of produce, forage, and horses by the army was done in a businesslike manner. To augment Wayne's Continental forces, he ordered out half of the militia, approximately three hundred men, and did his best to provide them with food and horses. Very little provisions and forage existed in Georgia, and Martin begged South Carolina's governor Rutledge for rice.[47] Governor Martin apologized many times to both Wayne and Greene between January and July for the slowness with which the militia quotas filled and his inability to provide adequate provisions and forage for the army.

Wayne relied on what local militia Governor Martin could supply him with to supplement his Continental troops, and these at first were partisan bands with reputations for plundering. Royal governor Wright referred to these groups as "small straggling parties of rebel militia who were going about the country murdering and plundering the loyal inhabitants in cold blood."[48] Wayne had little if any control over them, and their officers apparently had none.

Major Joseph Habersham of the Georgia militia tried unsuccessfully to keep his force in control during a mission into Indian country to meet with the Choctaws in late January and February 1782. He had little authority over the 120 men, who regularly threatened to desert and to plunder and ignored his orders not to kill Indians. The mission failed, for their attempt to trick the Choctaws into believing they were British soldiers did not work and the Indians left camp. Habersham ordered the militia to pursue them, but the men refused, claiming the fight would not be worth their effort for the Indians had nothing of value to plunder. Instead, all but six officers and two men rode off to plunder the white settlement of St. Andrew, killing three Indians along the way. They plundered the settlement and killed eleven settlers.[49]

Concerned for the effect the irregular rebel troops might have on Wayne's attitude toward the state militia, Martin apologized to him for having sent the volunteer or irregular corps of James McKay and Patrick Carr when he first entered Georgia. Martin wrote again that he never would have sent McKay's and Carr's volunteer corps if there had been any militia available.

He further explained that he had reduced these corps and had retained "a few under proper restrictions as a scout during the present alarm on the frontiers of Burke and Effingham Counties." He then offered, in a placating way, to send Wayne's troops a supply of tobacco, "as nothing contributes more to health in this climate than that plant." [50]

State militia colonel Elijah Clarke, himself raiding independently in Georgia until the advent of Continental troops, returned from raiding the Cherokees to take command of the Georgia militia. He requested that Carr and his men join him. Martin explained to General Wayne that "as a Volunteer Corps they are broke, and now go under the denomination of mounted militia." He suggested that, with the Georgia men subject to Wayne's orders, he might consider using them to reconnoiter the enemy, or perhaps send them out on an expedition to collect the large number of slaves, horses, cattle, and other items accumulated by McGirth and his gang. Martin suggested that if retrieved, McGirth's plunder could be used as bounty for enlistments. [51] Experienced plunderers such as Carr and Clarke would know where to look, and as long as Continental officers supervised the process, chances were good that the property could be retrieved.

The British forces at Savannah greatly outnumbered Wayne's, including approximately 970 fit for duty. Despite the efforts of Governor Martin to get militia into the field, very few joined Wayne. Luckily for the rebels, the British determined to evacuate Georgia and limited their military action to the defense of Savannah. Had they attacked the modest rebel troops assembled in Georgia, in all likelihood the British would have driven them away.

Wayne issued a general order on July 10, 1782, alerting the Continental troops and Georgia militia that Savannah would soon be evacuated of British troops and those loyalist citizens wishing to leave. He wanted state and Continental forces to maintain order and protect the plentiful supply of goods and provisions available in Savannah from plunderers. He ordered his men to appear in clean clothes and keep the camp followers out of Savannah until the army took possession. Lieutenant Colonel James Jackson accepted the keys to the gates of Savannah from a committee of British officers and had the job of keeping "a patrole in town to apprehend stragglers who may steal in with the hopes of plunder." Wayne warned that "Marauders may assure themselves of the most severe and exemplory punishment." [52]

In addition to protecting property, civil and military authorities began the lengthy and nearly impossible task of sorting out property claims. Of immediate concern were evacuees, who needed as much of their property as they could take to build a new life for themselves in East Florida or the West Indies, while those remaining or returning to Georgia needed slaves, supplies, and equipment to rebuild their farms and plantations. A chaotic scene ensued, and slave property proved particularly problematic to locate and claim. An eyewitness estimated that more than five thousand slaves left Savannah with loyalist evacuees and the army. These may well have included those slaves who had served the British troops and were considered loyalists entitled to be evacuated, as well as those promised their freedom by the army.[53]

Governor Martin also monitored public property in possession of the military and that which had been removed illegally from the state. In August he ordered Major Cornelius Collins, commandant at Augusta, to procure a boat and men to take the public arms and ammunition away from General John Twiggs, who presumably had prevented their transport to Savannah. Although Martin hoped that Twiggs "had not proceeded upon so unjustifiable a measure," he was prepared to take whatever measures might be necessary to retrieve the state's supplies, for they were "much wanted" in Savannah.[54]

The governor also worked with Lieutenant Colonel Edward Carrington, deputy quartermaster of the southern army, to determine the forage supplied to General Wayne and his army by the state. Although very little grain had been delivered, Martin noted that rice and corn fields had been destroyed by the army's horses, and these losses "must be valued by indifferent persons, in order to ascertain the same, to do justice to the proprietors." The Commissioners of the Forfeited Estates appointed a Mr. Lindsay agent to collect public property now in Virginia and North and South Carolina. Governor Martin wrote to the respective governors of these states, soliciting their support in recovering the property that had been illegally removed from Georgia.[55] After years of requisitioning and plundering, Martin began to reestablish civilian/military property issues on a legal basis.

By drawing on the expertise of former rebel raiders as well as the militia, Governor Martin tried to curb widespread outlaw activities. He wrote to Captain Patrick Carr informing him that "our roads have been of late so much infested by that fellow Moore and his gang." He hoped Carr would "clear the country of those scoundrels" as well as round up former loyalists who had fled Savannah rather than join Habersham's battalion. Martin asked Colonel Stephen Johnson to try to put a stop to the "scoundrels infesting our roads" in Effingham County and directed Colonel John Cooper, stationed at Midway, to catch marauding horse thieves and to investigate the reported plundering activities of "one Captain Fulton with his company" in the southern part of the state.[56]

Captain Carr offered his assistance as well. He reported to Martin in early August 1782 that fear of plunderers and Indians drove settlers from the Ogeechee River area of Burke County. He suggested the formation of a regiment of former loyalists, now coming in from the Indian Territory in large numbers, to protect the settlers in this area. He also pointed out that the Indian Territory contained a population of slaves hidden there by traders and plunderers while Georgia's coastal area badly needed a labor supply. He suggested to the governor that he ask the Spanish in West Florida to stop purchasing slaves coming from this area until Carr could get them out.[57]

The evacuation of the British had not put an end to violence. Lachlan McIntosh commented to General Greene in late October 1782 that the continued depredations of a "Lawless Savage and unprincipled Banditti" threatened to depopulate the state. He lamented that "no man is Safe one Night in his House in any part of this State or even in the Town [of] Savannah, or traveling a Mile upon the Roads."[58]

CHAPTER SEVEN

Aftermath of the British Evacuation

A Second Crop of Violence

I agree to forgive every body now the War is at an end.—
John Wereat, de facto governor of Georgia in 1779

Although the state needed people on the land to support a militia and a sufficient slave labor force to begin rebuilding the shattered agricultural system, legislation passed in early May 1782 pushed thousands of loyalists and their slaves out of Georgia. The Confiscation and Banishment Act declared 277 individuals guilty of treason and ordered them out of the state in sixty days. All of their land and debts held on April 19, 1775, were to be confiscated by the state. The act also included categories of unnamed individuals whose property would also be confiscated by the state, such as those who had traitorously abetted and participated in treasonable acts, those who had been declared guilty or convicted of offenses that had induced the confiscation of their estates, and those British subjects who possessed or were entitled to property the state wanted. While the state provided the option of joining the militia and serving until the war ended as a way to become a citizen and thereby save one's property from confiscation, for many this proved an impossible choice.[1]

For those who chose to align with Great Britain, it meant leaving their land, status, friends, and way of life. Many of the civil and military authorities, as well as other loyalists who evacuated Georgia, lived in the Savannah area and owned large numbers of slaves. Although the task of arranging at short notice for the transportation of their families and their slaves must have been daunting, many succeeded. Eyewitness accounts for early July indicate that eight hundred whites and between five and six thousand slaves gathered at Tybee Island, and this was just the beginning of the evacuation. While Georgia had the largest percentage of the population of any colony to make claims to the Royal Commission and Savannah had the largest percentage of any city's population to do so, the claimants' reported loss of slaves took up a very small portion of their cases. Real estate and other property losses predominate in the Georgia claims presented to the Royal Commission, indicating that most claimants got their valuable slave property out.[2]

It is difficult to determine the number of people, black and white, evacuated from Georgia, before and during the formal exodus of July 1782. What is known is that most loyalists and slaves who left Savannah went to East Florida, either by ship or overland. The Bahamas were temporarily under the control of Spain and thus not an option for settlement, so the second largest group went to Jamaica. A few Georgians went north to Charleston, knowing that it would be evacuated next, and from there they traveled to East Florida or farther north. Most who went to New York continued on to England, and a very few went to Nova Scotia.[3] During 1782 many more blacks and whites left Georgia than have been documented.

East Florida had been a place of refuge for loyalists throughout the Revolutionary War and continued to serve that purpose as long as the British held it. Georgia refugees, probably arriving on the very first transports or already in St. Augustine, stated in a July 31 memorial to Sir Guy Carleton that at least four thousand people, black and white, had come from Georgia. John Winmitte, commissary or inspector of the refugees at St. Augustine, listed the number of Georgia blacks and whites who arrived in East Florida between July and December 31, 1782, at 1,693 whites and 3,445 blacks for a total of 5,138. Governor Tonyn estimated the number of whites at 1,500 and the number of slaves at 1,000 in October 1782. Quite probably large numbers of Georgians, documented and undocumented, traveled to East Florida with their slaves before and during the evacuation of Savannah and then headed to Jamaica before the end of the year.[4]

Governor Wright and a group of some ten to fifteen wealthy property owners convinced General Alexander Leslie, commander of the British forces in the South, to provide them with a convoy of ships to sail directly from Savannah to Jamaica. The general provided six vessels, which transported ten families and between 1,568 and 2,000 slaves in early August. Wright no doubt had privileged information regarding the British proposal to surrender East Florida to Spain as part of the peace negotiations and so arranged for his valuable slave property, as well as that of his elite planter friends, to be transported to Jamaica instead. Sir Archibald Campbell, governor of Jamaica, who, as Lieutenant Colonel Campbell, had led the British invasion of Georgia in December 1778, greeted the Georgia loyalists. The historian Wallace Brown states that probably 400 whites and 5,000 blacks reached Jamaica after evacuating Savannah, indicating that additional Georgians transported their slaves there, possibly after a quick stop in St. Augustine.[5]

Because royal Georgia civil government rather than the military had control of the pioneer slaves, few slaves accompanied army personnel evacuating Georgia. Of all the soldiers who traveled from Savannah to New York and on to Nova Scotia between November 1782 and November 1783, very few brought Georgia slaves with them, nor did many civilians. The Georgia group formed a modest percentage of the total number of slaves and free blacks on board these vessels: of the 1,388 men, 955 women, and 559 children, the Georgians numbered only 55 men, 32 women, and 12 children.

From details taken down by commissioners regarding each black passenger before departure it can be learned that the presence of British troops in Georgia had influenced the movement of these people. Twenty of the Georgia slaves ran away from their masters at the time of the British invasion in late 1778, and twenty-one ran away from their masters at the time of the siege of Savannah, during October 1779. An additional eight, including three women, ran specifically to the British army during 1778 and 1779.

Army personnel owned seven men, eleven women, and four children on board the vessels. Among them were three Knoblauch Regimental drummers, all men in their twenties named George, who traveled under the care of Dr. William Munter, possibly to continue their journey to Hesse. Hessian regiments recruited blacks, paid them in specie, and apparently maintained a tolerant racial attitude. Eight ship captains owned one male slave each, and eight men, six women, and one child did not have an owner identified. The commissioners noted that four men, six women, and one child were free, among them Patty Stokes, formerly owned by Chief Justice Anthony Stokes, and Rachel and her daughter Sally, formerly owned by Lieutenant Governor John Graham.[6] Army personnel and civilians took few Georgia slaves to Nova Scotia between 1782 and 1783.

One can only estimate the number of slaves transported during the evacuation. Estimates range from three thousand to between five and six thousand. The enumerations made by John Winmitte at St. Augustine indicate that a total of 3,445 slaves arrived at that port from Georgia between July and December 31, 1782.[7] Add to this the approximate number that went directly from Savannah to Jamaica in the late July convoy arranged by Governor Wright (1,568–2,000) and the total reaches 5,013–5,445. Considering Wallace Brown's estimate of 5,000 Georgia slaves eventually reaching Jamaica and the sum increases by 3,000 to 8,013–8,445, although some of these slaves could have first evacuated to St. Augustine. Colonel James Jackson, an eyewitness to the mass of humanity gathered on Tybee Island in July 1782, provided the figure of not less than 5,000 and 6,000 for the number of slaves evacuated from Georgia by ship alone. These figures take into account only two well-documented points of disembarkation, and no doubt slaves left Georgia on undocumented vessels and by land, before and during the evacuation, and arrived at their destinations undocumented as well. It is possible that between 7,000 and 8,000 slaves left Georgia during 1782.

The state government made every effort to retain or regain slaves. On July 3 and 16, it attempted to purchase slaves from departing loyalists before their evacuation. On July 15, the council established a committee to search for "numbers of negroes and other property . . . now secreted in and about the town and Garrison of Savannah." On August 23 the council ordered Captain Samuel Goodhue to condemn the prize sloop *Swift*, which he had captured and brought to Savannah, to give the owners of slaves on board the opportunity to claim them. Evidently the prize contained "a number of negroes, part of which appear to be the property of some of the good citizens of this, and the next State." As before and during the war, the extensive and unpatrolled coastline and numerous rivers and creeks facilitated smuggling. Government efforts to retrieve Georgia slaves from East Florida dragged on for years, with little effect.[8]

In addition to a reduction in the slave population, the rebuilding of Georgia's agriculture suffered because plundering bands continued to operate between East Floria and Georgia as a result of a weak military presence on both sides of the border. With the Revolutionary War essentially over in the South, East Florida and Georgia discovered they had a common enemy in plunderers and established relations with each other in an effort to secure civil peace.

Governor John Martin described Colonel James Jackson's Legion, the only state troops in Georgia, as "annihilated" because the men's enlistment period had nearly expired; Major John Habersham's Georgia Battalion, made up of loyalist recruits, was "not to be much depended on at present." These limited troops could not contend with the cross-border raiding unassisted. On August 15 Martin wrote to Tonyn suggesting the two work together to "put an entire stop to and prevent all plundering and marauding parties in the future and for carrying on the war upon a more liberal plan." The executive council sent Colonel William McIntosh to St. Augustine, along with Samuel Stirk and John Wereat, as commissioners "with full and sufficient powers to treat for that purpose."[9]

Tonyn had his own problems. Many inhabitants rightly feared the eventual cession of East Florida to the Spanish and plotted to wrest the colony away from the British before this happened. Loyalist officer John Linder Jr., appointed by Tonyn to lead a troop of horse along the St. Johns River to stop plunderers, wrote to General Anthony Wayne on June 25, 1782, requesting that he send two hundred men to assist the inhabitants in taking East Florida from the British. Linder claimed that four-fifths of the population "declare in favor of America." After this effort at insurrection failed, Linder joined his father, John Linder Sr., in plundering with Daniel McGirth and others between the St. Johns and St. Marys Rivers. Most of the slave population of the colony, which before July 1782 had numbered approximately three thousand, lived here, as did many Georgia and South Carolina refugees; Tonyn had no control of the area. When in early December 1782 the governor formally announced that Britain would cede East Florida to Spain as part of the peace treaty, bands of marauders increased their activities, necessitating the formation of two troops of horse.[10]

Although the commissioners did not negotiate with Tonyn, they delivered Martin's sealed letter of August 15 and discussed the plundering situation. Tonyn described the plunderers as "a set of men who set themselves down between the two countrys and pay no obedience to the laws of either." He expressed particular concern that people from other states might come through Georgia or along the coast to plunder East Florida, and he urged that "every step should be taken to secure and punish such offenders." The Georgia commissioners told him that "our State was not competent to take notice of or punish them."[11]

Nevertheless, Tonyn hoped that Governor Martin would be forthcoming with help and sent him a letter to that end. Tonyn endorsed Martin's desire for cooperation between the two governments to curtail plundering activity and stated that he would immediately put this plan into effect. He added that each government must stop its own citizens from committing depredations and hostilities upon the other and that, until the signing of a peace treaty between Great Britain and the United States, "we shall conduct the contest with becoming moderation and as little as possible to the disadvantage of industrious, peaceable inhabitants of both countries." The two governors determined that each government would be responsible for preventing plundering bands from crossing the St. Marys River. They also agreed to an exchange of supplies, and Tonyn intended to procure provisions from South Carolina as well. Martin, in his October 19 reply to Tonyn's letter, pledged that "nothing shall be wanting on my part to promote and carry on a friendly intercourse between the two countries consistent with my duty and the laws of nations."[12]

The arrangement between Georgia and East Florida did not preclude British plundering activities or an attack from the West Indies, and Georgia civil and military authorities did their best to provide a defense. On September 7, Martin wrote to General Wayne in South Carolina requesting assistance should the British attack by sea, once "their particular purposes are answered in the West Indies." He stated, "We are preparing a couple of galleys and look-out boats, as speedily as possible, for the protection of this town and harbor." A week later he ordered Captain Robert Greer to retrieve the cannon on board the wrecked ship *Defiance* for the Savannah garrison and urged him to take every precaution not to be captured by the enemy.[13] Fortunately, no British attack occurred to put Georgia's meager coastal defenses to a test.

While rebels viewed East Florida as containing "refugees all instigated by a Spirit of revenge, and a wish to repair their broken fortunes" by going back into Georgia to recover property, Georgians themselves attempted to retrieve slave and other property in the royal colony. When in April 1783 it became officially known that the province was to be evacuated, Tonyn and his council refused to cooperate any longer with Georgians seeking their property until the confiscation laws in Georgia had been lifted and property restored to loyalist owners. This action met with the support of John Mulryne Tatnall, a Georgia loyalist evacuee living in St. Augustine. He wrote on July 4, 1783, that the "Americans" prevented "all and every" refugee from landing in the United States, while "they have had the assurance to come hither claiming Negroes and other property. This is now put a stop to by our governor who from the general claymore of the people was under the necessity of doing it."[14]

Near riotous conditions in St. Augustine put a further strain on civil authority. The province had contained approximately one thousand whites and three thousand blacks before the evacuations of Savannah and Charleston. Now, thousands of refugees and their slaves, loyalist provincial units from Georgia and the Carolinas, thousands of Indian warriors, and numerous sailors from the British transports crowded the city and province. The provincial corps at St. Augustine, consisting of nine hundred men from the Royal North Carolina Regiment, the South Carolina Royalists, and the King's Carolina Rangers, nearly mutinied on May Day 1783 because they did not know at what location they would be discharged. The arrival of the prospective Spanish governor, Manuel de Zespesdes, in June 1784 did not strengthen civil authority but made it more ambiguous. The chaotic conditions in East Florida no doubt spilled over the border into Georgia.[15]

According to Tonyn, many of the white Georgia refugees and their slaves remaining in East Florida depended on government assistance to survive. In a letter to Lord Shelburne dated November 14, 1782, he noted that "General Leslie has sent six months provisions but no necessary implements of agriculture or wherewithal to purchase, and many are without clothing." He described many of the refugees as indolent backwoodsmen and thought only four hundred of the Georgians capable of bearing arms, possibly to form a militia unit, and about five hundred slaves trustworthy enough to be armed. Tonyn anticipated that "when His Majesty's daily bounty to the refugees cease to be granted they will become exceeding clamourous and impatient and the worst is to be expected from the lower sort." He feared that now, with all the provincial troops either evacuated or discharged, the "lower sort" would unite with "an abandoned set of men collected together in the back countries of this and Georgia" and attempt "to ravage this country and insult government in its feeble disabled condition." Tonyn also worried about the "licentious disbanded" soldiers remaining in the province, who displayed a tendency toward "rapine and plunder."[16]

In addition to the "lower sort," East Florida offered refuge to prosperous if not elite families who bitterly resented abandoning their property in Georgia. Some had purchased and developed holdings in East Florida during the colonial era or during the early days of the Revolution and made a relatively easy transition. Others arrived with only the possessions they had managed to bring with them at the time of the evacuation but with the financial resources to begin again. In either case, these Georgians began to reestablish their customary lives of privilege, which centered primarily around agriculture and slave labor. When it became clear that the British government would give up East Florida to the Spanish, these steadfast loyalists learned that they had few places to choose where they might reestablish their way of life yet again. Georgian John Mulryne Tatnall referred to himself and other elites as "vagrants" whom Parliament had "plunged in the torrent of misery and despair."[17]

Governor Tonyn made every attempt to plan for the evacuation of East Florida but found it difficult. He wrote to General Sir Guy Carleton in September 1783 that he estimated ten thousand inhabitants would evacuate but "in the perplexing and fluctuating state of their minds it is impossible to judge what shipping may be absolutely wanted." Tonyn reported that government officials and their families, as well as others with families, had decided to evacuate to England while those with slaves preferred Jamaica, the Windward Islands, and the Bahamas. While some refugees in East Florida formally requested permission from the Georgia state government to settle in Georgia during 1784, others had quietly begun to go north across the border beginning in 1783. Governor Tonyn estimated that five thousand backcountry people returned overland to the United States before the formal evacuation of East Florida.[18]

William Brown, Tonyn's assistant, kept a formal though incomplete count of the number of whites and blacks who left East Florida during the lengthy evacuation that took place between April 1784 and November 1785. These people included evacuees from Georgia, South Carolina, and other states as well as residents of the province of East Florida. Brown listed a total of 3,398 white and 6,540 black evacuees. Brown's records indicate that the highest number of whites, 1,033, went to the Bahamas and took with them the second highest number of blacks, 2,214. The second highest number of whites, 725, evacuated to Nova Scotia with 155 slaves. The third highest number of whites, 462, returned to the United States with the highest number of blacks, 2,561. In addition, 450 whites and 200 slaves remained in East Florida, 246 whites and 35 blacks went to Europe, 225 whites and 444 blacks went to Dominica, 196 whites and 714 blacks went to Jamaica and the Spanish Main, and 61 whites and 217 blacks went to other foreign parts.[19] If Tonyn's estimate of 5,000 whites returning to the United States with an unestimated number of slaves before the evacuation is added to the 462 whites Brown counted, the approximate total of 5,462 whites returning to the United States from East Florida is a great deal more than the total number of whites who evacuated East Florida for all other places combined, 2,936. It may be supposed that thousands of undocumented white and black Georgians came into East Florida during 1782 and unofficially returned to the United States between 1783 and 1785.

Loyalists continued to move about after 1785. One study has traced white

Georgians both named and not named in the Confiscation and Banishment Act to the following locations after the completion of the East Florida evacuation in 1785: thirty-three named and forty-nine not named to the Bahamas; thirty named to Great Britain; twelve named to Jamaica; five named and four not named to Nova Scotia. This same study estimated that approximately one thousand whites left the state permanently. Loyalist Thomas Brown, living in the Bahamas, estimated in 1802 that more than three thousand loyalists emigrated from there to southern Georgia following a series of cotton crop failures.[20]

The Georgia Assembly began to adjust its response to refugee loyalists named in the Confiscation and Banishment Act almost immediately after the state was retaken from the British, and it also accommodated other loyalists not so named. In August 1782 the assembly removed forty-eight names from the Confiscation and Banishment Act and placed them on the Amercement Act. If these particular people paid their amercement tax to the state, generally not more than 12 percent of their property holdings, they would receive all their political privileges back, except for the right to vote or hold office, which would be returned to them three years after the war officially ended. The assembly also established county committees to gather the names of residents not named in the Banishment and Confiscation Act but who had pledged their allegiance to the British. Should they renounce their allegiance to the king and swear allegiance to Georgia and the United States, they would receive their political rights. Apparently neither the state government nor its citizens put very much effort into hunting down banished individuals who returned to the state after 1783, with the exception of loyalist military personnel.[21] As had been the case during the Revolutionary War, the civil government needed settlers to farm the land and fill the ranks of the militia. Thus many people who had aligned themselves with the British, particularly during the last part of the war, were able to pledge their allegiance to the United States without political ramifications.

Governor Tonyn watched the Georgia Assembly's treatment of confiscated estates and banished individuals with interest. He observed to officials in London during the spring and summer of 1783 that Georgia effected moderation while, in comparison, the state of South Carolina "is more violent. The populace has been let loose upon the loyalists, some of whom have been severely treated."[22] Although Georgia's moderation lay partly in its need for population, the contrast between South Carolina's and Georgia's legislatures may have been related to the fact that Georgians benefited from royal civil government during three years of the Revolutionary War, at a time when the rebel civil government ceased to function or barely existed.

South Carolina, in contrast, had no civil government between 1780 and 1782, although Lieutenant Governor William Bull and other civil officials lived in Charleston awaiting formal appointment. During this time South Carolinians lived under British martial law and rebel anarchy. After the high-ranking British civil and military authorities and loyalist militia officers were evacuated, Georgians chose to take a lenient approach when considering the various petitions of loyalists for special consideration. The South Carolina legislature responded regionally to the petitions of various individuals who wished to be removed from the confiscation and amercement acts of that state, with the coastal members taking a more lenient view than the backcountry representatives.[23]

A group of thirty-two former rebel soldiers and Georgia citizens signed a petition to the assembly in 1783 asking that loyalist Thomas Young, recently removed from the Confiscation and Banishment Act, now have his estate freed from the fines accrued by amercement. The petitioners built a case for Young based on their gratitude for the kindness and respect he had shown them while prisoners of war at Sunbury. Additionally, Young had helped effect the exchange of Raymond Demere, Daniel Roberts, and Joseph Rice during the Battle of the Rice Boats in 1776 and had also assisted those individuals who had their rice taken by the British navy in achieving compensation for their loss. Young had served in the militia of South Carolina and paid for a substitute to serve in his place in the Georgia line and then remained neutral. He assisted in locating runaway slaves and returning them to their owners at the evacuations of Savannah and Charleston and sent a group of forty slaves back to Savannah during these chaotic times. He lost a great deal of property through impressment and had been forced into exile when placed on the confiscation and banishment list. He filed a claim with the Loyalist Claims Commission that reported the loss of thirty-f.tagsive slaves and asked for an award of £19,590.7. The petitioners, among them Lachlan McIntosh Jr., Raymond Demere, Seth John Cuthbert, and John Wereat, stressed Young's "acts of friendship received in Their hours of adversity" as bearing considerable weight in pleading his case. On February 21, 1785, the assembly amerced Young's property at 12 percent and did not allow him to vote, hold office, or be eligible for a seat in government for fourteen years.[24] They did not hold to this restriction, however, for on February 10, 1787, they gave him full citizenship.

Although not named in the Confiscation and Banishment Act, Dr. Donald M'Leod sent a memorial to the assembly through Colonel John McIntosh seeking citizenship in Georgia, apparently as a British subject. A committee formed to review his memorial and received numerous petitions for and against his request, which the *Georgia Gazette* published. M'Leod had cared for the sick and wounded after the British took Savannah in late December 1778, tending to many of the rebels on land as well as on the prison ships. Colonel George Walton and General Samuel Elbert, among others, testified to M'Leod's professional care and kindness. A Continental soldier, James White, testified that as he lay in the hospital recovering from having his arm amputated, "he was greatly in want of a shirt and a pair of overalls and that John Newman was also in the same condition." M'Leod, "unasked, went and purchased necessaries to cover their nakedness." M'Leod arranged for a separate hospital ship to provide quarantine for prisoners taken ill while on board the prison ships. Despite his apparent professionalism, a Dr. Rehm and Mordecai Sheftall, among others, accused M'Leod of mixing fine, broken, or pulverized glass in "a parcel of medicines sent by him" to the prison ships, evidently to kill the prisoners. Other individuals sent memorials testifying that M'Leod at no time mixed medicines, and on July 31 1782, the committee recommended that his request be supported. Nevertheless, the assembly did not grant citizenship to M'Leod at that time, by a vote of eighteen to sixteen.[25] On August 1, 1783, however, the assembly voted to permit him to reside in Georgia for six months, granted him full citizenship on February 21, 1785, and allowed him to repossess whatever of his property remained unsold by the state on December 19, 1794.

Levi Sheftall's name appeared on the Confiscation and Banishment Act, for he had moved his family to Charleston in late 1778 and sworn allegiance to the king during the summer of 1780. His brother Mordecai returned to Savannah in December 1782 and encouraged the assembly to reinstate Levi, who returned to Savannah in August 1784.[26] On February 21, 1785, the assembly amerced Levi Sheftall's property at 12 percent and did not allow him to vote, hold office, or be eligible for a seat in government for fourteen years, but in February 1787 it restored him to full citizenship.

Francis Levett held property in Georgia but lived in East Florida during the Revolutionary War, owning a plantation along the St. Johns River and a town lot in St. Augustine. In 1783 he played a role in the capture of plunderer Daniel McGirth: Colonel William Young, who led a ranger corps established by Governor Tonyn to combat the growing lawlessness in East Florida, imprisoned McGirth for stealing Levett's horses. Upon the evacuation of East Florida, Levett went first to Jamaica and then the Bahamas with his family and one hundred slaves. Levett eventually gained permission to return to his sea island property in Georgia. Again, he played a role in the history of Georgia for there he became one, if not the first, to grow Pernambuco cottonseed. He announced its success in 1789, and thus began the cultivation of sea island cotton in Georgia.[27]

While accommodating returning loyalists, the state government at the same time dispensed land bounties to soldiers and civilians. The state had offered land as a bounty to attract soldiers and encourage backcountry settlers to join the militia after June 1781. Between February 17, 1783, and February 22, 1785, it gave several classes of men the opportunity to apply for bounty land grants in the Bounty Reserve, an area within the two newly formed counties of Franklin and Washington. The men qualified to apply included those who had fought with the Georgia Line attached to the Continental Army between January 1776 and December 1783; officers and enlisted men from the three Minute Battalions, all nonresidents of Georgia who came to the state between June 1777 and March 1778; members of the state militia from February 1776; refugees who fled Georgia but joined the militia regiments of either South or North Carolina; residents of Georgia who between August 1781 and July 1782 joined the militia and did not plunder; and British deserters.

The application process required these men to obtain a voucher from their commanding officer, if they had served, or the commanding officer of their district, if they had remained on their land, and present it to the executive council for verification. The council then issued a numbered warrant which the petitioner gave to the county surveyor, who surveyed the chosen land and made several plats. The surveyor general and secretary of state received the plat and executed the warrant, respectively, and recorded the information. After February 1785, the state opened the ungranted land in the Bounty Reserve to headright settlers and gave no preference to veterans. Many unqualified people ended up with Bounty Reserve land.[28]

The desire for land compelled some men to commit fraud. Officers and officials, among them Elijah Clarke and Edward Telfair, signed the initial vouchers for the soldiers and settlers and then purchased them from the men. They had the land grants issued to themselves and accumulated thousands of acres in the process. In addition, a riot in the land office on May 29,

1784, resulted in the removal and scattering of the warrants, which had yet to be numbered and distributed. This deliberate destruction of records resulted in the duplication of many warrants, thus enabling those in the possession of both to acquire two grants of land and others to claim they had received vouchers for larger claims than they actually had. Once distributed, others sold their numbered warrants and certificates to people not entitled to the land bounty.[29]

James Jackson noted bitterly that many staunch rebels had been "reduced from opulent fortunes to a condition little superior to beggary" while the British government compensated loyalists banished from the state for their losses. Parliament established the Loyalist Commission in 1783 to inquire into the losses, services, and claims of American loyalists, and it operated until 1790. The commissioners chose to limit compensation to the loss of lands, buildings, personal property, and slaves. When determining compensation, they did not consider uncultivated lands, debts owed to refugee loyalists by Americans, work done for the government, or material or money supplied to the military during the Revolutionary War. Governor Wright, who sailed to England on July 6, 1782, represented many Georgians before the Loyalist Commission in London until his death in 1785.[30] Back in Georgia, John Wereat, briefly governor of rebel Georgia in 1779, served as auditor general of the state from 1782 to 1793 and provided refugees with information regarding the value of their property losses. Loyalists and state citizens disputed prewar debts and confiscated property for years; one such case became the topic of the Supreme Court justices' first set of published opinions in *Georgia v. Brailsford* on August 11, 1792.[31]

Georgia had the highest percentage of its population of any former British colony to make claims to the Loyalist Commission, and 49 percent of these consisted of claims made by military personnel. This may have been the case partly because a large group of loyalists stayed together, moving from Georgia to East Florida and then to the Bahamas, and they may have encouraged and assisted one another with their claims. Additionally, the commission facilitated the filing of their claims by establishing branch offices in the Bahamas and in London and extending the filing date deadline by two and a half years, from January 1, 1787, to October 6, 1789. More than one hundred loyalists who had either evacuated to East Florida or who already lived there began to organize their claims before the 1785 evacuation of that province, and the branch office in Nassau filed approximately eighty claims. Although difficult to determine, the number of Georgians filing claims appears to be between 140 and 150.[32]

As loyalists attempted to receive compensation from the British govern-ment for their losses of real and personal property brought about by the evacuation of Georgia and East Florida, the Georgia state government set up a board of commissioners to organize the sale of confiscated loyalist estates to bring in badly needed money. At the end of the Revolutionary War the state had an accumulated debt of approximately $1.5 million in specie. This amount resulted from the total accumulation of the various forms of paper issued by the state, the Continental Congress, and the army to pay debts. Confiscated loyalist properties available for sale by the state included 200,000 acres of land, approximately 250 town dwellings and busi-ness properties, 200 vacant town lots, and a considerable number of slaves and other property.[33]

In addition to helping the state fiscally, these sales offered Georgians a chance to purchase valuable property and recoup some of the losses they had suffered after the return of the British in late 1778. The government held the first three sales before the British evacuated Georgia, offering choice tidal rice land and plantations as well as lots, businesses, and wharves in Savannah and Sunbury. Between June 13 and October 21, 1782, eight sales of loyalist property brought to the state a recorded £344,980.[34]

Deputy Paymaster Joseph Clay purchased property at these early sales. He had fled Georgia in 1779, taking his large family and as many slaves and possessions as he could into South Carolina. He relocated on the Ashley River and later took a house in Charleston. He left twelve or thirteen of his best slaves in Georgia, as well as household goods, cattle, hogs, and sheep, never expecting to see them again. He hoped that "it will be in my power (sooner or later) to make it up when I get back, out of the property of some of their [the British army's] loyal friends."[35] He did just that. Clay pur-chased five hundred acres of Governor Wright's plantation between the Ogeechee and Canoochee Rivers on June 13, 1782, while the governor was still in Georgia. He later purchased five hundred acres of Lieutenant Gov-ernor Graham's estate on the Ogeechee River. Including these two pur-chases, Clay bought nearly four thousand acres of land from the confiscated estates by July 1782.

Unlike Clay, however, many buyers of property at these early sales could not pay the state for the land. Over the next few years, the legislature insti-tuted various changes in the procedure to sell the confiscated estates which limited the number of buyers to those more able to pay. Sales for 1783–4 equaled £55,800, and the last large sale initiated by the state, in Sep-tember 1785, brought in £8,963. The state had essentially finished with selling loyalist property by 1787, though a small amount of money came in after that. Money generated from the sale of confiscated property, like previous sales in 1776–1778, did not meet expectations.[36]

The state, having set up a board of commissioners for confiscated properties in 1782, relied on it to make sense out of the chaos of public and private debt for the next forty years. Initially set up to retire the wartime debt, the funds from confiscated property sales also went to establish educational institutions in Georgia and pay operating expenses for the state government.[37] Those citizens who had been able to retain or regain their land, augment or replace their holdings, or acquire land for the first time during the war continued to be in a strong position after hostilities ceased, whereas the state experienced financial distress for several years. As before and during the Revolutionary War, land continued to be the best investment of all.

Many threads tie the Georgia of the 1760s with the Georgia of the 1780s, for they run straight through the Revolutionary War period without a break. A chronic lack of specie and an unreliable tax base remained the same for the population of Georgia. Factionalism among government leaders continued to exist. New lands opened up for settlement and emigrants threatened civil order by pushing into Indian territory. Marauders continued to plunder and kill. As the province and revolutionary state had begged for regular army defense knowing they could not rely on the militia, so too the postwar state looked in vain to the federal government for defense against the Indians. Despite requesting regular army protection, the population did not want federal government intervention regarding Georgia's claim to Indian land.[38] Georgia remained a violent frontier, sparsely populated by predominantly poor settlers with a minority of prosperous slave owners.

Georgians had learned the value of local and provincial civil government during colonial days and managed to keep some form of civil authority functioning at all times during the Revolutionary War. They were motivated to do so in hope of protecting their property rights. Reminiscing long after the war, William Few recalled in his autobiography how in January 1784, the assembly met in Savannah to establish "law, order and government, which had been nearly annihilated." With the civil government reestablishing authority yet again, the citizens, he continued, "now turned their attention to their various occupations and pursuits for the acquisition of property."[39]

NOTES

Chapter One. Poor Settlers on the Southern Frontier

1. Lee Ann Caldwell, "Women Landholders of Colonial Georgia," in *Forty Years of Diversity: Essays on Colonial Georgia*, eds. Harvey H. Jackson and Phinizy Spalding (Athens: University of Georgia Press, 1984), 185, 188.

2. The facts of Georgia's colonial history, the sequence of crucial events and the people and locales involved, have been treated in detail in such sources as: Allen D. Candler, ed., *Colonial Records of Georgia*, vol. 12: *Proceedings and Minutes of the Governor and Council, August 6, 1771–February 13, 1782* (Atlanta: Franklin-Turner, 1907), *The Revolutionary Records of Georgia*, vol. 1: *Proceedings of the Council of Safety* (Atlanta: Franklin-Turner, 1908); *Proceedings and Minutes of the Governor and Council of Georgia, October 4, 1774 through November 7, 1775 and September 6, 1779 through September 20, 1780*, Collections of the Georgia Historical Society (Savannah, Georgia Historical Society, 1952); Kenneth Coleman, *Colonial Georgia: a History* (Milwood, New Jersey: KTO Press, 1989), *The American Revolution in Georgia, 1763–1789* (Athens: University of Georgia Press, 1958); Kenneth Coleman and Charles Stephen Gurr, eds., *Dictionary of Georgia Biography* (Athens: University of Georgia Press, 1983); and Harold E. Davis, *The Fledgling Province: Social and Cultural Life in Colonial Georgia, 1733–1776* (Chapel Hill: University of North Carolina Press, 1976). All of these works inform the factual framework of this chapter.

3. John J. McCusker and Russel R. Menard, *The Economy of British America, 1607–1789* (Chapel Hill and London: University of North Carolina Press, 1985), 172.

4. John Martin Boltzius, "Johann Martin Bolzius Answers a Questionnaire on Carolina and Georgia," trans. and ed. Klaus G. Loewald, Beverly Starika, and Paul Taylor, *William and Mary Quarterly*, 3d ser., 14 (April 1957), 226–28, 232–33, 237–38, 244–46, 249.

5. George Fenwick Jones, ed., "A German Surgeon on the Flora and Fauna of Colonial Georgia: Four Letters of Johann Christoph Bornemann, 1753–1755," *Georgia Historical Quarterly* 76 (Winter 1992).

6. Alan Gallay, *The Formation of a Planter Elite: Jonathan Bryan and the Southern Colonial Frontier* (Athens: University of Georgia Press, 1989), 101, 90, 97.

7. Julia Floyd Smith, *Slavery and Rice Culture in Low Country Georgia, 1750–1860* (Knoxville: University of Tennessee Press, 1985), 15, 20–21.

8. Gallay, *The Formation of a Planter Elite*, 71, 90–92, 162.

9. Betty Wood, *Slavery in Colonial Georgia, 1730–1775* (Athens: University of Georgia Press, 1984), 96–97, 107; Sylvia R. Frey, *Water from the Rock: Black Resistance in a Revolutionary Age* (Princeton: Princeton University Press, 1991), 10.

10. Smith, *Slavery and Rice Culture*, 21, 23, 27 footnote 23.

11. Harry Roy Merrens, *Colonial North Carolina in the Eighteenth Century: A Study in Historical Geography* (Chapel Hill: University of North Carolina Press, 1964), 54; McCusker and Menard, *The Economy of British America*, 172.

12. Harold E. Davis, *The Fledgling Province: Social and Cultural Life in Colonial Georgia, 1733–1776* (Chapel Hill: University of North Carolina Press, 1976), 158.

13. Jack P. Greene, *The Quest for Power: The Lower Houses of Assembly in the Southern Royal Colonies, 1689–1776* (Chapel Hill: University of North Carolina Press, 1963), 45; Davis, Harold, *Fledgling Province*, 252; Jackson Turner Main, *The Social Structure of Revolutionary America* (Princeton: Princeton University Press, 1965), 280–81.

14. E. R. R. Green, "Queensborough Township: Scotch-Irish Emigration and the Expansion of Georgia, 1763–1776," *William and Mary Quarterly*, 3d ser., 17 (April 1960), 198.

15. Ralph C. Scott, Jr., "The Quaker Settlement of Wrightsborough, Georgia," *Georgia Historical Quarterly* 56 (Summer 1972), 211–13, 217; Edward J. Cashin, *Lachlan McGillivray, Indian Trader: The Shaping of the Southern Colonial Frontier* (Athens: University of Georgia Press, 1992), 235.

16. Rachel Klein, *Unification of a Slave State: The Rise of the Planter Class in the South Carolina Backcountry, 1760–1808* (Chapel Hill and London: University of North Carolina Press, 1990), 64–66.

17. Richard Maxwell Brown, *Strain of Violence: Historical Studies of American Violence and Vigilantism* (New York: Oxford University Press, 1975), 72–73.

18. Anthony Stokes, *A View of the Constitution of the British Colonies, in North America and the West Indies at the Time the Civil War Broke Out on the Continent of America* (London, 1783), 140–41.

19. Louis De Vorsey, Jr., *The Indian Boundary in the Southern Colonies, 1763–1775,* (Chapel Hill: University of North Carolina Press, 1961), 160–61.

20. *Documents of the American Revolution 1770–1783*, ed. K. G. Davies, Colonial Office Series, 25 vols. (Dublin: Irish University Press, 1974), vol. 5, James Habersham to the Earl of Hillsborough, 24 April, 1772, 77. Unless otherwise noted, all quoted correspondence to and from James Wright, John Stuart, Frederick Haldimand and the Earl of Dartmouth is from *Documents of the American Revolution*.

21. De Vorsey, *Indian Boundary*, 163–65.

22. J. Russel Snapp, *John Stuart and the Struggle for Empire on the Southern Frontier* (Baton Rouge: Louisiana State University Press, 1996), 116.

23. William Bartram, *Travels through North and South Carolina, Georgia, East and West Florida* (London, 1792; reprint ed. Charlottesville: University Press of Virginia, 1980), 37–38, 46.

24. Davies, *Documents of the American Revolution*, vol. 6, James Wright to the Earl of Dartmouth, 27 December 1773, 267.

25. Smith, *Slavery and Rice Culture*, 22; Elisha P. Douglass, *Rebels and Democrats: The Struggle for Equal Political Rights and Majority Rule During the American Revolution* (Chapel Hill: University of North Carolina Press, 1955), 340.

26. Percy Scott Flippin, "The Royal Government in Georgia, 1752–1776: The Military System, Part II," *Georgia Historical Quarterly* 13 (June 1929), 142.

27. James M. Johnson, *Militiamen, Rangers and Redcoats: The Military in Georgia, 1754–1776* (Macon: Mercer University Press, 1992), 91–92, 96–97; Davies, *Documents of the American Revolution*, vol. 8, John Stuart to the Earl of Dartmouth, 13 February 1774, 48, James Wright to the Earl of Dartmouth, 31 January 1774, 30, John Stuart to Frederick Haldimand, 3 February 1774, 34, Alexander Cameron to John Stuart, 1 March 1774, 57.

28. Davies, *Documents of the American Revolution*, vol. 8, John Stuart to the Earl of Dartmouth, 13 February 1774, 48–49.

29. Ibid., John Stuart to Frederick Haldimand, 3 February 1774, 35, John Stuart to the Earl of Dartmouth, 13 February 1774, 49.

30. Ibid., 92, 95; Johnson, *Militiamen, Rangers and Redcoats*, 100.

31. Percy Scott Flippin, "The Royal Government in Georgia, 1752–1776: The Financial System and Administration," *Georgia Historical Quarterly* 9 (September 1925), 188–89; Joseph Albert Ernst, *Money and Politics in America, 1755–1775: A Study in the Currency Act of 1764 and the Political Economy of Revolution* (Chapel Hill: University of North Carolina, 1973), 171; Percy Scott Flippin, "The Royal Government in Georgia, 1752–1776: The Commons House of Assembly," *Georgia Historical Quarterly* 8 (December 1924), 259; Percy Scott Flippin, "The Royal Government in Georgia, 1752–1776: Governor Wright," *Georgia Historical Quarterly* 8 (June 1924), 83.

32. Flippin, "The Financial System," 204; Beverly W. Bond, Jr., *The Quit-Rent System in the American Colonies* (New Haven: Yale University Press, 1919), 353–54.

33. Flippin, "The Financial System," 218; Ernest, *Money and Politics in America*, 172; Simon L. Adler, "Money and Money Units in the American Colonies" (Paper presented at the Rochester Historical Society, 8 January 1900), 2, 7–9; Alice Hanson Jones, *Wealth of a Nation to Be: The American Colonies on the Eve of the Revolution* (New York: Columbia University Press, 1980), 132–33; Ralph Volney Harlow, "Aspects of Revolutionary Finance, 1775–1783," *American Historical Review* 35 (October 1929), 49; Milton Sydney Heath, *Constructive Liberalism: The Role of the State in*

Economic Development in Georgia to 1860 (Cambridge: Harvard University Press, 1954) 61.

34. Gallay, *Formation of a Planter Elite*, 81, 97.

35. Heath, *Constructive Liberalism*, 58; Ernst, *Money and Politics in America*, 173.

36. James Habersham, *The Letters of the Hon. James Habersham, 1756–1775*, Collections of the Georgia Historical Society, vol. 6 (Savannah: Georgia Historical Society, 1904), James Habersham to Bella Wright, February 27, 1772, 168; Bartram, *Travels*, 64.

37. Douglass, *Rebels and Democrats*, 34, 75.

38. Gallay, *Formation of a Planter Elite*, 62–63, 72.

39. Jack P. Greene, "Legislative Turnover in British America, 1696 to 1775: A Quantitative Analysis," *William and Mary Quarterly*, 3d ser., 38 (July 1981), 461; Greene, *Quest for Power*, 382; Douglass, *Rebels and Democrats*, 74–80; Stokes, *A View of the Constitution*, 126; Harvey H. Jackson, "Consensus and Conflict: Factional Politics in Revolutionary Georgia," *Georgia Historical Quarterly* 59 (Winter 1975), 389–391.

40. Greene, *Quest for Power*, 380–81, 384; Flippin, "The Commons House" (James Wright to the Board of Trade, December 26, 1768), 245–46.

41. Stokes, *View of the Constitution*, 128.

42. Gallay, *Formation of a Planter Elite*, 112–14, 233–34 note 17; William W. Abbott, *Royal Governors of Georgia, 1754–1775* (Chapel Hill: University of North Carolina Press, 1959), 105–21.

43. Habersham, *Letters*, James Habersham to James Wright, February 17, 1772, 166.

44. Gallay, *Formation of a Planter Elite*, p. 122, 124–25.

45. Frances Harrold, "Colonial Siblings: Georgia's Relationship with South Carolina During the Pre-Revolutionary Period," *Georgia Historical Quarterly* 72 (Winter 1989), 716–17; Robert M. Weir, *"The Last of American Freemen": Studies in the Political Culture of the Colonial and Revolutionary South* (Macon: Mercer University Press, 1986), 164.

46. Jackson, "Consensus and Conflict," 390–91; Harvey H. Jackson, "Georgia Whiggery: The Origins and Effects of a Many-Faceted Movement," in *Forty Years of Diversity: Essays on Colonial Georgia*, eds. Harvey H. Jackson and Phinizy Spalding (Athens: University of Georgia Press, 1984), 260.

47. Frances Harrold, "Colonial Siblings: Georgia's Relationship with South Carolina During the Pre-Revolutionary Period," *Georgia Historical Quarterly* 72 (Winter 1989), 739; Abbot, *Royal Governors*, 159.

48. Leonard L. Mackall, "Edward Langworthy and the First Attempt to Write a Separate History of Georgia, with Selections from the Long Lost Langworthy Papers," *Georgia Historical Quarterly* 7 (March 1923), 2–3.

49. Habersham, *Letters*, James Habersham to Countess of Huntingdon, April 19, 1775, 238, James Habersham to John Edwards, May 25, 1775, 245.

50. Robert A. Olwell, "'Domestick Enemies'" Slavery and Political Independence in South Carolina, May 1775 – March 1776," *Journal of Southern History* 60 (February 1989), 30–31; Snapp, *John Stuart,* 158.

51. Colin G. Calloway, *The American Revolution in Indian Country: Crisis and Diversity in Native American Communities* (Cambridge: Cambridge University Press, 1995), 23; Snapp, *John Stuart,* 158–161.

52. *Letters from Governor Sir James Wright to the Earl of Dartmouth and Lord George Germain, Secretaries of State for America from August 24, 1774 to February 16, 1782* (Savannah: Georgia Historical Society, 1901), vol. 3, pt. 4, James Wright to the Earl of Dartmouth, June 20, 1775, 189.

53. Stokes, *A View of the Constitution,* 129; Douglass, *Rebels and Democrats,* 343.

54. Olwell, "'Domestick Enemies,'" 35, 39–40; Johnson, *Militiamen, Rangers and Redcoats,* 141.

55. Paul H. Smith, Gerard W. Gawalt, and Ronald M. Gephart, eds., *Letters of Delegates to Congress,* vols. 1–19 (Washington, D.C.: Library of Congress, 1976), vol. 1, John Hancock to George Washington, July 24, 1775, 663–64, vol. 2, John Adams' Diary, September 16, 1775, 18.

56. *Letters of James Wright,* James Wright to the Earl of Dartmouth, June 17, 1775, 184, James Wright to the Earl of Dartmouth, November 16, 1775, 222; William Moultrie, *Memoirs of the American Revolution,* 2 vols. (New York: David Longworth, 1802), vol. 1, Mr. Corbet to William Moultrie [n.d.], 59–61.

57. *Letters of James Wright,* James Wright to the Earl of Dartmouth, October 14, 1775, 217, November 1, 1775, 218–19, August 16, 1775, 206, September 23, 1775, 213, November 3, 1775, 220, James Wright to the Lords of Trade, November 3, 1775, 220.

58. *Letters of James Wright,* James Wright to the Earl of Dartmouth, July 8, 1775, 192, August 7, 1775, 205; *A Narrative of the Official Conduct of Anthony Stokes of the Inner Temple, London, Barrister at Law; His Majesty's Chief Justice and One of His Council of Georgia and of the Dangers and Distresses He Underwent in the Cause of Government: Some Copies of Which are Printed for the Information of His Friends* (London: 1784), 9–10.

59. [Stokes], *A Narrative,* 9–10; *Letters of James Wright,* James Wright to the Earl of Dartmouth, December 9, 1775, 223–24.

60. [Stokes], *A Narrative,* 10, 12–19, 25–26.

61. Ibid., *A Narrative,* 22–25.

62. Gordon B. Smith, "The Georgia Grenadiers," *Georgia Historical Quarterly* 64 (Winter 1980), 409.

63. *Letters of James Wright,* James Wright to the Earl of Dartmouth, August 17, 1775, 208; Edward J. Cashin, *The King's Ranger: Thomas Brown and the American Revolution on the Southern Frontier* (Athens: University of Georgia Press, 1989), 26–29.

64. Johnson, *Militiamen, Rangers and Redcoats,* 125.

65. *Letters of James Wright,* James Wright to the Earl of Dartmouth, September 23, 1775, 212.

66. Ibid., James Wright to the Earl of Dartmouth, October 14, 1775, 215.

67. Brown, Richard Maxwell, *Strain of Violence,* 73–74.

68. Douglass, *Rebels and Democrats,* 341; Greene, *Quest for Power,* 45–46.

69. Gallay, *Formation of a Planter Elite,* 71–2, 108.

70. *Letters of James Wright,* James Wright to the Earl of Dartmouth, December 11, 1775, 227.

71. Ibid., James Wright to the Earl of Dartmouth, March 10, 1776, 234.

Chapter Two. Rebels Take Charge

1. The facts of Georgia's revolutionary history, the sequence of crucial events and the people and locales involved, have been treated in detail in such sources as: Allen D. Candler, ed., *The Revolutionary Records of Georgia,* vol. 1: *Proceedings of the Council of Safety, Journal of the Council of Safety, Journal of the Provincial Congress* (Atlanta: Franklin-Turner, 1908); Kenneth Coleman, *The American Revolution in Georgia, 1763–1785* (Athens: University of Georgia Press, 1958); and Kenneth Coleman and Charles Stephen Gurr, eds., *Dictionary of Georgia Biography* (Athens: University of Georgia Press, 1983). All of these works inform the factual framework of this chapter.

2. Elizabeth Lightenstone Johnston, *Recollections of a Georgia Loyalist* (New York: M.F. Mansfield and Company, 1901), 44.

3. Unless otherwise noted, all quoted correspondence to and from James Wright, the Earl of Dartmouth and Lord George Germain is from *Letters from Governor Sir James Wright to the Earl of Dartmouth and Lord George Germain, Secretaries of State for America from August 24, 1774 to February 16, 1782,* Collections of the Georgia Historical Society (Savannah: Georgia Historical Society, 1901), vol. 3, pt. 4.

4. Ibid., James Wright to the Earl of Dartmouth, September 16, 1775, 209.

5. Ibid., James Wright to the Earl of Dartmouth, August 7, 1775, 169.

6. Paul H. Smith, Gerard W. Gawalt and Ronald M. Gephart, eds., *Letters of Delegates to Congress* , vols. 1–19 (Washington, D. C.: Library of Congress, 1976), vol. 2, Richard Smith's Diary, September 14, 1775, 11.

7. [Stokes], *A Narrative of the Official Conduct of Anthony Stokes of the Inner Temple, London, Barrister at Law; His Majesty's Chief Justice and One of His Council of Georgia and of the Dangers and Distresses He Underwent in the Cause of Government: Some Copies of Which Are Printed for the Information of His Friends* (London: 1784), 26; Harvey H. Jackson, "The Battle of the Rice Boats: Georgia Joins the Revolution," *Georgia Historical Quarterly* 58 (Summer 1974), 231.

8. "The Narrative of Henry Preston of Savannah, Joint Prothonotary and Clerk of

the Crown for the Province," in *Setting Out to Begin a New World: Colonial Georgia*, ed. Edward J. Cashin (Savannah: Beehive Press, 1995), 167; Jackson, "Battle of the Riceboats," 232.

9. Jackson, "Battle of the Riceboats," 231, 234, 237–38; James M. Johnson, *Militiamen, Rangers and Redcoats: The Military in Georgia, 1754–1776*, (Macon: Mercer University Press, 1992), 129.

10. Johnson, *Militiamen, Rangers and Redcoats*, 141; *Letters of James Wright*, James Wright to Lord George Germain, April 26, 1776, 243, Memorial of Lieutenant Governor Grahame [Read January 1, 1777], 376; Jackson "Battle of the Rice Boats," 231; *The Royal Commission on the Losses and Services of American Loyalists 1783–1785. Being the Notes of Mr. Daniel Parker Coke, M.P. One of the Commissioners During that Period*, ed. Hugh Edward Egerton (New York: Arno Press and The New York Times, 1969), 246–47; Johnston, *Recollections*, 46–47.

11. Lilla M. Hawes, ed., "Letter Book of Lachlan McIntosh, 1776–1777 Part I," *Georgia Historical Quarterly* 38 (June 1954), Lachlan McIntosh to George Washington, March 8, 1776, 150.

12. Ibid.

13. Smith, Gawalt, and Gephart, *Letters of Delegates*, vol. 2, Diary of John Adams, September 23, 1775, 50–51.

14. Silvia R. Frey, *Water from the Rock: Black Resistance in a Revolutionary Age* (Princeton: Princeton University Press, 1991), 45–80, 85.

15. Hawes, "Letter Book of Lachlan McIntosh, 1776–1777 Part I," Lachlan McIntosh to George Washington, March 8, 1776, 150.

16. Ibid., 151.

17. Jackson, "Battle of the Riceboats," 238–39; Hawes, "Letter Book of Lachlan McIntosh, 1776–1777 Part I," Lachlan McIntosh to George Washington, March 8, 1776, 152.

18. [Stokes], *A Narrative*, 32; "Georgia Council of Safety to the South Carolina Council of Safety," in *Setting Out to Begin a New World: Colonial Georgia*, ed. Edward J. Cashin (Savannah: Beehive Press, 1995), 171–2; Alan Gallay, *The Formation of a Planter Elite: Jonathan Bryan and the Southern Colonial Frontier* (Athens: University of Georgia Press, 1989), 71; *Letters of James Wright*, James Wright to Lord George Germain, March 20, 1776, 240; Egerton, *Royal Commission*, 318–19; Edward J. Cashin, *Lachlan McGillivray, Indian Trader: The Shaping of the Southern Colonial Frontier* (Athens: University of Georgia Press, 1992) 270, 315.

19. [Stokes], *A Narrative*, 28–29, 31; *Letters of James Wright*, James Wright to Lord George Germain, March 20, 1776, 240.

20. *Letters of James Wright*, James Wright to Lord George Germain, March 20, 1776, 239–40.

21. Martha Condray Searcy, "The Introduction of African Slavery into the Creek Indian Nation," *Georgia Historical Quarterly* 66 (Spring 1982), 27; Robert A. Olwell,

"'Domestick Enemies,': Slavery and Political Independence in South Carolina, May 1775–March 1776," *Journal of Southern History* 60 (February 1989), 45.

22. [Stokes], *A Narrative*, 31–34.

23. Hawes, "Letter Book of Lachlan McIntosh, 1776–1777 Part I," Lachlan McIntosh to George Washington, April 28, 1776, 153.

24. Johnson, *Militiamen, Rangers and Redcoats*, 155; Hawes, "Letter Book of Lachlan McIntosh, 1776–1777 Part I," Lachlan McIntosh to George Washington, April 28, 1776, 153.

25. Ibid., 154.

26. Albert Berry Saye, *A Constitutional History of Georgia 1732–1945* (Athens: University of Georgia Press, 1948), 92–95; Milton Sydney Heath, *Constructive Liberalism: The Role of the State in Economic Development in Georgia to 1860* (Cambridge: Harvard University Press, 1954), 78.

27. Smith, Gawalt, and Gephart, *Letters of Delegates*, vol. 3, Samuel Adams to Samuel Cooper, April 30, 1776, 601, vol. 8, James Lovell to William Whipple, November 3, 1777, vol. 10, Henry Laurens to John Houstoun, July 18, 1778, 304, vol. 11, James Duane to Mary Duane, January 23, 1779, 506, vol. 17, Artemas Ward to Thomas Ward, April 30, 1781, 201.

28. Heath, *Constructive Liberalism*, 58, 72, 120, 125, 126.

29. Curtis P. Nettels, *The Emergence of a National Economy, 1775–1815*, vol. 2: *The Economic History of the United States* (New York: Holt, Rinehart and Winston, 1962), 24–25; Ralph Volney Harlow, "Aspects of Revolutionary Finance, 1775–1783," *American Historical Review* 35 (October 1929), 50.

30. Heath, *Constructive Liberalism*, 78.

31. Robert S. Davis, Jr., "The Last Colonial Enthusiast: Captain William Manson in Revolutionary Georgia," *Atlanta Historical Journal* 28 (1984), 23–27.

32. *Letters of James Wright*, James Wright to the Lords of Trade, November 3, 1775, 220, James Wright to Lord George Germain, March 20, 1776, 240, James Wright to Lord Dartmouth, November 1, 1775, 219; Egerton, *Royal Commission*, 61–63.

33. *Letters of James Wright*, James Wright to Lord George Germain, April 26, 1776, 243–44.

34. Egerton, *Royal Commission*, 14–19.

35. *Letters of James Wright*, Memorial of Lieutenant Governor Grahame [Read January 1, 1777], 377.

36. [Stokes], *A Narrative*, 38–45.

37. Egerton, *Royal Commission*, 66–67; Johnston, *Recollections*, 45–47.

38. Lorenzo Sabine, *Biographical Sketches of the Loyalists of the American Revolution, with an Historical Essay*, (Boston: Little, Brown, 1864), 200–201, 553, 111; *Letters of James Wright*, James Wright to Lord Dartmouth, January 3, 1776, 229, November 1, 1775, 219; Martha Condray Searcy, *The Georgia-Florida Contest in the Ameri-*

can Revolution, 1776–1778 (Tuscaloosa: University of Alabama Press, 1985), 66; Gallay, *Formation of a Planter Elite*, 71, 235 n. 26; Cashin, *Lachlan McGillivray*, 291, 293.

39. Egerton, *Royal Commission*, 246–47; 318–19; 61–63; *Letters of Joseph Clay, Merchant of Savannah 1776–1793*, Collections of the Georgia Historical Society (Savannah: Georgia Historical Society, 1913), vol. 8, Joseph Clay to Bright and Pechin and Mr. Rice, May 3, 1777, 28.

40. Heard Robertson, ed., "Georgia's Banishment and Expulsion Act of September 16, 1777," *Georgia Historical Quarterly* 55 (Summer 1971), 277.

41. Egerton, *Royal Commission*, 61–63, 341–42.

42. Ibid., 249–50, 318–19, 243–47.

43. Saye, *Constitutional History*, pp. 95–96.

44. Harvey H. Jackson, "Georgia Whiggery: The Origins and Effects of a Many-Faceted Movement," in *Forty Years of Diversity: Essays on Colonial Georgia*, eds. Harvey H. Jackson and Phinizy Spalding (Athens: University of Georgia Press, 1984), 266; Harvey H. Jackson, *Lachlan McIntosh and the Politics of Revolutionary Georgia* (Athens: University of Georgia Press, 1979), 52–54.

45. "The Case of George McIntosh," *Georgia Historical Quarterly* 3 (1919), 132.

46. Searcy, *Georgia-Florida Contest*, 21; Wilbur Henry Siebert, *Loyalists in East Florida, 1774 to 1785: The Most Important Documents Pertaining Thereto*, vol. 2: *Records of Their Claims for Losses of Property in the Province* (Deland: Florida State Historical Society, 1929; reprint ed., Boston: Greg Press, 1972), 365–66; *The Case of George McIntosh, Esquire, a Member of the Late Council and Convention of the State of Georgia, with the Proceedings Thereon in the Hon. the Assembly and Council of That State* (Savannah, 1777; reprint ed., Photostat Americana, 2nd ser., no. 16, August 15, 1942), 4, 19.

47. *The Case of George McIntosh, Esquire*, 3–4, 15.

48. Ibid., Affidavit of James Johnston, June 23, 1777, 15.

49. *Papers of the Continental Congress*, microfilm, M247 r87, Edward Langworthy, August 8, 1777, 125; Smith, Gawalt and Gephart, *Letters of Delegates*, vol. 6, John Hancock to George Washington, July 24, 1775, 664.

50. Lilla M. Hawes, ed., "The Papers of Lachlan McIntosh, 1774–1799: Miscellaneous Papers Part IV," *Georgia Historical Quarterly* 39 (March 1955), Resolve of the St. Andrews Parochial Committee, September 10, 1776, 58–59.

51. *Papers of the Continental Congress*, microfilm, M247 r87, Patrick Tonyn to Lord George Germain, July 19, 1776, 36.

52. Bradley Chapin, "Colonial and Revolutionary Origins of the American Law of Treason," *William and Mary Quarterly*, 3d ser., 17 (January 1960), 15, 17.

53. Harvey H. Jackson, *Lachlan McIntosh and the Politics of Revolutionary Georgia* (Athens: University of Georgia Press, 1979), 56–57; *Papers of the Continental Congress*, microfilm, M247 r87, John Adam Treutlen to John Hancock, June 19, 1777, 43–44.

54. *The Case of George McIntosh, Esquire*, 27–28.

55. Lilla M. Hawes, ed., "The Papers of Lachlan McIntosh, 1774–1799: Miscellaneous Papers Part V," *Georgia Historical Quarterly* 39 (June 1955), John Wereat to George Walton, August 30, 1777, 178.

56. "The Case of George McIntosh," 137.

57. Searcy, *Georgia-Florida Contest*, 16, 23, 37–38, 40, 72.

58. Smith, Gawalt and Gephart, *Letters of Delegates*, vol. 11, Cornelius Harnett to Richard Caswell, November 24, 1778, 251.

59. Searcy, *Georgia-Florida Contest*, 36, 46, 50, 55, 138; Lilla M. Hawes, ed. "The Papers of Lachlan McIntosh, 1774–1799: Miscellaneous Papers Part VII," *Georgia Historical Quarterly* 39 (December 1955), John Brickell to Lachlan McIntosh, October 11, 1781, 360–61.

60. Hawes, "Letter Book of Lachlan McIntosh Part I," Lachlan McIntosh to Robert Howe, November 19, 1776, 168.

61. Hawes, Miscellaneous Papers of Lachlan McIntosh Part IV," Lachlan McIntosh, Jr. to Lachlan McIntosh, July 22, 1776, 54.

62. Lilla M. Hawes, ed., "Miscellaneous Papers of James Jackson, 1781–1798," *Georgia Historical Quarterly* 37 (March 1953), 67; Hawes, "Miscellaneous Papers of Lachlan McIntosh Part IV," Lachlan McIntosh to Archibald Bulloch, November 1, 1776, 60.

63. Searcy, *Georgia-Florida Conflict*, 35.

64. Ibid., 50, 61.

65. Hawes, "Letter Book of Lachlan McIntosh Part I," Lachlan McIntosh to Valantine Beard, October 1, 1776, 160, Lachlan McIntosh to Robert Howe, October 29, 1776, 157, Lachlan McIntosh to [Major Leonard Marbury?], November 25, 1776, 168–69; Cashin, *King's Ranger*, 56.

66. Hawes, "Letter Book of Lachlan McIntosh, 1776–1777 Part I," Lachlan McIntosh to Robert Howe, between October 8 and October 22, 1776, 163; Searcy, *Georgia-Florida Contest*, 39, 68.

67. Hawes, "Letter Book of Lachlan McIntosh, 1776–1777 Part I," Lachlan McIntosh to Robert Howe, November 19, 1776, 167, Lachlan McIntosh to Robert Howe, October 29, 1776, 167.

Chapter Three. Things Fall Apart

1. Martha Condray Searcy, *The Georgia-Florida Contest in the American Revolution, 1776–1778* (Tuscaloosa: University of Alabama Press, 1985), 87–88.

2. The facts of Georgia's revolutionary history, the sequence of crucial events and the people and locales involved, have been treated in detail in such sources as: Kenneth Coleman, *The American Revolution in Georgia, 1763–1785* (Athens: University of Georgia Press, 1958); Kenneth Coleman and Charles Stephen Gurr, eds., *Dictionary of Georgia Biography* (Athens: University of Georgia Press, 1983); Albert Berry Saye,

A Constitutional History of Georgia 1732–1945 (Athens: University of Georgia Press, 1948); Allen D. Candler, *The Revolutionary Records of Georgia*, vol. 1: *House of Assembly, Proceedings of the Council of Safety*, vol. 2: *Minutes of the Executive Council* (Atlanta: Franklin-Turner, 1908); and Lilla M. Hawes, ed., "Collections of the Georgia Historical Society and Other Documents: Minutes of the Executive Council, May 7 through October 14, 1777," *Georgia Historical Quarterly* (December 1949), (March 1950), (June 1950). All of these works inform the factual framework of this chapter.

3. *Letters from Governor Sir James Wright to the Earl of Dartmouth and Lord George Germain, Secretaries of State for America from August 24, 1774 to February 16, 1782*, Collections of the Georgia Historical Society (Savannah: Georgia Historical Society, 1901) vol. 3, pt. 4, James Wright to the Earl of Dartmouth, December 19, 1775, 228; Elizabeth Lightenstone Johnston, *Recollections of a Georgia Loyalist* (New York: M. F. Mansfield and Company, 1901), 45.

4. Unless otherwise noted, all quoted correspondence to and from Joseph Clay and Henry Laurens, Robert Howe, Josiah Smith, the firm of Bright & Pechin, and Ralph Izzard, Jr. are from *Letters of Joseph Clay, Merchant of Savannah 1776–1793*, Collections of the Georgia Historical Society (Savannah: Georgia Historical Society, 1913), vol. 8.

5. Elisha P. Douglass, *Rebels and Democrats: The Struggle for Equal Political Rights and Majority Rule During the American Revolution* (Chapel Hill: University of North Carolina Press, 1955), 345; Anthony Stokes, *A View of the Constitution of the British Colonies, in North America and the West Indies at the Time the Civil War Broke Out on the Continent of America* (London: 1783), 129, 131, 137.

6. Stokes, *A View of the Constitution*, 119–21.

7. Douglass, *Rebels and Democrats*, 344–45; Stokes, *A View of the Constitution*, 119–121.

8. Milton Sydney Heath, *Constructive Liberalism: The Role of the State in Economic Development in Georgia to 1860* (Cambridge: Harvard University Press, 1954), 126; *Papers of the Continental Congress*, microfilm, M247 r87, John Adam Treutlen to the President of Congress, August 6, 1777, 102–103.

9. Lilla M. Hawes, ed., "The Papers of Lachlan McIntosh, 1774–1779: Letter Book of Lachlan McIntosh, 1774–1779 Part III," *Georgia Historical Quarterly* 38 (December 1954), Lachlan McIntosh to George Washington, April 3, 1777, 366.

10. Heath, *Constructive Liberalism*, 122; Ralph Volney Harlow, "Aspects of Revolutionary Finance, 1775–1783," *American Historical Review* 35 (October 1929), 66.

11. *Letters of Joseph Clay*, Joseph Clay to John Lewis Gervais, July 26, 1778, 96, Joseph Clay to Henry Laurens, May 30, 1778, 78.

12. *Papers of the Continental Congress*, microfilm, M247 r94 v. 8, Officers to Samuel Elbert, September 5, 1778, 296–97, Samuel Elbert to the Continental Congress, September 5, 1778, 291; *Letters of Joseph Clay*, Joseph Clay to Henry Laurens, Septem-

ber 9, 1778, 105, May 30, 1778, 76–77; E. Wayne Carp, *To Starve the Army at Pleasure: Continental Army Administration and American Political Culture, 1775–1783* (Chapel Hill: University of North Carolina Press, 1984), 71, 163, 165; Heath, *Constructive Liberalism,* 120.

13. Edward J. Cashin, "'But Brothers, It is Our Land We Are Talking About', Winners and Losers in the Georgia Backcountry," in *An Uncivil War: The Southern Backcountry During the American Revolution,* eds Ronald Hoffman, Thad W. Tate, and Peter J. Albert (Charlottesville: University Press of Virginia, 1985), 255; *Letters of Joseph Clay,* Joseph Clay to Edward Telfair, August 10, 1777, 37–38.

14. Paul H. Smith, Gerard W. Gawalt, and Ronald M. Gephart, eds, *Letters of Delegates to Congress,* vols. 1–19 (Washington, D.C.: Library of Congress, 1976), vol. 7, Henry Laurens to Joseph Clay, August 20, 1777, 519, vol. 11, Henry Laurens to Rawlins Lowndes, January 29, 1779, 533–34, Henry Laurens to John Wereat, August 30, 1777, 576, vol. 7, Henry Laurens to Joseph Clay, September 2, 1777, 593–94.

15. Heath, *Constructive Liberalism,* 71, 79, 84.

16. *Letters of Joseph Clay,* Joseph Clay to Henry Laurens, September 29, 1777, 41.

17. Harvey H. Jackson, *Lachlan McIntosh and the Politics of Revolutionary Georgia* (Athens: University of Georgia Press, 1979), 54–59; Searcy, *Georgia-Florida Conflict,* 100, 235, fn. 10; Smith, Gawalt and Gephart, *Letters of Delegates,* vol. 6, George Walton to Lachlan McIntosh, April 18, 1777, 615 note 2.

18. *Papers of the Continental Congress,* microfilm, M247 r87, Button Gwinnett to John Hancock, March 28, 1777, item 21 p. 2; Searcy, *Georgia-Florida Contest,* 89–97; Alexander A. Lawrence, "General Lachlan McIntosh and His Suspension from Continental Command During the Revolution," *Georgia Historical Quarterly* 38 (June 1954), 112–13, 115–16.

19. Lilla M. Hawes, ed., "The Papers of Lachlan McIntosh, 1774–1799: Miscellaneous Papers Part V," *Georgia Historical Quarterly* 39 (June 1955), John Wereat to George Walton, August 30, 1777, 174.

20. Smith, Gawalt and Gephart, *Letters of Delegates to Congress,* vol. 7, George Walton to George Washington, August 5, 1777, 431, 432 note 1; Alexander A. Lawrence, "General Lachlan McIntosh and His Suspension from Continental Command During the Revolution," *Georgia Historical Quarterly* 38 (June 1954), 118–19.

21. Hawes, "Miscellaneous Papers of Lachlan McIntosh, Part V," John Wereat to George Walton, August 30, 1777, 172, 177–78.

22. Searcy, *Georgia-Florida Contest,* 104–5, 81.

23. Samuel Elbert, *Order Book of Samuel Elbert, Colonel and Brigadier General in the Continental Army, October 1776 to November 1778,* Collections of the Georgia Historical Society, vol. 5 (Savannah: Georgia Historical Society, 1902), John A. Treutlen to the officers commanding the first and second minute Battalions, August 25, 1777, 52, Samuel Elbert to Hatten Middleton, September 9, 1777, 54; Searcy, *Georgia-Florida Contest,* 113.

24. Elbert, *Order Book,* Samuel Elbert to Lachlan McIntosh, August 27, 1777, 53; Robert S. Davis, Jr., *Georgia Citizens and Soldiers in the American Revolution* (Easley, South Carolina: Southern Historical Press, Inc., 1979; reprint ed., 1983), 164–65.

25. Elbert, *Order Book,* Samuel Elbert to Lachlan McIntosh, May 26, 1777, 31, Samuel Elbert to Robert Howe, July 18, 1777, 45.

26. Smith, Gawalt and Gephart, *Letters of Delegates,* vol. 15, Richard Howley to Horatio Gates, July 28, 1780, 518.

27. Heard Robertson, ed., "Georgia's Banishment and Expulsion Act of September 16, 1777," *Georgia Historical Quarterly* 55 (Summer 1971), 278–81.

28. *The Royal Commission on the Losses and Services of American Loyalists 1783–1785. Being the Notes of Mr. Daniel Parker Coke, M.P. One of the Commissioners during that Period,* ed. Hugh Edward Egerton (New York: Arno Press and The New York Times, 1969), 318–19, 61–63.

29. John Joachim Zubly, "Rev. J. J. Zubly's Appeal to the Grand Jury, October 8, 1777," *Georgia Historical Quarterly* 1 (June 1917), 161–65.

30. Egerton, *Royal Commission,* 61–65, 318–19; Wilbur Henry Siebert, *Loyalists in East Florida, 1774 to 1785: The Most Important Documents Pertaining Thereto,* vol. 1: *The Narrative,* 75; Zubly, "Appeal to the Grand Jury," 165.

31. Egerton, *Royal Commission,* 341–42, 48.

32. Ibid., 339–40, 243–46.

33. Searcy, *Georgia-Florida Contest,* 118.

34. Siebert, *Loyalists in East Florida,* vol. 1: *The Narrative,* 61–62.

35. Searcy, *Georgia-Florida Contest,* 120–121.

36. Elbert, *Order Book,* Copy of a letter from Richard Eastmead to Mordecai Sheftall, October 17, 1777, 65, Samuel Elbert to Colonel [James] Screven, October 19, 1777, 64–65, Samuel Elbert to [Joseph] Habersham, December 5, 1777, 75–76, Samuel Elbert to Lieutenant-Colonel Harris, October 19, 1777, 66.

37. Ibid., Samuel Elbert to Robert Howe, December 5, 1777, 76–77.

38. Fred Shelley, ed., "The Journal of Ebenezer Hazard in Georgia, 1778," *Georgia Historical Quarterly* 41 (September 1957), 316, 318.

39. Ibid., 317–19.

40. *Papers of the Continental Congress,* microfilm, M247 r87, Robert Howe to John Houstoun, February 3, 1778, 153; Elbert, *Order Book,* August 28, 1778, 183, September 19, 1778, 185.

41. *Papers of the Continental Congress,* microfilm, M247 r87, Robert Howe to [John Houstoun?], February 27, 1778, 215, Robert Howe to the Georgia Assembly, [February, 1778?], 203.

42. Ibid., Robert Howe to John Houstoun, February 3, 1778, 152.

43. *Letters of Joseph Clay,* Joseph Clay to John Lewis Gervais, July 26, 1778, 96.

44. Egerton, *Royal Commission,* 193–94.

45. *Letters of Joseph Clay,* Joseph Clay to Josiah Smith, [May 1778?], 69–70.

46. Heath, *Constructive Liberalism*, 80.

47. William Few, "Autobiography of Col. William Few of Georgia," *Magazine of American History* 7 (November 1881), 347; *Papers of the Continental Congress*, microfilm, M247 r177 v. 2, William Moultrie to Henry Laurens, July 27, 1778, 469; Searcy, *Georgia-Florida Contest*, 146; Smith, Gawalt and Gephart, *Letters of Delegates*, vol. 10, Henry Laurens to John Houstoun, June 1, 1778, 9–10, note 2, [?] to [?], 696; *Letters of Joseph Clay*, Joseph Clay to Henry Laurens, September 9, 1778, 106, October 16, 1777, 50.

48. *Letters of Joseph Clay*, Joseph Clay to Josiah Smith, Jr., [May 1778?], 70.

49. *Papers of the Continental Congress*, microfilm, M247 r87, John Houstoun to Henry Laurens, August 20, 1778, 228–29; Searcy, *Georgia-Florida Contest*, 154–55.

50. Edward J. Cashin, *The King's Ranger: Thomas Brown and the American Revolution on the Southern Frontier* (Athens: University of Georgia Press, 1989), 75; Searcy, *Georgia-Florida Contest*, 131.

51. *Papers of the Continental Congress*, microfilm, M247 r177 v. 2, William Moultrie to Henry Laurens, April 20, 1778, 456; Searcy, *Georgia-Florida Contest*, 132 ; *Papers of the Continental Congress*, microfilm, M247 r87, Speaker of the Assembly Whitefield to the Continental Congress, May 6, 1778, 208–209.

52. Searcy, *Georgia-Florida Contest*, 161, 163; William Moultrie, *Memoirs of the American Revolution*, 2 vols. (New York: David Longworth, 1802) vol. 1, Robert Howe to William Moultrie, December 8, 1778, 247; *Papers of the Continental Congress*, microfilm, M247 r177 v. 1, Benjamin Lincoln to Henry Laurens, December 19, 1778, 175–76.

53. Searcy, *Georgia-Florida Contest*, 159–60; Randall Miller, "Back Country Loyalist Plan to Retake Georgia and the Carolinas, 1778," *South Carolina Historical Magazine* (1974), 208–214.

54. Smith, Gawalt and Gephart, *Letters of Delegates*, vol. 10, Henry Laurens to George Washington, September 23, 1778, 690–91; Henry Laurens to Richard Caswell, September 26, 1778, 698.

55. Ibid., vol. 11, Henry Laurens to Patrick Henry, November 16, [1778], 217–18; Cashin, "'But Brothers,'" 257–59.

56. Smith, Gawalt and Gephart, *Letters of Delegates*, vol. 11, Henry Lauren's Notes on a Georgia Campaign, January 20, [1779], 494–95.

57. Moultrie, *Memoirs*, vol. 1, William Moultrie to Robert Howe, November 28, 1778, 244–45, Robert Howe to William Moultrie, December 8, 1778, 247–48, Isaac Huger to William Moultrie, December 28, 1778, 251–52; *Papers of the Continental Congress*, microfilm, M247 r177 v.1, Benjamin Lincoln to the President of Congress, December 19, 1778, 175.

58. *Papers of the Continental Congress*, microfilm, M247 r177 v. 1, Benjamin Lincoln to the President of Congress, December 31, 1778, 181.

Chapter Four. Stalemate

1. George Fenwick Jones, *The Georgia Dutch: From the Rhine and Danube to the Savannah 1733–1783* (Athens and London: University of Georgia Press, 1992), 188; Archibald Campbell, *Journal of an Expedition Against the Rebels of Georgia in North America under the Orders of Archibald Campbell Esquire Lieutenant Colonel of His Majestys Regiment 1778*, ed. Colin Campbell (Darien: Ashantilly Press, 1981), December 5, 1778, 12–13, November 10, 1778, vii, 9, 11, December 24, 1778, 19; Richard C. Cole, "The Siege of Savannah and the British Press, 1779–1780," *Georgia Historical Quarterly* 65 (Fall 1981), 195.

2. *Papers of the Delegates to Congress*, microfilm, M247 r102 i78 v. 20, 631; Campbell, *Journal of an Expedition*, December 29, 28–29; footnote 66, 110–111; footnote 67, 111.

3. Campbell, *Journal of an Expedition*, January 15, 1779, 40; footnote 93, 114–45; footnote 93a, 115.

4. Elizabeth Lightenstone Johnston, *Recollections of a Georgia Loyalist* (New York: M.F. Mansfield and company, 1901), 48; Edith Duncan Johnston, *The Houstouns of Georgia* (Athens: University of Georgia Press, 1950), 223; *Papers of the Delegates to Congress*, microfilm, M247 r87, John Houstoun to the President of Congress, January 2, 1779, 238.

5. Campbell, *Journal of an Expedition*, December 22, 1778, 15.

6. "Letter from Savannah January 16, 1779," trans. Ray Waldron Pettengill, *Letters from America 1776–1779* (Boston: Houghton Mifflin Company, 1924), 202; William Moultrie, *Memoirs of the American Revolution*, 2 vols. (New York: David Longworth, 1802), vol. 1, William Moultrie to Charles Pinckney, January 10, 1779, 259, from a friend to Benjamin Lincoln, some time in February, 1779, 333–34; "Stephen DeLancey Writes to His Wife," in *The Price of Loyalty: Tory Writings from the Revolutionary Era*, ed. Catherine S. Crary (New York: McGraw-Hill Book Company, 1973), 272; Campbell, *Journal of an Expedition*, November 3, 1778, 6.

7. Campbell, *Journal of an Expedition*, January 3, 1779, 35–36.

8. "Letter from Savannah," 202; "Stephen DeLancey Writes to His Wife," 272; Moultrie, *Memoirs*, vol. 1, William Moultrie to Charles Pinckney, January 14, 1779, 177–78.

9. Campbell, *Journal of an Expedition*, January 8, 1779, 38–39.

10. The facts of Georgia's revolutionary history, the sequence of crucial events and the people and locales involved, have been treated in detail in such sources as : Kenneth Coleman, *The American Revolution in Georgia, 1763–1789* (Athens: University of Georgia Press, 1958); Kenneth Coleman and Charles Stephen Gurr, eds., *Dictionary of Georgia Biography* (Athens: University of Georgia Press, 1983); Allen D. Candler, ed., *The Revolutionary Records of Georgia*, vol. 1, *British Disqualifying Act, British Act of Attainder*, vol. 2, *Minutes of the Executive Council*, vol. 15, *Journal of the Commons*

House (Atlanta: Franklin-Turner, 1908); *Proceedings and Minutes of the Governor and Council of Georgia, October 4, 1774 through November 7, 1775 and September 6, 1779 through September 20, 1780.* Collections of the Georgia Historical Society (Savannah: Georgia Historical Society, 1952); Alexander A. Lawrence, *Storm over Savannah: The Story of Count d'Estaing and the Siege of the Town in 1779* (Athens: University of Georgia Press, 1951). All of these works inform the factual framework of this chapter.

11. James Ingram, *Proceedings of a Council of War Held at Burke Jail, Georgia, January 14th, 1779; with a Narrative of the Subsequent Proceedings, and the Proclamation Issued,* ed. Paul Leicester Ford (Brooklyn: Historical Printing Club, 1890); Edward J. Cashin, *The King's Ranger: Thomas Brown and the American Revolution on the Southern Frontier* (Athens and London: University of Georgia Press, 1989), 85; Robert S. Davis, Jr., *Georgia Citizens and Soldiers in the American Revolution* (Easley, South Carolina: Southern Historical Press, Inc., 1979: reprint ed., 1983), 64.

12. *The Royal Commission on the Losses and Services of American Loyalists 1783–1785. Being the Notes of Mr. Daniel Parker Coke, M.P. One of the Commissioners During that Period,* ed. Hugh Edward Egerton (New York: Arno Press and The New York Times, 1969), 246–47, 360–61; Campbell, *Journal of an Expedition,* 116, note 104, 105, December 30, 1778 30, January 20, 1779, 44.

13. Lilla M. Hawes, "Minute Book, Savannah Board of Police, 1779," *Georgia Historical Quarterly* 45 (September 1961), February 4, 1779, 249.

14. Hawes, "Minute Book, Savannah Board of Police," March 3, 1779, 254–56, February 13, 1779, 250, February 16, 1779, 251, January 30, 1779, 250, February 4, 1779, 249, February 5, 1779, 249.

15. Hawes, "Minute Book, Savannah Board of Police," March 8, 1779, January 5, 1779, January 6, 1779, 256–57; *Letters from Governor Sir James Wright to the Earl of Dartmouth and Lord George Germain, Secretaries of State for America from August 24, 1774 to February 16, 1782.* Collections of the Georgia Historical Society (Savannah: Georgia Historical Society, 1901) vol. 3, pt. 4, Report of the Board of Police, May 20, 1780, 290–91.

16. Campbell, *Journal of an Expedition,* January 20, 1779, 44, 116, notes 104–105, March 13, 1779, 79.

17. *Documents of the American Revolution 1770–1783,* ed. K. G. Davies, Colonial Office Series, 25 vols. (Dublin: Irish University Press, 1974), vol. 17, James Mark Prevost to Lord George Germain, 14 April 1779, 103–104.

18. Moultrie, *Memoirs,* vol. 1, William Moultrie to Charles Pinckney, April 6, 1779, 364–65; *Papers of the Continental Congress,* microfilm, M247 r177 v. 1, Benjamin Lincoln to the President of Congress, April 2, 1779, 247.

19. Davies, *Documents of the American Revolution,* vol. 17, Patrick Tonyn to Lord George Germain, 3 July 1779, 156–57; Martha Condray Searcy, *The Georgia-Florida*

Contest in the American Revolution, 1776–1778 (Tuscaloosa: University of Alabama Press, 1985), 6.

20. *Papers of the Continental Congress*, microfilm, M247 r177 v. 1, Benjamin Lincoln to the President of Congress, January 5–6, 1779, 185, Benjamin Lincoln to the President of Congress, February 6, 1779, 197; Moultrie, *Memoirs*, vol. 1, Benjamin Lincoln to William Moultrie, February 8, 1779, 301.

21. Campbell, *Journal of an Expedition*, January 31, 1779, 54, February 3, 1779, 58–59; Doyce Nunis, Jr., ed., "Memorandums of the Road, and the March of a Corps of Troops from Savannah to Augusta, and some Subsequent Occurences" in "Colonel Archibald Campbell's March from Savannah to Augusta, 1779," *Georgia Historical Quarterly* 45 (September 1961), 286.

22. Nunis, Jr., "March from Savannah," 282, 286; Cashin, *The King's Ranger*, 94, 98; J. Russell Snapp, *John Stuart and the Struggle for Empire on the Southern Frontier* (Baton Rouge: Louisiana State University Press, 1996), 200, 203; Campbell, *Journal of an Expedition*, February 10, 1779, 60.

23. *Papers of the Continental Congress*, microfilm, M247 r177 v. 1, Benjamin Lincoln to the President of Congress, February 6, 1779, 197; Moultrie, *Memoirs*, vol. 1, William Moultrie to Charles Pinckney, February 10, 1779, 309–10; William Few, "Autobiography of Col. William Few of Georgia," *Magazine of American History* 7 (November 1881), 348.

24. Campbell, *Journal of an Expedition*, February 14, 1779, 64; Moultrie, *Memoirs*, vol. 1, William Moultrie to Charles Pinckney, February 27, 1779, 318; Edward J. Cashin, Jr., and Heard Robertson, *Augusta and the American Revolution: Events in the Georgia Backcountry 1773–1783* (Darien: Ashantilly Press, 1975), 28.

25. Moultrie, *Memoirs*, vol. 1, (narration), 321–22; Campbell, *Journal of an Expedition*, February 23, 1779, 69, February 25, 1779, p. 70, March 3, 1779, 77.

26. Moultrie, *Memoirs*, vol. 1, John Ash to William Moultrie, March 3, 1779, 323–24, (narration), 325–26; Campbell, *Journal of an Expedition*, March 6, 1779, 77–78.

27. Moultrie, *Memoirs*, vol. 1, (narrative), 326.

28. "Letter from Savannah," 203; Campbell, *Journal of an Expedition*, footnote 94, 115.

29. *The Siege of Savannah in 1779, As Described in Two Contemporaneous Journals of French Officers in the Fleet of Count D'Estaing* (Albany: Joel Munsell, 1874; reprint ed., New York: The New York Times and Arno Press, 1968), 51–52, 57, 60–63.

30. *Letters of James Wright*, Report of the Board of Police, May 20, 1780, 292; Davies, *Documents of the American Revolution*, vol. 17, Augustine Prevost to Henry Clinton, 21 May 1779, 127, Patrick Tonyn to Lord George Germain, 3 July 1779, 156–57; Cashin, *King's Rangers*, 97.

31. *A Narrative of the Official Conduct of Anthony Stokes of the Inner Temple, London, Barrister at Law; His Majesty's Chief Justice and One of His Council of Georgia and of*

the Dangers and Distresses He Underwent in the Cause of Government: Some Copies of which are Printed for the Information of His Friends (London: 1784), 49.

32. Unless otherwise noted, all quoted correspondence to and from James Wright and Lord George Germain is from *Letters of James Wright.*

33. Davies, *Documents of the American Revolution,* vol. 17, Lord George Germain to James Wright, 31 March 1779, 92, vol. 18, Lord George Germain to James Wright, 19 January 1780, 39.

34. Sylvia R. Frey, *Water from the Rock: Black Resistance in a Revolutionary Age* (Princeton: Princeton University Press, 1991), 95; *Letters of James Wright,* Report of the Commissioners of Claims, May 20, 1780, 298.

35. *Letters of James Wright,* James Wright to Lord George Germain, July 31, 1779, 254–55.

36. Harvey Jackson, "Rise of the Western Members: Revolutionary Politics and the Georgia Backcountry," in *An Uncivil War: The Southern Backcountry During the American Revolution,* eds. Ronald Hoffman, Thad W. Tate, and Peter J. Albert (Charlottesville: University Press of Virginia, 1985), 304.

37. Alexander A. Lawrence, "General Lachlan McIntosh and His Suspension from Continental Command During the Revolution," *Georgia Historical Quarterly* 38 (June 1954), 101, 121; Jackson, "Rise of the Western Members," 309.

38. Edward J. Cashin, "'The Famous Colonel Wells': Factionalism in Revolutionary Georgia," *Georgia Historical Quarterly* 58 (Supplement 1974), 136, 140, 146–47.

39. Edward J. Cashin, "George Walton and the Forged Letter," *Georgia Historical Quarterly* 62 (1978), 139; Moultrie, *Memoirs,* vol. 2, William Moultrie to Benjamin Lincoln, September 26, 1779, 35.

40. *Papers of the Continental Congress,* microfilm, M247 r87, William Glascock to the President of Congress, July 10, 1779, 241.

41. "The Siege of Savannah by Count D'Estaing, in 1779," in *The Siege of Savannah in 1779, As Described in Two Contemporaneous Journals of French Officers in the Fleet of Count D'Estaing* (Albany: Joel Munsell, 1874; reprint ed., New York: The New York Times and Arno Press, 1968), 17–18, footnote 2.

42. *Letters of James Wright,* James Wright to Lord George Germain, November 5, 1779, 262; Egerton, *Royal Commission,* 18.

43. Stokes, Anthony, "Anthony Stokes, Chief Justice of Georgia to His Wife, November 9, 1779," in *Muskets Cannon Balls and Bombs: Nine Narratives of the Siege of Savannah in 1779,* trans. and ed. Benjamin Kennedy (Savannah: Beehive Press, 1974), 109.

44. "The Siege of Savannah," p. 51 footnote 1; "Extract from the Journal of a Naval Officer in the Fleet of Count D'Estaing, 1782," in *The Siege of Savannah in 1779, As Described in Two Contemporaneous Journals of French Officers in the Fleet of Count D'Estaing* (Albany: Joel Munsell, 1874; reprint ed., New York: The New York Times and Arno Press, 1968), 63; "Francois d'Auber de Peyrelongue, Lieutenant of Artil-

lery," in *Muskets, Cannon Balls and Bombs: Nine Narratives of the Siege of Savannah in 1779*, trans. and ed. Benjamin Kennedy (Savannah: Beehive Press, 1974), 35; Johnston, *Recollections*, 57–59; Davies, *Documents of the American Revolution*, vol. 17, Augustine Prevost to Lord George Germain, 1 November 1779, 245–46; Stokes, "To His Wife," 114.

45. Stokes, "To His Wife," 113; "Extract from the Journal of a Naval Officer," 63–64; Johnston, *Recollections*, 58, 62.

46. "The Siege of Savannah," 27–28, footnote 3; Davies, *Documents of the American Revolution*, vol. 17, Augustine Prevost to Lord George Germaine, 1 November 1779, 246.

47. "The Siege of Savannah," 47; "Anonymous Naval Officer, British Commander," in *Muskets, Cannon Balls and Bombs: Nine Narratives of the Siege of Savannah in 1779*, trans. and ed. Benjamin Kennedy (Savannah: Beehive Press, 1974), October 11, 1779, 86.

48. *Papers of the Continental Congress*, microfilm, M247 r177 v. 2, Benjamin Lincoln to the President of Congress, October 22, 1779, 279, Benjamin Lincoln to Committee of Correspondence, December 2, 1779, 306; Moultrie, *Memoirs*, vol. 2, (narrative), 43.

49. Cole, "The Siege of Savannah and the British Press, 1779–1789," 190–91, 193, 195–96, 198–200; Stokes, "To His Wife," 114.

50. Johnston, *Recollections*, 63; Davies, *Documents of the American Revolution*, vol. 17, Augustine Prevost to Lord George Germain, 1 November 1779, 245; *Letters of James Wright*, Report of the Commissioners of Claims, May 20, 1780, 298.

51. [Stokes], *A Narrative*, 67–70; Egerton, *Royal Commission*, 339–41, 249–250, 193–94.

52. Cashin, "George Walton and the Forged Letter," 138; Edward J. Cashin, "Colonel Wells," 146–47.

53. Cashin, "Colonel Wells," 147, 149; Cashin, "George Walton and the Forged Letter," 139–40; Smith, Gawalt and Gephart, *Letters of Delegates*, vol. 16, George Walton's memorial, September 7, 1780, 38.

54. George R. Lamplugh, "'To Check and Discourage the Wicked and Designing': John Wereat and the Revolution in Georgia," *GHQ* 61 (Winter 1977), 300; Jackson, "Rise of the Western Members," 312; Cashin, "Colonel Wells," 148; Cashin, "George Walton and the Forged Letter," 141.

55. Cashin, "Colonel Wells," 148–49.

56. William O. Foster, "James Jackson in the American Revolution," *Georgia Historical Quarterly* 31 (December 1947), 254; Cashin, "Colonel Wells," 151; Smith, Gawalt and Gephart, *Letters of Delegates*, vol. 14, Samuel Huntington to Lachlan McIntosh, February 15, 1780.

57. Lilla M. Hawes, ed., "The Papers of Lachlan McIntosh, 1774–1799: Miscellaneous Papers Part VI," *Georgia Historical Quarterly* 39 (September 1955), 258–63.

58. Hawes, "Miscellaneous Papers of Lachlan McIntosh, Part VI," 262–63.

59. Smith, Gawalt and Gephart, *Letters of Delegates,* vol. 14, Samuel Huntington to Richard Howley, February 29, 1780, note 1, 47, March 3, 1780, 228; Davis, Jr., *Citizens and Soldiers,* 158–60.

60. Alan Gallay, *Formation of a Planter Elite: Jonathan Bryan and the Southern Colonial Frontier* (Athens: University of Georgia Press, 1989), 82, 90.

61. Lilla M. Hawes, ed., "Miscellaneous Papers of James Jackson, 1781–1798," *Georgia Historical Quarterly* 37 (1953), 68–69; Davis, Jr., *Citizens and Soldiers,* 168; Foster, "James Jackson," 254.

62. Heard Robertson, "The Second British Occupation of Augusta, 1780–1781," *Georgia Historical Quarterly* 58 (1974), 425; Patrick J. Furlong "Civilian-Military Conflict and the Restoration of the Royal Province of Georgia, 1778–1782," *Journal of Southern History* 38 (August 1972), 436.

63. Betsy Knight, "Prisoner Exchange and Parole in the American Revolution," *William and Mary Quarterly,* 3d ser., 48 (April 1991), 208–9, 213–14; Moultrie, *Memoirs,* vol. 2 (narrative), 209–10.

64. Johnston, *The Houstouns,* 300–304.

65. Moultrie, *Memoirs,* vol. 2, (narrative), 210.

66. Furlong, "Civilian-Military Conflict," 436–37; Davis, Jr., *Citizens and Soldiers,* 76–77.

67. Stokes, *A View of the Constitution,* 131–32, 126–27.

68. Cashin, *The King's Ranger,* 105.

69. Robertson, "Second British Occupation," 264; Cashin and Robertson, *Augusta and the American Revolution,* 42–43.

70. Davis, Jr., *Citizens and Soldiers,* 168; Cashin and Robertson, *Augusta and the American Revolution,* 44.

71. Robertson, "Second British Occupation," 432; Cashin, *The King's Ranger,* p. 113, 115–19; Moultrie, *Memoirs,* vol. 2 (narrative), 238.

72. Robertson, "Second British Occupation," 436.

73. *Letters of James Wright,* James Wright to Lord George Germain, October 27, 1780, 321; Robertson, "Second British Occupation," 436; Gary D. Olson, "Thomas Brown, Loyalist Partisan, and the Revolutionary War in Georgia, 1777–1782 Part II," *Georgia Historical Quarterly* 54 (Summer 1970), 191.

74. Hawes, "Miscellaneous Papers of James Jackson," 73.

75. Henry Lee, *Memoirs of the War in the Southern Department of the United States* (Philadelphia: Bradford and Inskeep; New York: Inskeep and Bradford, 1812; reprint ed., New York, 1869), 94, 115; Moultrie, *Memoirs,* vol. 2 (narrative), 336.

76. Moultrie, *Memoirs,* vol. 2, (narrative), 235.

77. Cashin and Robertson, *Augusta and the American Revolution,* 47–48.

78. *Letters of James Wright,* James Wright to Lord George Germain, December 1, 1780, 322–23.

79. Ibid., James Wright to Lord George Germain, December 20, 1780, 327.

80. Davies, *Documents of the American Revolution*, vol. 18, James Wright to Lord George Germain, 20 December 1780, 260.

Chapter Five. Land and Allegiance

1. *Papers of Nathanael Greene*, ed. Richard Showman, et al. (Chapel Hill and London: University of North Carolina Press, 1991), vol. 6: *1 June 1780 – 25 December 1780*, 385; William Moultrie, *Memoirs of the American Revolution*, 2 vols, (New York: David Longworth, 1802), vol. 2, (narrative), 273.

2. *Papers of Nathanael Greene*, vol. 6: *1 June 1780 – 25 December 1780*, xvii–xviii, Nathanael Greene to Francis Marion, December 24, 1780, 607, Nathanael Greene to Lord Cornwallis, December 17, 1780, 592, Nathanael Greene to Daniel Morgan, December 16, 1780, 589 – 90; John S. Pancake, *This Destructive War: The British Campaign in the Carolinas, 1780 – 1782* (University, Alabama: University of Alabama Press, 1985), 190.

3. Edward J. Cashin, *The King's Ranger: Thomas Brown and the American Revolution on the Southern Frontier* (Athens and London: University of Georgia Press, 1989), 126 – 27, 129 – 30; Heard Robertson, "The Second British Occupation of Augusta, 1780 – 1781," *Georgia Historical Quarterly* 58 (Summer 1974), 437; *Documents of the American Revolution 1770 – 1783*, ed. K. G. Davies, Colonial Office Series, 25 vols. (Dublin: Irish University Press, 1974), vol. 20, James Wright to Lord Cornwallis, 23 April 1781, 118.

4. *Letters from Governor Sir James Wright to the Earl of Dartmouth and Lord George Germain, Secretaries of State for America from August 24, 1774 to February 16, 1782*, Collections of the Georgia Historical Society (Savannah: Georgia Historical Society, 1901), vol. 3, pt. 4, James Wright to Lord George Germain, December 20, 1780, p. 327, Address of the Council of Georgia to James Wright, December 1, 1780; Davies, *Documents of the American Revolution*, James Wright to Lord George Germain, 5 March 1781, p. 74. Unless otherwise noted, all quoted correspondence to and from James Wright, Lord George Germain, the Lords of Trade and William Knox is from *Letters from Governor Sir James Wright to the Earl of Dartmouth and Lord George Germain, Secretaries of State for America from August 24, 1774 to February 16, 1782.*

5. *Letters of James Wright*, James Wright to Lord George Germain, March 5, 1781, 336 – 37, April 24, 1781, 346 – 47, May 5, 1781, 350.

6. Ibid., James Wright to Lord George Germain, April 24, 1781, 346, April 2, 1781, 343, May 25, 1781, 351, May 5, 1781, 349 – 50; Cashin, *The King's Ranger*, 138.

7. *Letters of James Wright*, Memorial of James Wright to the Lords of the Treasury, June 14, 1781, 357, James Wright to Lord George Germain, May 5, 1781, 349.

8. Henry Lee, *The Campaign of 1781 in the Carolinas* (Philadelphia: E. Littell, 1824; reprint ed., Spartanburg: Reprint Company, 1975), Henry Lee to Nathanael Greene, February 3, 1781, xxviii–xxix, Appendix.

9. Edward J. Cashin, Jr. and Heard Robertson, *Augusta and the American Revolution: Events in the Georgia Backcountry 1773–1783* (Darien: Ashantilly Press, 1975) 59.

10. Davies, *Documents of the American Revolution*, vol. 21, Narrative of James Wright, September 3, 1782, 117, James Wright to Lord George Germain, June 14, 1781, 358–59.

11. Ibid., vol. 18, James Wright to Lord George Germain, 30 December 1780, 261.

12. Lilla M. Hawes, ed., "Some Papers of the Governor and Council of Georgia, 1780–1781," *Georgia Historical Quarterly* 46 (September–December 1962), April 25, 1781, May 1, 1781, 401–402.

13. *Letters of James Wright*, James Wright to Lord George Germain, March 9, 1781, 341–42.

14. "Memorial of the Merchants of London Trading to South Carolina and Georgia to the Board of Trade [London]," in *Colonial Records of the State of Georgia*, eds. Kenneth Coleman and Milton Ready (Athens: University of Georgia Press, 1979), vol. 28, pt. 2, 404–406.

15. Edward Telfair, "A Letter to J. Y. Noel Relative to William Telfair's Claim," in "Basil Cowper's Remarkable Career in Georgia" by William Harden, *Georgia Historical Quarterly* 1 (March 1917), 30.

16. *The Royal Commission on the Losses and Services of American Loyalists 1783–1785. Being the Notes of Mr. Daniel Parker Coke, M.P. One of the Commissioners During that Period*, ed. Hugh Edward Egerton (New York: Arno Press and The New York Times, 1969), 243–46, 360–61.

17. Telfair, "A Letter," 31–33.

18. Alexander A. Lawrence, "General Lachlan McIntosh and His Suspension from Continental Command During the Revolution," *Georgia Historical Quarterly* 38 (June 1954), 130–31; Lilla M. Hawes, ed., "The Papers of Lachlan McIntosh, 1774–1799: Miscellaneous Papers Part VII," *Georgia Historical Quarterly* 39 (December 1955), Robert Baillie to Lachlan McIntosh, July 17, 1781, 358–59; "The Case of George McIntosh," *Georgia Historical Quarterly* 3 (1919) 189.

19. Lilla M. Hawes, "Some Papers of the Governor and Council of Georgia, 1780–1781," *Georgia Historical Quarterly* 46 (September–December 1962), July 25, 1781, 406–407.

20. The facts of Georgia's revolutionary history, the sequence of crucial events and the people and locales involved, have been treated in detail in such sources as: *Proceedings and Minutes of the Governor and Council of Georgia, October 4, 1774 through November 7, 1775 and September 6, 1779 through September 20, 1780*, Collections of the Georgia Historical Society (Savannah: Georgia Historical Society, 1952), vol. 10; Allen D. Candler, *The Revolutionary Records of Georgia* vol. 2, *Minutes of the Executive Council*, vol. 3, *Journal of the House of Assembly* (Atlanta: Franklin-Turner, 1908); Allen D. Candler, *The Colonial Records of Georgia*, vol. 15, *Journal of the House of Assembly* (Atlanta: Franklin-Turner, 1904–16); Kenneth Coleman, *The American*

Revolution in Georgia, 1763–1789 (Athens: University of Georgia Press, 1958); Kenneth Coleman and Charles Stephen Gurr, eds., *Dictionary of Georgia Biography* (Athens: University of Georgia Press, 1983). All of these sources inform the factual framework of this chapter.

21. William Bacon Stevens, *A History of Georgia, from Its First Discovery by Europeans to the Adoption of the Present Constitution in MDCCXCVIII* (New York: Appleton and co.; Savannah: W. T. Williams, 1847; reprint ed., Philadelphia: E. H. Butler and Co., 1859), vol. 2, 376–78; Philip D. Morgan, "Black Society in the Lowcountry," in *Slavery and Freedom in the Age of the American Revolution*, eds. Ira Berlin and Ronald Hoffman (Charlottesville: University Press of Virginia, 1983), 139.

22. Paul H. Smith, Gerard W. Gawalt and Ronald H. Gephart, eds., *Letters of Delegates to Congress*, vols. 1–19 (Washington, D.C.: Library of Congress, 1976), vol. 17, Georgia Delegates to Nathanael Greene, April 26, 1781, 186–87; Harvey Jackson, "Rise of the Western Members," in *An Uncivil War: The Southern Backcountry During the American Revolution*, eds. Ronald Hoffman, Thad W. Tate and Peter J. Albert (Charlottesville: University Press of Virginia, 1985), 315.

23. Theodore Thayer, *Nathanael Greene, Strategist of the American Revolution* (New York: Twayne Publishers, 1960) 357–58; Lilla M. Hawes, ed., "Miscellaneous Papers of James Jackson 1781–1798," *Georgia Historical Quarterly* 37 (March 1953) 74; Smith, Gawalt and Gephart, *Letters of Delegates*, vol. 17, Georgia Delegates to Nathanael Greene, April 26, 1781, 187; Edward J. Cashin, "Nathanael Greene's Campaign for Georgia in 1781," *Georgia Historical Quarterly* 62 (Spring 1977), 51.

24. Cashin, "Nathanael Greene," 5; *The Century Dictionary of the English Language*, William Dwight Whitney, ed., 24 vols. (New York: The Century Co., 1884), vol. 23, 6678; Smith, Gawalt and Gephart, *Letters of Delegates*, vol. 16, Georgia Delegates proposed Resolution, [November 18, 1780], 349; Georgia Delegates "Observations," [January 8, 1781], 561–66.

25. William Few, "Autobiography of Col. William Few of Georgia," *Magazine of American History* 7 (November 1881), 351; Smith, Gawalt and Gephart, *Letters of Delegates*, vol. 17, Georgia Delegates to the Speaker of the Georgia Assembly, July 18, 1781, 421 note 1.

26. Cashin, "Nathanael Greene," 51.

27. Smith, Gawalt and Gephart, *Letters of Delegates*, vol. 17, Georgia Delegates to Nathanael Greene, April 26, 1781, 187 note 1; Cashin, "Nathanael Greene," 52–54; Few, "Autobiography," 351; Hawes, "Miscellaneous Papers of Lachlan McIntosh, Part VII," John Brickell to Lachlan McIntosh, October 11, 1781, 360.

28. Cashin and Robertson, *Augusta and the American Revolution*, 61.

29. Milton Sydney Heath, *Constructive Liberalism: The Role of the State in Economic Development in Georgia to 1860* (Cambridge: Harvard University Press, 1954), 78; Robert and George Watkins, *A Digest of the laws of the state of Georgia. From its first establishment as a British province down to the year 1798, inclusive, and the principal acts*

of 1799: in which is comprehended the Declaration of Independence; the state constitutions of 1777 and 1789, with the alterations and amendments in 1794 (Philadelphia: Printed by R. Aitken, No. 22, Market Street, 1800), 238.

30. William O. Foster, "James Jackson in the American Revolution," *Georgia Historical Quarterly* 31 (December 1947), 265, 268, 271–72; Hawes, "Papers of James Jackson," 75–76; *Papers of the Continental Congress,* microfilm, M247 r175 v. 2, Nathanael Greene to the President of Congress, December 9, 1781, 375.

31. Cashin and Robertson, *Augusta and the American Revolution,* 65; Cashin, *King's Ranger,* x, 17–19.

32. Hawes, "Papers of James Jackson," 77.

33. Smith, Gawalt and Gephart, *Letters of Delegates,* vol. 16, William Sharpe to Nathanael Greene, June 21, 1781, 340, Thomas McKean to William Bingham, et al., July 25, 1781, 447; Moultrie, *Memoirs,* vol. 2 (commentary), 297–98.

34. *Papers of the Continental Congress,* microfilm, M247 r175 v. 2, 242.

35. Heath, *Constructive Liberalism,* 80–81; footnote 65.

36. "Official Letters of Governor John Martin, 1782–1783," *Georgia Historical Quarterly* 1 (December 1917), John Martin to the Georgia Delegates, March 14, 1782, 294; Cashin and Robertson, *Augusta and the American Revolution,* 69–70; Moultrie, *Memoirs,* vol. 2, (narrative), 337; Harry Emerson Wildes, *Anthony Wayne, Trouble Shooter of the American Revolution* (Westport: Greenwood Press, 1969), 278; *Letters of James Wright,* James Wright to William Knox, February 12, 1782, 367.

37. "Letters of John Martin," John Martin to Anthony Wayne, March 14, 1782, 296, John Martin to the Governor of South Carolina, March 14, 1782, 297.

38. Ibid., John Martin to Nathanael Greene, April 10, 1782, 303–304, John Martin to Anthony Wayne, April 10, 1782, 304.

39. Ibid., John Martin to Anthony Wayne, May 6, 1782, 309, John Martin to the Speaker and the Assembly, April 30, 1782, 308.

40. *A Narrative of the Official Conduct of Anthony Stokes of the Inner Temple, London, Barrister at Law; His Majesty's Chief Justice and One of His Council of Georgia and of the Dangers and Distresses He Underwent in the Cause of Government: Some Copies of Which Are Printed for the Information of His Friends* (London: 1784), 91.

41. Davies, *Documents of the American Revolution,* vol. 21, Narrative of Governor Sir James Wright, September 3, 1782, 117–118; Wilbur Henry Siebert, *Loyalists in East Florida, 1774 to 1785: The Most Important Documents Pertaining Thereto,* vol. 1: *The Narrative,* 115–16.

42. *Letters of James Wright,* James Wright to the Lords of Trade, January 23, 1782, 364, James Wright to Lord George Germain, January 18, 1782, 362, February 12, 1782, 365; James Wright to William Knox, February 23, 1782, 373–74.

43. *Letters of James Wright,* James Wright to William Knox, March 5, 1782, 374; *Papers of the Continental Congress,* microfilm, M247 r171 v. 11, Enclosure in Anthony

Wayne to George Washington, November 1, 1783, 575–77, no. 2; Wildes, *Anthony Wayne,* 278.

44. Jones, George, *The Georgia Dutch,* 189–90; George Fenwick Jones, "The Black Hessians: Negroes Recruited by the Hessians in South Carolina and Other Colonies," *South Carolina Historical Magazine* 83 (1982), 297, footnotes 20–21; Wildes, *Anthony Wayne,* 278; *Letters of James Wright,* James Wright to William Knox, February 23, 1782, 373; Cashin, *The King's Ranger,* 148.

45. "Letters of John Martin," John Martin to Anthony Wayne, May 6, 1782, 309.

46. Robert G. Mitchell, "The Losses and Compensation of Georgia Loyalists," *Georgia Historical Quarterly* 68 (Summer 84), 233–34.

47. "Letters of John Martin," John Martin to John Habersham [?], June 27, 1782, 312.

48. Robert S. Lambert, "The Confiscation of Loyalist Property in Georgia, 1782–1786," *William and Mary Quarterly,* 3d ser., 20 (January 1963), 80–94.

49. Egerton, *Royal Commission,* 249–50, 243–46; Hawes, "Some Papers of the Governor and Council," 295.

50. Robert S. Lambert, "The Flight of the Georgia Loyalists," *Georgia Review* 7 (Winter 1963), 447.

51. [Stokes], *A Narrative,* 92; *Papers of the Continental Congress,* M247 r171 v. 10, Extract of a letter to George Washington of intelligence, one of several sent May 28, 1782 by George Washington to the Continental Congress, 575.

52. Davies, *Documents of the American Revolution,* vol. 21, Narrative of Governor Sir James Wright, September 3, 1782, 118–19.

53. Ibid., 119; [Stokes], *A Narrative,* 92–93.

54. Clyde R. Ferguson, "Functions of the Partisan-Militia in the South During the American Revolution: An Interpretation," in *The Revolutionary War in the South: Power, Conflict, and Leadership,* ed. W. Robert Higgins (Durham: Duke University Press, 1979), 266–68; Davies, *Documents of the American Revolution,* vol. 22, narrative, 17–18; Charlene Kozy, "Tories Transplanted: The Caribbean Exile and Plantation Settlement of Southern Loyalists," *Georgia Historical Quarterly* 75 (Spring 1991), 19.

55. Ira D. Gruber, "Britain's Southern Strategy," in *The Revolutionary War in the South: Power, Conflict, and Leadership,* ed. W. Robert Higgins (Durham: Duke University Press, 1979), 268–69; Hawes, "Papers of James Jackson," 79.

56. *Papers of the Continental Congress,* microfilm, M247 r175 v. 2, Anthony Wayne to Nathanael Greene, July 12, 1782, 503–4, Anthony Wayne's Orders, July 11, 1782, 507–8.

57. Ibid., Anthony Wayne to Nathanael Greene, October 5, 1782, 541–42; Smith, Gawalt and Gephart, *Letters of Delegates,* vol. 19, James Madison's Notes of Debates, December 30, 1782, 521–22.

58. Foster, "James Jackson," 279; Hawes, "Papers of James Jackson," 79; Smith,

Gawalt and Gephart, *Letters of Delegates,* vol. 18, Georgia Delegates to John Martin, July 13, 1782, 634; *Papers of the Continental Congress,* microfilm, M247 r175 v. 2, Nathanael Greene to the President of Congress, August 13, 1782, 513.

Chapter Six. Pillaged, Plundered, and Carried Off

1. Lilla M. Hawes, "Minute Book, Savannah Board of Police, 1779," *Georgia Historical Quarterly,* 45 (September 1961), February 17–19, 1779, 251–53.

2. Sylvia R. Frey, *Water from the Rock: Black Resistance in a Revolutionary Age* (Princeton: Princeton University Press, 1991), 86; Paul H. Smith, Gerard W. Gawalt and Ronald M. Gephart, eds., *Letters of Delegates to Congress,* vols. 1–19 (Washington, D.C.: Library of Congress, 1976), vol. 11, Henry Laurens' Notes on a Georgia Campaign, January 20, [1779], 494–95.

3. *Documents of the American Revolution 1770–1783,* ed. K. G. Davies, Colonial Office Series, 25 vols. (Dublin: Irish University Press, 1974), vol. 16, Memorial to Lord George Germain, 6 January 1779, 16.

4. Smith, Gawalt and Gephart, *Letters of Delegates,* vol. 12, Thomas Burke's Draft Committee Report, [ante March 25, 1779], 243, John Collins to William Greene, March 30, 1779, 263, vol. 13, Henry Laurens to John Laurens, September 21, 1779, 522; *Papers of the Continental Congress,* microfilm, M247 r29 v. 2, Delivered December 8, 1780, 443–444.

5. *Papers of the Continental Congress,* microfilm, M247, r86, Rawdon Loundes to the President of Congress, January 15, 1779, 478; William Moultrie, *Memoirs of the American Revolution,* 2 vols, (New York: David Longworth, 1802) vol. 1, Stephen Bull to William Moultrie, February 12, 1779, 313, William Moultrie to Charles Pinckney, April 6, 1779, 364; Archibald Campbell, *Journal of an Expedition Against the Rebels of Georgia in North America under the Orders of Archibald Campbell Esquire Lieutenant Colonel of His Majesty's Regiment 1778,* ed. Colin Campbell (Darien: Ashantilly Press, 1981), January 30, 1779, 53; February 11, 1779, 63.

6. Doyce Nunis, Jr., ed. "Memorandums of the Road, and the March of a Corps of Troops from Savannah to Augusta, and some Subsequent Occurences," in "Colonel Archibald Campbell's March from Savannah to Augusta, 1779," *Georgia Historical Quarterly* 45 (September 1961), 286.

7. Campbell, *Journal of an Expedition,* January 1, 1779, 32–33.

8. Ibid., January 25, 1779, 48, January 30, 1779, 52; Davies, *Documents of the American Revolution,* vol. 17, Archibald Campbell to Henry Clinton, March 4, 1779, 74.

9. Campbell, *Journal of an Expedition,* January 26, 1779, 49, February 3, 1779, 57–58, February 10, 1779, 60, 123, footnote 157.

10. Moultrie, *Memoirs,* vol. 1, William Moultrie to John Rutledge, April 16, 1779, 368.

11. Edward J. Cashin, *The King's Ranger: Thomas Brown and the American Revo-*

lution on the Southern Frontier (Athens and London: University of Georgia Press, 1989), 93–94; William Few, "Autobiography of Col. William Few of Georgia," *Magazine of American History* 7 (November 1881), 349–50; Campbell, *Journal of an Expedition,* 90–91 Appendix III; J. Russell Snapp, *John Stuart and the Struggle for Empire on the Southern Frontier* (Baton Rouge: Louisiana State University Press, 1996), 200.

12. *Letters from Governor Sir James Wright to the Earl of Dartmouth and Lord George Germain, Secretaries of State for America from August 24, 1774 to February 16, 1782,* Collections of the Georgia Historical Society (Savannah: Georgia Historical Society, 1901), vol. 3, pt. 4, Report of the Board of Police to Governor Wright, 20 May 1780, 293. Unless otherwise noted, all quoted correspondence to and from James Wright and Lord George Germain is from the above source.

13. Ibid., 291–293.

14. Ibid., Report of the Commissioners of Claims, 20 May, 1780, 294, Report of the Board of Police to Governor Wright, 20 May 1780, 291–93.

15. Martha Condray Searcy, "The Introduction of African Slavery into the Creek Indian Nation," *Georgia Historical Quarterly* 66 (Spring 1982), 29; Wilbur Henry Siebert, *Loyalists in East Florida, 1774 to 1785: The Most Important Documents Pertaining Thereto* (Deland: Florida State Historical Society, 1929; reprint ed. Boston: Greg Press, 1972), vol. 1: *The Narrative,* 45.

16. Siebert, *Loyalists in East Florida,* vol. 1: *The Narrative,* 72–73.

17. *Letters of James Wright,* Report of the Commissioners of Claims, May 20, 1780, 295–96.

18. Ibid., 296.

19. Siebert, *Loyalists in East Florida,* vol. 1: *The Narrative,* 76; Frey, *Water from the Rock,* 91–93.

20. Moultrie, *Memoirs,* vol. 1, William Moultrie to John Rutledge, May 3, 1779, 397, vol. 2, John Rutledge to William Moultrie, June 26, 1779, 5; Siebert, *Loyalists in East Florida,* vol. 1: *The Narrative,* 76–78; Frey, *Water from the Rock,* 92; George Fenwick Jones, *The Georgia Dutch: From the Rhine and Danube to the Savannah, 1733–1783* (Athens and London: University of Georgia Press, 1992), 188; Lilla M. Hawes, ed., "Miscellaneous Papers of James Jackson, 1781–1798," *Georgia Historical Quarterly* 37 (March 1953), 65.

21. Searcy, "The Introduction of African Slavery," 30, 27–28.

22. Patrick J. Furlong, "Civilian-Military Conflict and the Restoration of the Royal Province of Georgia, 1778–1782," *Journal of Southern History* 38 (August 1972), 435.

23. Searcy, "The Introduction of African Slavery," 29–30.

24. Frey, *Water from the Rock,* 96–98; *Letters of James Wright,* James Wright to Lord George Germain, November 5, 1779, 262, Report of the Commissioners of Claims, May 20, 1780, 299.

25. *Letters of Joseph Clay, Merchant of Savannah, 1776–1793,* Collections of the Georgia Historical Society (Savannah: Georgia Historical Society, 1913), vol. 8, Joseph Clay to John Lewis Gervais, September 28, 1779, 146–147; *Letters of James Wright,* Commissioners of Claims, May 20, 1780, 299.

26. The facts of Georgia's colonial history, the sequence of crucial events and the people and locales involved, have been treated in detail in such sources as: Allen D. Candler, ed., *The Revolutionary Records of Georgia,* vol. 2, *Minutes of the Executive Council* (Atlanta: Franklin-Turner, 1908); Allen D. Candler, ed., *The Colonial Records of Georgia,* vol. 15, *Journal of the House of Assembly* (Atlanta: Franklin-Turner, 1904–1916); *Proceedings and Minutes of the Governor and Council of Georgia, October 4, 1774 through November 7, 1775 and September 6, 1779 through September 20, 1780,* Collections of the Georgia Historical Society (Savannah: Georgia Historical Quarterly, 1952); Kenneth Coleman, *The American Revolution in Georgia, 1763–1789* (Athens: University of Georgia Press, 1958). All of these works inform the factual framework of this chapter.

27. Robert S. Davis, Jr., *Georgia Citizens and Soldiers in the American Revolution* (Easley, South Carolina: Southern Historical Press, Inc., 1979; reprint ed., 1983), 75.

28. Edward McCrady, *The History of South Carolina* (New York: Russell and Russell, 1901–1902; reprint ed., 1969), vol. 1: *1775–1780,* 333–35, 342–43; Moultrie, *Memoirs,* vol. 1, (narration) 276.

29. *Letters of Joseph Clay,* Joseph Clay to Joseph Carlenton, March 23, 1779, 132, June 9, 1779, 138–39; Moultrie, *Memoirs,* vol. 2, Benjamin Lincoln to William Moultrie, July 11, 1979, 23.

30. George Smith McCowen, Jr., *The British Occupation of Charleston, 1780–1782* (Columbia, South Carolina: University of South Carolina Press, 1972), 54–55; Moultrie, *Memoirs,* vol. 1, (narrative), 276–77.

31. Smith, Gawalt and Gephart, *Letters of Delegates,* vol. 15, Richard Howley to Horatio Gates, July 28, 1780, 518; Jac Weller, "The Irregular War in the South," *Military Affairs* 24 (Fall 1960) 135; Lilla M. Hawes, ed., "Miscellaneous Papers of James Jackson 1781–1798," *Georgia Historical Quarterly* 37 (March 1953), 75; William O. Foster, "James Jackson in the American Revolution," *Georgia Historical Quarterly* 31 (December 1947), 250.

32. *Papers of Nathanael Greene,* ed. Richard Showman, et al. (Chapel Hill and London: University of North Carolina Press, 1991), vol. 6: *1 June 1780 – 25 December 1780,* 586–87, note 1; Foster, "James Jackson," 255–68; George F. Scheer and Hugh F. Rankin, *Rebels and Redcoats* (New York: World Publishing Company, 1963), 479, 485–486.

33. Edward J. Cashin, Jr. and Heard Robertson, *Augusta and the American Revolution: Events in the Georgia Backcountry 1773–1783* (Darien: Ashantilly Press, 1975), 53.

34. Cashin, *The King's Ranger,* 125–26; Cashin and Robertson, *Augusta and the American Revolution,* 61.

35. Davis, Jr., *Citizens and Soldiers,* 70–71.

36. Cashin, *The King's Ranger,* 130.

37. Ralph C. Scott, Jr., "The Quaker Settlement of Wrightsborough, Georgia," *Georgia Historical Quarterly* 56 (Summer 1972), 220; Cashin and Robertson, *Augusta and the American Revolution,* 54–55, 60.

38. Davis, Jr., *Citizens and Soldiers,* 71–73, 66.

39. Ibid, 177.

40. Ibid, 178.

41. Hawes, "Papers of James Jackson," 63–64.

42. Kenneth Coleman, "Restored Colonial Georgia, 1779–1782," *Georgia Historical Quarterly* 40 (March 1956), 12; Davis, Jr., *Citizens and Soldiers,* 176; Lilla M. Hawes, ed., "The Papers of Lachlan McIntosh, 1774–1799: Miscellaneous Papers Part VII," *Georgia Historical Quarterly* 39 (December 1955), 360–61.

43. "Official Letters of Governor John Martin, 1782–1783," *Georgia Historical Quarterly* 1 (December 1917), John Martin to Anthony Wayne, January 19, 1782, 285–287; John Martin to Nathanael Greene, February 9, 1782, 290–292.

44. Ibid., John Martin to Anthony Wayne, January 19, 1782, 285–87, John Martin to Anthony Wayne, March 14, 1782, 298, John Martin to Nathanael Greene, March 15, 1782, 300.

45. Ibid., John Martin to Nathanael Greene, February 9, 1782, 292, John Martin to the Georgia Delegates, March 14, 1782, 295, John Martin to Elijah Clarke, March 22, 1782, 301–302, John Martin to Anthony Wayne, March 14, 1782, 295–96; Cashin, *King's Ranger,* 148–49.

46. Davis, Jr., *Citizens and Soldiers,* 64; "Letters of John Martin," John Martin to Anthony Wayne, March 14, 1782, 298, John Martin to Nathanael Greene, February 9, 1782, 291.

47. "Letters of John Martin," John Martin to Anthony Wayne, January 19, 1782, 287, John Martin to Anthony Wayne, February 3, 1782, 289.

48. Davies, *Documents of the American Revolution,* vol. 21, Narrative of Governor Sir James Wright to Thomas Townsend, 3 September 1782, 118.

49. Harry Emerson Wildes, *Anthony Wayne, Trouble Shooter of the American Revolution* (Westport: Greenwood Press, 1969), 276–78.

50. "Letters of John Martin," John Martin to Anthony Wayne, March 14, 1782, 298, John Martin to Anthony Wayne, March 22, 1782, 298–99.

51. Ibid, 302.

52. "Papers of James Jackson," 60, 78.

53. Ibid., 78.

54. "Letters of John Martin," John Martin to Cornelius Collins, August 13, 1782, 317.

55. Ibid., John Martin to Edward Carrington, October 2, 1782, 329–30, John Martin to "Sir," August 9, 1782, 327.

56. Ibid., John Martin to Patrick Carr, August 28, 1782, 323, John Martin to Stephen Johnson, August 26, 1782, 321, John Martin to John Cooper, September 4, 1782, 324, John Martin to John Cooper, September 17, 1782, 328.

57. Ibid., Patrick Carr to John Martin, August 11, 1782, 338, August 22, 1782, 339.

58. Hawes, "Miscellaneous Papers of Lachlan McIntosh, Part VII," Lachlan McIntosh to Nathanael Greene, October 30, 1782, 363.

Chapter Seven. Aftermath of the British Evacuation

1. The facts of Georgia's revolutionary history, the sequence of crucial events and the people and locales involved, have been treated in detail in such sources as: Allen D. Candler, ed., *The Revolutionary Records of Georgia,* vol. 1, *Proceedings of the Council of Safety, Journal of the House of Assembly,* vol. 2, *Minutes of the Executive Committee* (Atlanta: Franklin-Turner, 1908); Kenneth Coleman, *The American Revolution in Georgia, 1763–1789* (Athens: University of Georgia Press, 1958); Kenneth Coleman and Charles Stephen Gurr, eds., *Dictionary of Georgia Biography* (Athens: University of Georgia Press, 1983). All of these works inform the factual framework of this chapter.

2. *Documents of the American Revolution 1770–1783,* ed. K. G. Davies, Colonial Office Series, 25 vols. (Dublin: Irish University Press, 1974), vol. 21, Narration of Governor Sir James Wright enclosed in Wright's letter of 3 September 1782 to Townshend, 116; Lilla M. Hawes, ed., "Miscellaneous Papers of James Jackson, 1781–1798," *Georgia Historical Quarterly* 37 (1953), 78; Charlene Kozy, "Tories Transplanted: the Caribbean Exile and Plantation Settlement of Southern Loyalists," *Georgia Historical Quarterly* 75 (Spring 1991), 27; Robert G. Mitchell, "Losses and Compensation of Georgia Loyalists," *Georgia Historical Quarterly* 68 (Summer 1984), 237–39.

3. Davies, *Documents of the American Revolution,* vol. 21, Thomas Townshend to General Sir Guy Clinton, 14 August 1782, 110; Kozy, "Tories Transplanted," 19.

4. William Henry Siebert, *Loyalists in East Florida 1774 to 1785: The Most Important Documents Pertaining Thereto,* 2 vols. (Deland: Florida State Historical Society, 1929; reprint ed., Boston: Greg Press, 1972), vol. 1: *The Narrative,* 108, 131.

5. Siebert, *Loyalists in East Florida,* vol. 2: *Records of Their Claims for Losses of Property in the Province,* 173, 351–52; Wallace Brown, *The Good Americans* (New York: William Morrow and Company, 1969), 217.

6. George Fenwick Jones, "The Black Hessians: Negroes Recruited by the Hessians in South Carolina and Other Colonies," *South Carolina Historical Magazine* 83 (1982), 300, 302; *Papers of the Continental Congress,* microfilm, M247 r7 Bk. 1, 6–49, Bk. 2, 54–70; M247 r66 i53 280–94.

7. Mitchell, "Losses and Compensation," 239; Clyde R. Ferguson, "Functions of the Partisan-Militia in the South During the American Revolution: An Interpretation," in *The Revolutionary War in the South: Power, Conflict, and Leadership,* ed.

W. Robert Higgins (Durham: Duke University Press, 1979), 267–68; Hawes, "Papers of James Jackson," 78; Siebert, *Loyalists in East Florida*, vol. 1: *The Narrative*, 124, 131.

8. *Papers of the Continental Congress*, microfilm, M247 r141 i124 v. 3, 183–90.

9. "Official Letters of Governor John Martin, 1782–1783," *Georgia Historical Quarterly* 1 (December 1917), John Martin to Nathanael Greene, August 8, 1782, 315; John Martin to Patrick Tonyn, August 15, 1782, 320–21.

10. *Papers of the Continental Congress*, microfilm, M247 r188 i169 v. 9, John Linder, Jr. to Anthony Wayne, June 25, 1782, 418–19; Carole Watterson Troxler, "Loyalist Refugees and the British Evacuation of East Florida, 1783–1785," *Florida Historical Quarterly* 60 (July 1981), 6, 16–17; Edward J. Cashin, *The King's Ranger: Thomas Brown and the American Revolution in the Southern Frontier* (Athens and London: University of Georgia Press, 1989), 156; Siebert, *Loyalists in East Florida*, vol. 1: *The Narrative*, p. 107.

11. "Letters of John Martin," Representation of the Deputies to Governor Martin, December 5, 1782, 343–44.

12. Ibid., Patrick Tonyn to John Martin, August 28, 1782, 341–43, John Martin to Colonel Cooper, September 17, 1782, 328, John Martin to Patrick Tonyn, October 18, 1782, 334; Davies, *Documents of the American Revolution*, vol. 21, Patrick Tonyn to Thomas Townshend, 24 December 1782, 145.

13. "Letters of John Martin," John Martin to Anthony Wayne, September 7, 1782, 326–27; John Martin to Captain Robert Greer, September 16, 1782, 328.

14. Paul H. Smith, Gerard W. Gawalt and Ronald M. Gephart, eds., *Letters of Delegates to Congress*, vols. 1–19 (Washington, D.C.: Library of Congress, 1976), vol. 19, David Ramsay to Nathanael Greene, September 10, 1782, 142–43; "Letters of John Martin," John Martin to Colonel Cooper, September 17, 1782, 328–29; Siebert, *Loyalists in East Florida*, vol. 1: *The Narrative*, 122–23; Davies, *Documents of the American Revolution*, vol. 21, M. Tatnall to John Street, 4 July 1783, 174.

15. Cashin, *The King's Ranger*, 156; Troxler, "Loyalist Refugees," 6–7, 15; Siebert, *Loyalists in East Florida*, vol. 1: *The Narrative*, 111, 131–33; vol. 2: *Records of Their Claims for Losses of Property in the Province*, 313, 329.

16. Davies, *Documents of the American Revolution*, vol. 21, Patrick Tonyn to the Earl of Shelburne (No. 2), November 14, 1782, 136, Patrick Tonyn to General Sir Guy Carleton, September 1783, 216; Siebert, *Loyalists in East Florida*, vol. 1: *The Narrative*, 108, 115; Troxler, "Loyalist Refugees," 9.

17. Davies, *Documents of the American Revolution*, vol. 21, M. Tatnall to John Street, 4 July 1782, 175.

18. Ibid., Patrick Tonyn to General Sir Guy Carleton, September 1783, 216–17, December 1783, 217; Troxler, "Loyalists Refugees," 20.

19. Troxler, "Loyalist Refugees," 20–21.

20. Robert S. Lambert, "The Flight of the Georgia Loyalists," *Georgia Review* 7 (Winter 1963), 447; Sandra Riley, *Homeward Bound: A History of the Bahama Islands*

to 1850 with a Definitive Study of Abaco in the American Loyalist Plantation Period (Miami: Island Research, 1983), 90.

21. Kozy, "Tories Transplanted," 42; Cashin, *The King's Ranger*, 171.

22. Davies, *Documents of the American Revolution*, vol. 21, Patrick Tonyn to Thomas Townshend, 15 May 1783, 169–70, Patrick Tonyn to Lord North, 21 August 1783, 211–12.

23. Ibid., Lt. Governor William Bull to Thomas Townshend 19 January 1783, 149; Rachel Klein, *Unification of a Slave State: The Rise of the Planter Class in the South Carolina Backcountry, 1760–1808* (Chapel Hill and London: University of North Carolina Press, 1990), 121, 123.

24. Mitchell, "Losses and Compensation," 239, 240 footnote 15; Robert S. Davis, Jr., *Georgia Citizens and Soldiers in the American Revolution* (Easley, South Carolina: Southern Historical Press, Inc., 1979; reprint ed., 1983), 81–82; *Papers of the Continental Congress*, microfilm, M247 r88 i76, House of Assembly, February 21, 1785, 170–71.

25. Davis, Jr., *Citizens and Soldiers*, 56–62.

26. John McKay Sheftall, "The Sheftalls of Savannah: Colonial Leaders and Founding Fathers of Georgia Judaism," in *Jews of the South: Selected Essays from the Southern Jewish Historical Society*, eds. Samuel Proctor and Louis Schmier with Malcolm Stern (Macon: Mercer University Press, 1984), 74–77.

27. Lorenzo Sabine, *Biographical Sketches of the Loyalists of the American Revolution, with an Historical Essay*, 2 vols. (Boston: Little, Brown and company, 1864), vol. 2, 14; Troxler, "Loyalist Refugees," 6; Siebert, *Loyalists in East Florida*, vol. 2: *Records of Their Claims for Losses of Property in the Province*, 328–29.

28. Alex M. Hitz, "Georgia Bounty Land Grants," *Georgia Historical Quarterly* 38 (December 1954), 339–43.

29. Ibid., 337–38.

30. *A Narrative of the Official Conduct of Anthony Stokes of the Inner Temple, London, Barrister at Law; His Majesty's Chief Justice and One of His Council of Georgia and of the Dangers and Distresses He Underwent in the Cause of Government: Some Copies of Which Are Printed for the Information of His Friends* (London: 1784), p. 97.

31. Bernard Schwartz, *A History of the Supreme Court* (New York and Oxford: Oxford University Press, 1993), 20.

32. Wallace Brown, *The King's Friends: The Composition and Motives of the American Loyalist Claimants* (Providence: Brown University Press, 1965), 240–41, 343; Cashin, *The King's Ranger*, 165, 178–79, 218; Kozy, "Tories Transplanted," 22–23, 25, 27–28; Troxler, "Loyalist Refugees," 3, 9; Mitchell, "Losses and Compensation," 234–35; Davis, Jr., *Citizens and Soldiers*, 222–27.

33. Milton Sydney Heath, *Constructive Liberalism: The Role of the State in Economic Development in Georgia to 1860* (Cambridge: Harvard University Press, 1954), 126, 70.

34. Robert S. Lambert, "The Confiscation of Loyalist Property in Georgia, 1782–1786," *William and Mary Quarterly*, 3d ser. 20 (January 1963), 80–94.

35. *Letters of Joseph Clay, Merchant of Savannah, 1776–1793,* Collections of the Georgia Historical Society (Savannah: Georgia Historical Society, 1913), vol. 8, Clay to Messrs. Bright & Pechin, March 23, 1779, 131, Clay to Nathaniel Rice, March 15, 1779, 127–28, Clay to Christopher Pechin, November 2, 1779, 156.

36. Lambert, "Confiscation," 80–94; Mitchell, "Losses and Compensation," 234.

37. Heath, *Constructive Liberalism,* 81–83.

38. George R. Lamplugh, *Politics on the Periphery: Factions and Parties in Georgia, 1783–1806* (Newark: University of Delaware Press, 1986), 28–29, 31, 200–201.

39. William Few, "Autobiography of Col. William Few of Georgia," *Magazine of American History* 7 (November 1881), 351–52.

BIBLIOGRAPHY

Abbot, William W. "Lowcountry, Backcountry: A View of Georgia in the American Revolution." In *An Uncivil War: The Southern Backcountry During the American Revolution,* edited by Ronald Hoffman, Thad W. Tate, and Peter Albert, 321–34. Charlottesville: University Press of Virginia, 1985.

———. *Royal Governors of Georgia, 1754–1775.* Chapel Hill: University of North Carolina Press, 1959.

Adler, Simon L. "Money and Money Units in the American Colonies." Paper presented at the Rochester Historical Society, January 8, 1900.

Alden, John Richard. *The South in the American Revolution, 1763–1789.* Baton Rouge: Louisiana State University Press, 1957.

Andrews, Israel Ward. "McMaster on Our Early Money." *Magazine of Western History* 4 (June 1886): 141–52.

"Anonymous Naval Officer, British Commander." In *Muskets, Cannon Balls and Bombs: Nine Narratives of the Siege of Savannah in 1779,* translated and edited by Benjamin Kennedy, 79–89. Savannah: Beehive Press, 1974.

Ashmore, Otis. "Wilkes County, Its Place in Georgia History." *Georgia Historical Quarterly* 1 (March 1917): 59–63.

Ashmore, Otis, and Olmstead, Charles H. "The Battles of Kettle Creek and Brier Creek." *Georgia Historical Quarterly* 10 (June 1926): 85–125.

Barrow, Thomas C. "The American Revolution as a Colonial War for Independence." *William and Mary Quarterly* 25 (July 1968): 452–64.

Bartram, William. *Travels Through North and South Carolina, East and West Florida.* 1792. Reprint, Charlottesville: University Press of Virginia, 1980.

Becker, Robert A. "Revolution and Reform: An Interpretation of Southern Taxation, 1763 to 1783." *William and Mary Quarterly* 3d ser., 32 (July 1975): 417–42.

Bellesiles, Michael A. *Revolutionary Outlaws: Ethan Allen and the Struggle for Independence on the Early American Frontier.* Charlottesville: University Press of Virginia, 1993.

Boltzius, John Martin. "Johann Martin Bolzius Answers a Questionnaire on Carolina and Georgia." Translated and edited by Klaus G. Loewald, Beverly Starika, and Paul Taylor. *William and Mary Quarterly* 3d ser., 14 (April 1957): 218–61.

Bond, Beverley W. Jr. *The Quit-Rent System in the American Colonies.* New Haven: Yale University Press, 1919.

Bonner, J. C. *A History of Georgia Agriculture, 1732–1860.* Athens: University of Georgia Press, 1964.

Brown, Richard Maxwell. *Strain of Violence: Historical Studies of American Violence and Vigilantism.* New York: Oxford University Press, 1975.

Bowers, Ray. "The American Revolution." *Military Review* 46 (July 1966): 64–72.

Brown, Wallace. *The Good Americans.* New York: William Morrow, 1969.

———. *The King's Friends: The Composition and Motives of the American Loyalist Claimants.* Providence: Brown University Press, 1965.

Caldwell, Lee Ann. "Women Landholders of Colonial Georgia." In *Forty Years of Diversity: Essays on Colonial Georgia,* edited by Harvey H. Jackson and Phinizy Spalding, 183–97. Athens: University of Georgia Press, 1984.

Calhoon, Robert McCluer. *The Loyalists in Revolutionary America, 1760–1781.* New York: Harcourt Brace Jovanovich, 1973. A volume in the series The Founding of the American Republic.

Calloway, Colin G. *The American Revolution in Indian Country: Crisis and Diversity in Native American Communities.* Cambridge: Cambridge University Press, 1995.

Campbell, Archibald. *Journal of an Expedition Against the Rebels of Georgia in North America Under the Orders of Archibald Campbell Esquire Lieutenant Colonel of His Majestys Regiment 1778.* Edited by Colin Campbell. Darien, Ga.: Ashantilly Press, 1981.

Candler, Allen D., ed. *The Colonial Records of Georgia.* Vol. 6: *The Legislature, Proceedings of the President and Assistants, October 12, 1741–October 30, 1754.* Atlanta: Franklin-Turner, 1906.

———. *The Colonial Records of Georgia.* Vol. 12: *Proceedings and Minutes of the Governor and Council, August 6, 1771–February 13, 1782.* Atlanta: Franklin-Turner, 1907.

———. *The Colonial Records of Georgia.* Vol. 15: *Journal of the Commons House.* Atlanta: Franklin-Turner, 1907.

———. *The Revolutionary Records of Georgia.* 3 vols. Atlanta: Franklin-Turner, 1908.

"Capture of Mordecai Sheftall, Deputy Commissary-General of Issues to the Continental Troops for the State of Georgia, viz., 1778, December 29th." In *Historical Collections of Georgia: Containing the Most Interesting Facts, Traditions, Biographical Sketches, Anecdotes, etc. Relating to Its History and Antiquities, from Its First Settlement to the Present Time.* Compiled from original records and official documents. Illustrated by nearly one hundred engravings. By the Rev. George White, 340–42. New York: Pudney & Russell, 1854.

Carp, E. Wayne. *To Starve the Army at Pleasure: Continental Army Administration and American Political Culture, 1775–1783.* Chapel Hill: University of North Carolina Press, 1984.

Carroll, B. R., comp. *Historical Collections of South Carolina Embracing Many Rare and Valuable Pamphlets, and Other Documents Relating to the History of That State, from Its First Discovery to Its Independence in the Year 1776.* New York: Harper and Brothers, 1836.

"The Case of George McIntosh." *Georgia Historical Quarterly* 3 (1919): 131–45.

The Case of George McIntosh, Esquire, a Member of the Late Council and Convention of the State of Georgia, with the Proceedings Thereon in the Hon. the Assembly and Council of that State. 1777. Reprint, Photostat Americana, 2d ser., no. 16, August 15, 1942.

Cashin, Edward J. "Book Review: William Bartram on the Southeastern Indians. Edited and annotated by Gregory A. Waselkov and Kathryn E. Holland Braund." *Journal of Southern History* 63 (February 1997): 148–49.

———. "'But Brothers, It Is Our Land We Are Talking About,' Winners and Losers in the Georgia Backcountry." In *An Uncivil War: The Southern Backcountry During the American Revolution,* edited by Ronald Hoffman, Thad W. Tate, and Peter J. Albert, 240–75. Charlottesville: University Press of Virginia, 1985.

———. "'The Famous Colonel Wells': Factionalism in Revolutionary Georgia." *Georgia Historical Quarterly* 58 (Supplement 1974): 137–56.

———. "George Walton and the Forged Letter." *Georgia Historical Quarterly* 62 (1978): 133–45.

———. *The King's Ranger: Thomas Brown and the American Revolution on the Southern Frontier.* Athens : University of Georgia Press, 1989.

———. *Lachlan McGillivray, Indian Trader: The Shaping of the Southern Colonial Frontier.* Athens: University of Georgia Press, 1992.

———. "Nathanael Greene's Campaign for Georgia in 1781." *Georgia Historical Quarterly* 62 (Spring 1977): 43–58.

———. "Sowing the Wind: Governor Wright and the Georgia Backcountry on the Eve of the Revolution." In *Forty Years of Diversity: Essays on Colonial Georgia,* edited by Harvey H. Jackson and Phinizy Spalding, 233–50. Athens: University of Georgia Press, 1984.

Cashin, Edward J. Jr., and Robertson, Heard. *Augusta and the American Revolution: Events in the Georgia Backcountry, 1773–1783.* Darien, Ga.: Ashantilly Press, 1975.

Chapin, Bradley. "Colonial and Revolutionary Origins of the American Law of Treason." *William and Mary Quarterly* 3d ser., 17 (January 1960): 3–21.

Chaplin, Joyce E. "Tidal Rice Cultivation and the Problem of Slavery in South Carolina and Georgia, 1760–1815." *William and Mary Quarterly* 3d ser., 49 (January 1992): 29–61.

Chappell, Absalom H. *Miscellanies of Georgia: Historical, Biographical, Descriptive, etc.* Atlanta: J. F. Meegan, [1874].

Charlton, Thomas Usher Pulaski. *The Life of Major General James Jackson.* Augusta: F. Randolph, 1809.

Clay, Joseph. *Letters of Joseph Clay, Merchant of Savannah, 1776–1793.* Collections of the Georgia Historical Society, vol. 8. Savannah: Georgia Historical Society, 1913.

Colcomb, Pierre. "Memoirs of a Revolutionary Soldier." *Collector* 63–64 (December 1950–January 1951): 198–201, 2–5.

Cole, Richard C. "The Siege of Savannah and the British Press, 1779–1780." *Georgia Historical Quarterly* 65 (Fall 1981): 189–202.

Coleman, Kenneth. *The American Revolution in Georgia, 1763–1789.* Athens: University of Georgia Press, 1958.

———. *Colonial Georgia: A History.* Millwood, N.J.: KTO Press, 1989.

———. "Restored Colonial Georgia, 1779–1782." *Georgia Historical Quarterly* 40 (March 1956): 1–20.

Coleman, Kenneth, and Charles Stephen Gurr, eds. *Dictionary of Georgia Biography.* Athens: University of Georgia Press, 1983.

Coleman, Kenneth, and Milton Ready, eds. *The Colonial Records of the State of Georgia.* Vol. 28, Part 2: *Original Papers of Governor Wright, President Habersham, and Others, 1764–1782.* Athens: University of Georgia Press, 1979.

Conway, Stephen. "To Subdue America: British Army Officers and the Conduct of the Revolutionary War." *William and Mary Quarterly* 3d ser., 43 (July 1986): 381–407.

Countryman, Edward. "'Out of the Bounds of the Law': Northern Land Rioters in the Eighteenth Century." In *The American Revolution: Explorations in the History of American Radicalism,* edited by Alfred F. Young, 37–69. De Kalb: Northern Illinois University Press, 1976.

Crow, Jeffrey J. "Liberty Men and Loyalists: Disorder and Disaffection in the North Carolina Backcountry." In *An Uncivil War: The Southern Backcountry During the American Revolution,* edited by Ronald Hoffman, Thad W. Tate, and Peter J. Albert, 125–78. Charlottesville: University Press of Virginia, 1985.

Daniel, Marjorie. "John Joachim Zubly: Georgia Pamphleteer of the Revolution." *Georgia Historical Quarterly* 19 (March 1935): 1–16.

Davies, K. G., ed. *Documents of the American Revolution, 1770–1783.* Colonial Office Series. 25 vols. Dublin: Irish University Press, 1974.

Davis, Harold E. *The Fledgling Province: Social and Cultural Life in Colonial Georgia, 1733–1776.* Chapel Hill: University of North Carolina Press, 1976.

Davis, Robert S. Jr. *Georgia Citizens and Soldiers in the American Revolution.* 1979. Reprint. Easley, S.C.: Southern Historical Press, 1983.

———. "The Last Colonial Enthusiast: Captain William Manson in Revolutionary Georgia." *Atlanta Historical Journal* 28 (1984): 23–38.

———. "The Other Side of the Coin: Georgia Baptists Who Fought for the King." *Viewpoints: Georgia Baptist History* 7 (1980): 47–57.

Dederer, John Morgan. *Making Bricks Without Straw: Nathanael Greene's Southern Campaign and Mao Tse-Tung's Mobile War.* Manhattan, Kan.: Sunflower University Press, 1983.

De Vorsey, Louis Jr. *The Indian Boundary in the Southern Colonies, 1763–1775.* Chapel Hill: University of North Carolina Press, 1961.

"Diary of Captain Johann Hinrichs, December 1779–February 10, 1780." In *The Siege of Charleston, with an Account of the Province of South Carolina: Diaries and Letters of Hessian Officers from the von Jungkenn Papers in the William L. Clements Library,* translated and edited by Bernhard A. Ulendorf, 104–77. Ann Arbor: University of Michigan Press, 1938.

Douglass, Elisha P. *Rebels and Democrats: The Struggle for Equal Political Rights and Majority Rule During the American Revolution.* Chapel Hill: University of North Carolina Press, 1955.

Egerton, Hugh Edward, ed. *The Royal Commission on the Losses and Services of American Loyalists, 1783–1785. Being the Notes of Mr. Daniel Parker Coke, M.P. One of the Commissioners During That Period.* New York: Arno Press and the New York Times, 1969.

Egnal, Marc. "The Economic Development of the Thirteen Continental Colonies." *William and Mary Quarterly* 3d ser., 32 (April 1975): 191–222.

Ekirch, A. Robert. "Whig Authority and Public Order in Backcountry North Carolina, 1776–1783." In *An Uncivil War: The Southern Backcountry During the American Revolution,* edited by Ronald Hoffman, Thad W. Tate, and Peter J. Albert, 99–124. Charlottesville: University Press of Virginia, 1985.

Elbert, Samuel. *Order Book of Samuel Elbert, Colonel and Brigadier General in the Continenal Army, October 1776 to November 1778.* Collections of the Georgia Historical Society, vol. 5. Savannah: Georgia Historical Society, 1902.

Ernst, Joseph Albert. *Money and Politics in America, 1755–1775: A Study in the Currency Act of 1764 and the Political Economy of Revolution.* Chapel Hill: University of North Carolina Press, 1973.

Ettinger, Amos Aschbach. *James Edward Oglethorpe, Imperial Idealist.* 1936. Reprint, Hamden, Conn.: Archon Books, 1968.

Ewald, Captain Johann. *Diary of the American War: A Hessian Journal.* Translated and edited by Joseph P. Tustin. New Haven: Yale University Press, 1979.

"Extract from the Journal of a Naval Officer in the Fleet of Count D'Estaing, 1782." In *The Siege of Savannah in 1779, as Described in Two Contemporaneous Journals of French Officers in the Fleet of Count D'Estaing,* 55–70. 1874. Reprint, New York: New York Times and Arno Press, 1968.

Faragher, John Mack, ed. *Encyclopedia of Colonial and Revolutionary America.* New York: Facts on File, 1990.

Ferguson, Clyde R. "Carolina and Georgia Patriot and Loyalist Militia in Action, 1778–1783." In *The Southern Experience in the American Revolution,* edited by Jeffrey J. Crow and Larry E. Tise, 174–99. Chapel Hill: University of North Carolina Press, 1978.

———. "Functions of the Partisan-Militia in the South During the American Revolution: An Interpretation." In *The Revolutionary War in the South: Power, Conflict, and Leadership,* edited by W. Robert Higgins, 239–58. Durham: Duke University Press, 1979.

Ferguson, E. James. "Currency Finance: An Interpretation of Colonial Monetary Practices." *William and Mary Quarterly* 3d ser., 10 (April 1953): 153–80.

Few, William. "Autobiography of Col. William Few of Georgia." *Magazine of American History* 7 (November 1881): 343–58.

Flanders, Ralph Betts. *Plantation Slavery in Georgia.* 1933. Reprint, Cos Cob, Conn.: John E. Edwards, 1967.

Flippin, Percy Scott. "The Royal Government in Georgia, 1752–1776: The Commons House of Assembly." *Georgia Historical Quarterly* 8 (December 1924): 243–91.

———. "The Royal Government in Georgia, 1752–1776: The Financial System and Administration." *Georgia Historical Quarterly* 9 (September 1925): 187–245.

———. "The Royal Government in Georgia, 1752–1776: Governor Wright." *Georgia Historical Quarterly* 8 (June 1924): 81–120.

———. "The Royal Government in Georgia, 1752–1776: The Land System." *Georgia Historical Quarterly* 10 (March 1926): 1–25.

———. "The Royal Government in Georgia, 1752–1776: The Military System." *Georgia Historical Quarterly* 12 (December 1928): 326–52.

———. "The Royal Government in Georgia, 1752–1776: The Military System, Part II." *Georgia Historical Quarterly* 13 (June 1929): 128–53.

Foster, William O. "James Jackson in the American Revolution." *Georgia Historical Quarterly* 31 (December 1947): 249–81.

"François d'Auber de Peyrelongue, Lieutenant of Artillery." In *Muskets, Cannon Balls and Bombs: Nine Narratives of the Siege of Savannah in 1779,* translated and edited by Benjamin Kennedy, 27–38. Savannah: Beehive Press, 1974.

Frey, Sylvia R. *Water from the Rock: Black Resistance in a Revolutionary Age.* Princeton: Princeton University Press, 1991.

Furlong, Patrick J. "Civilian-Military Conflict and the Restoration of the Royal Province of Georgia, 1778–1782." *Journal of Southern History* 38 (August 1972): 415–41.

Gallay, Alan. *The Formation of a Planter Elite: Jonathan Bryan and the Southern Colonial Frontier.* Athens: University of Georgia Press, 1989.

———, ed. *Colonial Wars of North America, 1512–1763, An Encyclopedia.* New York: Garland, 1996.

"Georgia Council of Safety to the South Carolina Council of Safety." In *Setting Out to Begin a New World: Colonial Georgia,* ed. Edward J. Cashin, 170–72. Savannah: Beehive Press, 1995.

Georgia Gazette, 1775–76, 1782–83.

Gray, Lewis Cecil. *History of Agriculture in the Southern United States.* New York: P. Smith, 1941.

Green, E. R. R. "Queensborough Township: Scotch-Irish Emigration and the

Expansion of Georgia, 1763–1776." *William and Mary Quarterly* 3d ser., 17 (April 1960): 183–99.

Greene, Jack P. "The Georgia Commons House of Assembly and the Power of Appointment to Executive Offices, 1765–1775." *Georgia Historical Quarterly* 46 (June 1962): 151–61.

———. "Legislative Turnover in British America, 1696 to 1775: A Quantitative Analysis." *William and Mary Quarterly* 3d ser., 38 (July 1981): 442–63.

———. *The Quest for Power: The Lower Houses of Assembly in the Southern Royal Colonies, 1689–1776.* Chapel Hill: University of North Carolina Press, 1963.

———. "William Knox's Explanation for the American Revolution." *William and Mary Quarterly* 3d ser., 30 (April 1973): 293–306.

Gruber, Ira D. "Britain's Southern Strategy." In *The Revolutionary War in the South: Power, Conflict, and Leadership,* edited by W. Robert Higgins, 205–38. Durham: Duke University Press, 1979.

Habersham, James. *The Letters of the Hon. James Habersham, 1756–1775.* Collections of the Georgia Historical Society, vol. 6. Savannah: Georgia Historical Society, 1904.

Harden, William. "Basil Cowper's Remarkable Career in Georgia." *Georgia Historical Quarterly* 1 (March 1917): 24–35.

Harlow, Ralph Volney. "Aspects of Revolutionary Finance, 1775–1783." *American Historical Review* 35 (October 1929): 46–68.

Harrold, Frances. "Colonial Siblings: Georgia's Relationship with South Carolina During the Pre-Revolutionary Period." *Georgia Historical Quarterly* 72 (Winter 1989): 707–44.

Hawes, Lilla M., ed. "Collections of the Georgia Historical Society and Other Documents: Minutes of the Executive Council, May 7 through October 14, 1777." *Georgia Historical Quarterly* 33 (December 1949): 318–30; 34 (March 1950): 19–35; (June 1950): 106–25.

———. "Letter Book of Lachlan McIntosh, 1776–1777 Part I." *Georgia Historical Quarterly* 38 (June 1954): 149–69.

———. "Minute Book, Savannah Board of Police, 1779." *Georgia Historical Quarterly* 45 (September 1961): 245–57.

———. "Miscellaneous Papers of James Jackson, 1781–1798." *Georgia Historical Quarterly* 37 (March 1953): 54–81.

———. "The Papers of Lachlan McIntosh, 1774–1799: Letter Book of Lachlan McIntosh, 1774–1799 Part III." *Georgia Historical Quarterly* 38 (December 1954): 356–68.

———. "The Papers of Lachlan McIntosh, 1774–1799: Miscellaneous Papers Part IV." *Georgia Historical Quarterly* 39 (March 1955): 52–67.

———. "The Papers of Lachlan McIntosh, 1774–1799: Miscellaneous Papers Part V." *Georgia Historical Quarterly* 39 (June 1955): 172–86.

———. "The Papers of Lachlan McIntosh, 1774–1799: Miscellaneous Papers Part VI." *Georgia Historical Quarterly* 39 (September 1955): 253–68.

————. "The Papers of Lachlan McIntosh, 1774–1799: Miscellaneous Papers Part VII." *Georgia Historical Quarterly* 39 (December 1955): 356–74.

————. "Some Papers of the Governor and Council of Georgia, 1780–1781." *Georgia Historical Quarterly* 46 (September–December 1962): 280–96, 395–417.

Heath, Milton Sydney. *Constructive Liberalism: The Role of the State in Economic Development in Georgia to 1860.* Cambridge, Mass.: Harvard University Press, 1954.

Hepburn, A. Barton. *History of Coinage and Currency in the United States and the Perennial Contest for Sound Money.* 1903. Reprint, New York: Greenwood Press, 1968.

Herndon, G. Melvin. "Forest Products of Colonial Georgia." *Journal of Forest History* 23 (July 1979): 130–35.

Higginbotham, Don. "The Early American Way of War: Reconnaisance and Appraisal." *William and Mary Quarterly* 3d ser., 44 (April 1987): 230–73.

Hitz, Alex M. "Georgia Bounty Land Grants." *Georgia Historical Quarterly* 38 (December 1954): 337–48.

Hoffman, Ronald. "The 'Disaffected' in the Revolutionary South." In *The American Revolution: Explorations in the History of American Radicalism,* edited by Alfred F. Young, 273–316. De Kalb: Northern Illinois University Press, 1976.

Ingram, James. *Proceedings of a Council of War Held at Burke Jail, Georgia, January 14th, 1779, with a Narrative of the Subsequent Proceedings, and the Proclamation Issued.* Edited by Paul Leicester Ford. Brooklyn: Historical Printing Club, 1890.

Isaac, Rhys. "Preachers and Patriots: Popular Culture and the Revolution in Virginia." In *The American Revolution: Explorations in the History of American Radicalism,* edited by Alfred F. Young, 125–56. De Kalb: Northern Illinois University Press, 1976.

Jackson, Harvey H. "'American Slavery, American Freedom' and the Revolution in the Lower South: The Case of Lachlan McIntosh." *Southern Studies* 19 (Spring 1980): 81–93.

————. "The Battle of the Riceboats: Georgia Joins the Revolution." *Georgia Historical Quarterly* 58 (Summer 1974): 229–43.

————. "Consensus and Conflict: Factional Politics in Revolutionary Georgia, 1774–1777." *Georgia Historical Quarterly* 59 (Winter 1975): 388–401.

————. "Georgia Whiggery: The Origins and Effects of a Many-Faceted Movement." In *Forty Years of Diversity: Essays on Colonial Georgia,* edited by Harvey H. Jackson and Phinizy Spalding, 251–73. Athens: University of Georgia Press, 1984.

————. *Lachlan McIntosh and the Politics of Revolutionary Georgia.* Athens: University of Georgia Press, 1979.

————."Rise of the Western Members: Revolutionary Politics and the Georgia Backcountry." In *An Uncivil War: The Southern Backcountry During the American Revolution,* edited by Ronald Hoffman, Thad W. Tate, and Peter J. Albert, 276–320. Charlottesville: University Press of Virginia, 1985.

Jensen, Merrill. *The Founding of a Nation: A History of the American Revolution, 1763–1776.* New York: Oxford University Press, 1968.

Johnson, James M. *Militiamen, Rangers and Redcoats: The Military in Georgia, 1754–1776.* Macon: Mercer University Press, 1992.

Johnson, Joseph. *Traditions and Reminiscences Chiefly of the American Revolution in the South.* 1851. Reprint, Spartanburg: Reprint Company, 1972.

Johnston, Edith Duncan. *The Houstouns of Georgia.* Athens: University of Georgia Press, 1950.

Johnston, Elizabeth Lightenstone. *Recollections of a Georgia Loyalist.* New York: M. F. Mansfield, 1901.

Jones, Alice Hanson. *Wealth of a Nation to Be: The American Colonies on the Eve of the Revolution.* New York: Columbia University Press, 1980.

Jones, Charles C. Jr. *Biographical Sketches of the Delegates from Georgia to the Continental Congress.* Boston: Houghton Mifflin, 1891.

———. *The Dead Towns of Georgia.* Collections of the Georgia Historical Society, vol. 4. Savannah: Morning News Steam Printing House, 1878.

———. *The History of Georgia.* Boston: Houghton Mifflin, 1883.

Jones, Eldon. "The British Withdrawal from the South, 1781–85." In *The Revolutionary War in the South: Power, Conflict, and Leadership,* edited by W. Robert Higgins, 259–86. Durham: Duke University Press, 1979.

Jones, George Fenwick. "The Black Hessians: Negroes Recruited by the Hessians in South Carolina and Other Colonies." *South Carolina Historical Magazine* 83 (1982): 287–302.

———. *The Georgia Dutch: From the Rhine and Danube to the Savannah, 1733–1783.* Athens: University of Georgia Press, 1992.

———. "Hessian Deserters." *Journal of the Johannes Schwalm Historical Association* 4 (1990): 54–58.

———, ed. "A German Surgeon on the Flora and Fauna of Colonial Georgia: Four Letters of Johann Christoph Bornemann, 1753–1755." *Georgia Historical Quarterly* 76 (Winter 1992): 891–914.

Jones, Thomas. *History of New York During the Revolutionary War and the Leading Events in the Other Colonies at That Period.* Edited by Edward Floyd DeLancey. New York: Printed for the New York Historical Society, 1879.

Killion, Ronald G., and Charles T. Waller. *Georgia and the Revolution.* Atlanta: Cherokee Publishing Co., 1975.

Kipping, Ernst. *The Hessian View of America, 1776–1783.* Monmouth Beach, N.J.: Philip Freneau Press, 1971.

Klein, Rachel N. "Frontier Planters and the Revolution: The Southern Backcountry, 1775–1782." In *An Uncivil War: The Southern Backcountry During the American Revolution,* edited by Ronald Hoffman, Thad W. Tate, and Peter J. Albert, 37–69. Charlottesville: University Press of Virginia, 1985.

————. "Ordering the Backcountry: The South Carolina Regulation." *William and Mary Quarerly* 3d ser., 38 (October 1981): 661–80.

————. *Unification of a Slave State: The Rise of the Planter Class in the South Carolina Backcountry, 1760–1808.* Chapel Hill: University of North Carolina Press, 1990.

Knight, Betsy. "Prisoner Exchange and Parole in the American Revolution." *William and Mary Quarterly* 3d ser., 48 (April 1991): 201–22.

Kozy, Charlene. "Tories Transplanted: The Caribbean Exile and Plantation Settlement of Southern Loyalists." *Georgia Historical Quarterly* 75 (Spring 1991): 18–49.

Lambert, Robert S. "The Confiscation of Loyalist Property in Georgia, 1782–1786." *William and Mary Quarterly* 3d ser., 20 (January 1963): 80–94.

————. "The Flight of the Georgia Loyalists." *Georgia Review* 7 (Winter 1963): 435–48.

Lamplugh, George R. *Politics on the Periphery: Factions and Parties in Georgia, 1783–1806.* Newark: University of Delaware Press, 1986.

————. "'To Check and Discourage the Wicked and Designing': John Wereat and the Revolution in Georgia." *Georgia Historical Quarterly* 61 (Winter 1977): 295–307.

————. "Up from the Depths: The Career of Thomas Gibbons, 1783–1789." *Atlanta Historical Journal* 25 (1981): 37–44.

Lawrence, Alexander A. "General Lachlan McIntosh and His Suspension from Continental Command During the Revolution." *Georgia Historical Quarterly* 38 (June 1954): 101–41.

————. "General Robert Howe and the British Capture of Savannah in 1778." *Georgia Historical Quarterly* 36 (1952): 303–27.

————. "James Jackson: Passionate Patriot." *Georgia Historical Quarterly* 34 (June 1950): 75–86.

————. *Storm Over Savannah: The Story of Count d'Estaing and the Siege of the Town in 1779.* Athens: University of Georgia Press, 1951.

Leamon, James S. *Revolution Downeast: The War for American Independence in Maine.* Amherst: University of Massachusettes Press, 1993.

Lee, Henry. *The Campaign of 1781 in the Carolinas.* 1824. Reprint, Spartanburg: Reprint Company, 1975.

————. *Memoirs of the War in the Southern Department of the United States, 1812.* Reprint, New York: Inskeep and Bradford, 1869.

"Letter from Eliza Wilkinson." In *The Spirit of 'Seventy-Six: The Story of the American Revolution as Told by Participants.* Edited by Henry Steele Commager and Richard B. Morris, 1121–22. New York: Harper & Row, 1967.

"Letter from Savannah January 16, 1779." In *Letters from America, 1776–1779.* Translated by Ray Waldron Pettengill, 197–204. Boston: Houghton Mifflin, 1924.

Letters from Governor Sir James Wright to the Earl of Dartmouth and Lord George Germain, Secretaries of State for America from August 24, 1774, to February 16, 1782. Collections of the Georgia Historical Society, vol. 3, part 4. Savannah: Georgia Historical Society, 1901.

"Letters of Patrick Carr, Terror to British Loyalists, to Governors John Martin and Lyman Hall, 1782–1783." *Georgia Historical Quarterly* 1 (1917): 337–41.

Levy, B. H. "Savannah's Old Jewish Community Cemeteries." *Georgia Historical Quarterly* 66 (Spring 1982): 1–20.

Lutz, Paul. "The Oath of Absolution." *Georgia Historical Quarterly* 53 (September 1969): 330–34.

Mackall, Leonard L. "Edward Langworthy and the First Attempt to Write a Separate History of Georgia, with Selections from the Long Lost Langworthy Papers." *Georgia Historical Quarterly* 7 (March 1923): 1–17.

Main, Jackson Turner. *The Social Structure of Revolutionary America.* Princeton: Princeton University Press, 1965.

———. *The Upper House in Revolutionary America 1763–1788.* Madison: University of Wisconsin Press, 1967.

McCowen, George Smith Jr., *The British Occupation of Charleston, 1780–1782.* Columbia: University of South Carolina Press, 1972.

McCrady, Edward. *The History of South Carolina in the Revolution.* 2 vols. 1901–2. Reprint, New York: Russell and Russell, 1969.

McCusker, John J., and Russell R. Menard. *The Economy of British America, 1607–1789.* Chapel Hill: University of North Carolina Press, 1985.

Menard, Russell R. "Slavery, Economic Growth, and Revolutionary Ideology in the South Carolina Low Country." In *The Economy of Early America: The Revolutionary Period, 1763–1790,* Edited by Ronald Hoffman, John J. McCusker, Russell Menard, and Peter J. Albert, 244–74. Charlottesville: University Press of Virginia, 1988.

Merrens, Harry Roy. *Colonial North Carolina in the Eighteenth Century: A Study in Historical Geography.* Chapel Hill: University of North Carolina Press, 1964.

Middlekaupf, Robert. *The Glorious Cause: The American Revolution, 1763–1789.* New York: Oxford University Press, 1982.

Miller, Randall. "Back Country Loyalist Plan to Retake Georgia and the Carolinas, 1778." *South Carolina Historical Magazine* 75 (1974): 207–14.

Mitchell, Robert G. "The Losses and Compensation of Georgia Loyalists." *Georgia Historical Quarterly* 68 (Summer 1984): 233–43.

———. "Sir James Wright Looks at the American Revolution." *Georgia Historical Quarterly* 53 (December 1969): 509–18.

Morgan, David T. "A New Look at Benjamin Franklin as Georgia's Colonial Agent." *Georgia Historical Quarterly* 68 (Summer 1984): 222–32.

Morgan, Philip D. "Black Society in the Lowcountry." In *Slavery and Freedom in the Age of the American Revolution,* edited by Ira Berlin and Ronald Hoffman, 83–141. Charlottesville: University Press of Virginia, 1983.

Moultrie, William. *Memoirs of the American Revolution.* 2 vols. New York: David Longworth, 1802.

Naisawald, L. Van Loan. "Major General Robert Howe's Activities in South Carolina and Georgia, 1776–1779." *Georgia Historical Quarterly* 35 (March 1951): 23–30.

"The Narrative of Henry Preston of Savannah, Joint Prothonotary and Clerk of the Crown for the Province." In *Setting Out to Begin a New World: Colonial Georgia*, ed. Edward J. Cashin, 167–69. Savannah: Beehive Press, 1995.

A Narrative of the Official Conduct of Anthony Stokes of the Inner Temple, London, Barrister at Law; His Majesty's Chief Justice and One of His Council of Georgia and of the Dangers and Distresses He Underwent in the Cause of Government: Some Copies of Which Are printed for the Information of His Friends. London, 1784.

Nelson, William H. *The American Tory.* Oxford: Clarendon Press, 1961.

Nettels, Curtis P. *The Emergence of a National Economy, 1775–1815.* Vol. 2: *The Economic History of the United States.* New York: Holt, Rinehart and Winston, 1962.

Norton, Mary Beth. *The British Americans.* London: Constable, 1974.

Nunis, Doyce Jr., ed. "Memorandums of the Road, and the March of a Corps of Troops from Savannah to Augusta, and some subsequent Occurences." In "Colonel Archibald Campbell's March from Savannah to Augusta, 1779." *Georgia Historical Quarterly* 45 (September 1961): 275–86.

"Official Letters of Governor John Martin, 1782–1783." *Georgia Historical Quarterly* 1 (December 1917): 281–344.

Olson, Gary D. "Thomas Brown, Loyalist Partisan, and the Revolutionary War in Georgia, 1777–1782 Part II." *Georgia Historical Quarterly* 54 (Summer 1970): 183–208.

Olwell, Robert A. "'Domestick Enemies': Slavery and Political Independence in South Carolina, May 1775–March 1776." *Journal of Southern History* 60 (February 1989): 21–48.

Pancake, John S. *This Destructive War: The British Campaign in the Carolinas, 1780–1782.* University: University of Alabama Press, 1985.

Papers of Nathanael Greene. Edited by Richard Showman et al. 10 vols. Chapel Hill: University of North Carolina Press, 1991.

Papers of the Continental Congress.

Pennypacker, Samuel W. "Anthony Wayne." *Pennsylvania Magazine of History and Biography* 32 (1908): 257–301.

Phillips, Ulrich B., ed. "Some Letters of Joseph Habersham, 1775–1790." *Georgia Historical Quarterly* 10 (June 1926): 145–63.

Pierce, William. "Letters of Major William Pierce to St. George Tucker." *Magazine of American History* 7 (1881): 431–45.

Presley, Delma E. "The Crackers of Georgia." *Georgia Historical Quarterly* 60 (Summer 1976): 102–16.

Prevost, Augustine. "Major General Augustine Prevost." In *Muskets, Cannon Balls and Bombs: Nine Narratives of the Siege of Savannah in 1779,* translated and edited by Benjamin Kennedy, 90–106. Savannah: Beehive Press, 1974.

Price, Jacob M. "Reflections on the Economy of Revolutionary America." In *The*

Economy of Early America: The Revolutionary Period, 1763–1790, edited by Ronald Hoffman, John J. McCusker, Russell R. Menard, and Peter J. Albert, 303–24. Charlottesville: University Press of Virginia, 1988.

Proceedings and Minutes of the Governor and Council of Georgia, October 4, 1774, through November 7, 1775, and September 6, 1779, through September 20, 1780. Collections of the Georgia Historical Society, vol. 10. Savannah: Georgia Historical Society, 1952.

Proceedings of the First Provincial Congress of Georgia, 1775. Collections of the Georgia Historical Society, vol. 5, part 1. Savannah: Georgia Historical Society, 1901.

Proceedings of the Georgia Council of Safety, 1775–1777. Collections of the Georgia Historical Society, vol. 5, part 1. Savannah: Georgia Historical Society, 1901.

Reese, Trevor Richard. *Colonial Georgia: A Study in British Imperial Policy in the Eighteenth Century.* Athens: University of Georgia Press, 1963.

Riley, Sandra. *Homeward Bound: A History of the Bahama Islands to 1850 with a Definitive Study of Abaco in the American Loyalist Plantation Period.* Miami: Island Research, 1983.

Robertson, Heard. "The Second British Occupation of Augusta, 1780–1781." *Georgia Historical Quarterly* 58 (1974): 422–46.

————, ed. "Georgia's Banishment and Expulsion Act of September 16, 1777." *Georgia Historical Quarterly* 55 (Summer 1971): 274–82.

Robson, Eric. *The American Revolution in Its Political and Military Aspects, 1763–1783.* New York: Oxford University Press, 1955.

Royal Georgia Gazette, 1779–82.

Sabine, Lornezo. *Biographical Sketches of the Loyalists of the American Revolution, with an Historical Essay.* 2 vols. Boston: Little, Brown, 1864.

Saye, Albert Berry. *A Constitutional History of Georgia, 1732–1945.* Athens: University of Georgia Press, 1948.

Scheer, George F., and Hugh F. Rankin. *Rebels and Redcoats.* New York: World, 1963.

Schmier, Louis. "This New Canaan: The Jewish Experience in Georgia." *Georgia Historical Quarterly* 73 (Winter 1989): 815–27.

Schwartz, Bernard. *A History of the Supreme Court.* New York: Oxford University Press, 1993.

Scott, Ralph C. Jr. "The Quaker Settlement of Wrightsborough, Georgia." *Georgia Historical Quarterly* 56 (Summer 1972): 210–23.

Scruggs, Carroll Proctor. *Georgia During the Revolution.* Norcross, Ga.: Bay Tree Grove, 1976.

Searcy, Martha Condray. *The Georgia-Florida Contest in the American Revolution, 1776–1778.* Tuscaloosa: University of Alabama Press, 1985.

————. "The Introduction of African Slavery into the Creek Indian Nation." *Georgia Historical Quarterly* 66 (Spring 1982): 21–32.

————. "1779: The First Year of the British Occupation of Georgia." *Georgia Historical Quarterly* 67 (Summer 1983): 168–88.

Sheftall, John McKay. "The Sheftalls of Savannah: Colonial Leaders and Founding

Fathers of Georgia Judaism." In *Jews of the South: Selected Essays from the Southern Jewish Historical Society,* edited by Samuel Proctor and Louis Schmier with Malcolm Stern, 65–78. Macon: Mercer University Press, 1984.

Sheftall, Mordecai. *Capture of Mordecai Sheftall, Deputy Commissary-General of Issues to the Continental Troops for the State of Georgia, vis., 1778, December 29th.* In *Historical Collections of Georgia,* ed. George White, 340–42. New York: Pudney and Russell, 1854.

Shelley, Fred, ed. "The Journal of Ebenezer Hazard in Georgia, 1778." *Georgia Historical Quarterly* 41 (September 1957): 316–18.

Shepherd, James F. "British America and the Atlantic Economy." In *The Economy of Early America: The Revolutionary Period, 1763–1790,* edited by Ronald Hoffman, John J. McCusker, Russell R. Menard, and Peter J. Albert, 3–44. Charlottesville: University Press of Virginia, 1988.

Shepherd, James F., and Samuel H. Williamson. "The Coastal Trade of British North American Colonies, 1768–1772." *Journal of Economic History* 32 (1972): 783–810.

Shy, John. "A New Look at Colonial Militia." *William and Mary Quarterly* 3d ser., 20 (January–October 1963): 175–85.

———. "The War for American Independence." In *The Southern Experience in the American Revolution,* edited by Jeffrey J. Crow and Larry E. Tise, 155–73. Chapel Hill: University of North Carolina Press, 1978.

Siebert, Wilbur Henry. *Loyalists in East Florida, 1774 to 1785: The Most Important Documents Pertaining Thereto.* 2 vols. 1929. Reprint, Boston: Greg Press, 1972.

"The Siege of Savannah by Count D'Estaing, in 1779." In *The Siege of Savannah in 1779, as Described in Two Contemporaneous Journals of French Officers in the Fleet of Count D'Estaing,* 7–52. 1874. Reprint, New York: New York Times and Arno Press, 1968.

Smith, Gordon B. "The Georgia Grenadiers." *Georgia Historical Quarterly* 64 (Winter 1980): 405–15.

Smith, Julia Floyd. *Slavery and Rice Culture in Low Country Georgia, 1750–1860.* Knoxville: University of Tennessee Press, 1985.

Smith, Paul H. *Loyalists and Redcoats: A Study in British Revolutionary Policy.* Chapel Hill: University of North Carolina Press, 1964.

Smith, Paul H., Gerald W. Gawalt, and Ronald M. Gephart, eds. *Letters of Delegates to Congress.* 19 vols. Washington, D.C.: Library of Congress, 1976.

Snapp, J. Russell. *John Stuart and the Struggle for Empire on the Southern Frontier.* Baton Rouge: Louisiana State University Press, 1996.

"Stephen DeLancey Writes to His Wife." In *The Price of Loyalty: Tory Writings from the Revolutionary Era,* ed. Catherine S. Crary, 271–74. New York: McGraw-Hill, 1973.

Stern, Malcolm H. "The Sheftall Diaries." *American Jewish Historical Quarterly* 54 (1965):243–77.

Stevens, William Bacon. *A History of Georgia, From Its First Discovery by Europeans to the Adoption of the Present Constitution in MDCCXCVIII.* 2 vols. 1847. Reprint, Philadelphia: E. H. Butler, 1859.

Stille, Charles J. *Major-General Anthony Wayne and the Pennsylvania Line in the Continental Army.* 1893. Reprint, Port Washington, N.Y.: Kennikat Press, 1968.

Stokes, Anthony. "Anthony Stokes, Chief Justice of Georgia to His Wife, November 9, 1779." In *Muskets, Cannon Balls and Bombs: Nine Narratives of the Siege of Savannah in 1779,* translated and edited by Benjamin Kennedy, 108–16. Savannah: Beehive Press, 1974.

———. *A View of the Constitution of the British Colonies, in North America and the West Indies at the Time the Civil War Broke Out on the Continent of America.* London, 1783.

Sutherland, Stella H. *Population Distribution in Colonial America.* 1936. Reprint, New York: AMS Press, 1966.

Telfair, Edward. "A Letter to J. Y. Noel Relative to William Telfair's Claim." In "Basil Cowper's Remarkable Career in Georgia" by William Harden, 30–33. *Georgia Historical Quarterly* 1 (March 1917): 24–35.

Thayer, Theodore. *Nathanael Greene, Strategist of the American Revolution.* New York: Twayne, 1960.

Treacy, M. F. *Prelude to Yorktown: The Southern Campaign of Nathanael Greene, 1780–1781.* Chapel Hill: University of North Carolina Press, 1963.

Troxler, Carole Watterson. "Loyalist Refugees and the British Evacuation of East Florida, 1783–1785." *Florida Historical Quarterly* 60 (July 1981): 1–28.

Tucker, Glenn. *Mad Anthony Wayne and the New Nation: The Story of Washington's Front-Line General.* Harrisburg: Stackpole Books, 1973.

Van Tyne, Claude Halstead. *The Loyalists in the American Revolution.* Gloucester: Peter Smith, 1959.

Ver Steeg, Clarence L. *Origins of a Southern Mosaic: Studies of Early Carolina and Georgia.* Athens: University of Georgia Press, 1975.

Watkins, Robert, and George Watkins. *A Digest of the Laws of the State of Georgia. From its first establishment as a British province down to the year 1798, inclusive, and the principal acts of 1799: in which is comprehended the Declaration of Independence; the state constitutions of 1777 and 1789, with the alterations and amendments in 1794.* Philadelphia: Printed by R. Aitken, 1800.

Wax, Darold D. "'New Negroes Are Always in Demand': The Slave Trade in Eighteenth-Century Georgia." *Georgia Historical Quarterly* 68 (Summer 1984): 193–220.

Weems, M. L. *A Reminiscence of the Bold and Successful Adventures of Small Scouting Parties of Revolutionary Patriots Against the British and Tories in South Carolina and*

Georgia During the Revolutionary War, as Related by One Who Took an Active Part in Many of the Scenes. New York, 1840.

Weigley, Russell F. *The Partisan War: The South Carolina Campaign of 1780–1782.* Columbia: University of South Carolina Press, 1970.

Weir, Robert M. *"The Last of American Freemen": Studies in the Political Culture of the Colonial and Revolutionary South.* Macon: Mercer University Press, 1986.

———. *"A Most Important Epocha": The Coming the Revolution in South Carolina.* Columbia: University of South Carolina Press, 1970.

Weiss, Roger. "The Issue of Paper Money in the American Colonies, 1720–1774." *Journal of Ecomonic History* 30 (1970): 770–84.

Weller, Jac. "The Irregular War in the South." *Military Affairs* 24 (Fall 1960): 124–36.

Whitney, William Dwight, ed. *The Century Dictionary of the English Language.* 24 vols. New York: Century, 1889.

Wiener, Frederick Bernays. *Civilians Under Military Justice: The British Practice Since 1689 Especially in North America.* Chicago: University of Chicago Press, 1967.

Wildes, Harry Emerson. *Anthony Wayne, Trouble Shooter of the American Revolution.* Westport: Greenwood Press, 1969.

Wood, Betty. *Slavery in Colonial Georgia, 1730–1775.* Athens: University of Georgia Press, 1984.

Zubly, John Joachim. "Rev. J. J. Zubly's Appeal to the Grand Jury, October 8, 1777." *Georgia Historical Quarterly* 1 (June 1917): 161–65.

INDEX